Happy Birthday, Honey

You have been my comfort
and joy through all our
changing!

Love,

Joanne

W9-AQU-339

Tidings of Comfort and Joy

Tidings of Comfort and Joy

by
Robert S. Spitzer, M.D.

Science and Behavior Books, Inc.
Palo Alto, California

Science and Behavior Books, Inc.
P.O. Box 11457
Palo Alto, California 94306

Copyright 1975 by Science and Behavior Books, Inc. Printed in the United States of America. All Rights Reserved. This book or parts thereof may not be reproduced in any form without written permission of the publisher.

Library of Congress Catalog Card Number: 75–7997
ISBN 0–8314–0039–X

To my joy and comfort,

Becky

and

To my friend, Peg Granger,
editor, *par excellance*.

Acknowledgements

I wish to thank the following people for reading my manuscript and for their comments and encouragement.

Alfred Bochner, Dan McCluney, Lucille Hurwitz, George Torzsay-Biber, Marilyn Yalom, James Hurwitz, Lucy McCluney, Virginia Satir, Jane Foster, Dan Spitzer, Raven Lang, Gene Belote, and Elaine Katz.

Preface

It has been said that politics makes strange bedfellows. There is some risk of a similar result when a publisher assembles the works of his own authors in an anthology—particularly when he identifies closely with their works and when the authors are also his friends. Nevertheless, I believe there is a unity in this anthology. Alexander Pope said, "The proper study of mankind is man." Virginia Satir, Fritz Perls, Raven Lang, and Sheldon Kopp are all students of man. They also have in common an intensity that comes from owning their own perceptions. Being with them or reading their works makes us more aware of our potentials and focuses our attention on how we are experiencing and changing our lives. My courage *(or is it chutzpah)* is in including my essay with their works, and in giving this anthology my title.

The basic idea of my essay is that it is very easy to lose sight of the rapid evolution of society. We are all so much caught up in our individual life stories that we forget that relatively a short time ago in the history of mankind slavery was accepted, women did not have the vote, children worked in the mines, and deviancy of all kinds was considered at least sick if not against the law. The last decade has seen great advances in changed attitudes toward racism, sexism and awareness of ecology. We still have a long way to go, and frequently in the face of various crises we question our progress and fear that all is about to be lost.

On this date, February 7, 1975, deepening economic depression and a new war in the Middle East are being predicted by many. These subjects are discussed in the essay, but are analyzed in more detail in the addendum that follows the essay.

Contents

Part I

Tidings of Comfort and Joy

by

Robert S. Spitzer, M.D.

Accept hope, all who enter here.

"After a lapse of two years, Pharaoh had a dream. He saw himself standing by the Nile, when up out of the Nile came seven cows, handsome and fat, they grazed in the reed grass. Behind them seven other cows, ugly and gaunt, came out of the Nile and standing on the bank of the Nile beside the others, the ugly gaunt cows ate up the seven handsome fat cows. The Pharaoh woke up.

"He fell asleep again and had another dream. He saw seven ears of grain fat and healthy growing on a single stalk. Behind them sprouted seven ears of grain thin and blasted by the east wind. And the seven thin ears swallowed up the seven fat healthy ears. Then Pharaoh woke up to find it was only a dream.

"Pharaoh therefore had Joseph summoned from the dungeon, and Joseph said unto Pharaoh, the seven healthy cows are seven years and the seven healthy ears are seven years. Seven years of great abundance are now coming throughout the land of Egypt, but these will be followed by seven years of famine.

"Pharaoh was pleased with Joseph and followed his advice and appointed him an overseer. During the seven years of plenty when the land produced abundant crops, Joseph husbanded all the food of these years of plenty and garnered grain quantities like the sands of the sea. When the seven years of abundance enjoyed by the land of Egypt came to an end, the seven years of famine set in just as Joseph had predicted. Although there was famine in all the other countries, food was available throughout the land of Egypt. In fact, all the world came to Joseph to obtain rations of grain for famine had gripped the whole world."

I recount this story from Genesis not as an example of divine intervention or of early dream interpretation, but rather to show man's concern for the future and his search for what I call trends and what Wall Street might call long range forecasts.

My interest in underlying trends first centered on foreign affairs under the influence of my grandmother, Sophie Weisstein, a small, gentle, gray-haired lady of great dignity. She had an intensity that under other circumstances might have made her a Golda Meir. Her life had literally depended on her ability to predict foreign affairs. An immigrant from Russia, the only survivor of sixteen children, she knew exciting stories about Cossacks and pogroms in the Ukraine. But she seldom spoke of the past, and I respected her sorrow and did not pester.

Her domain was the kitchen, where it seemed to me as a child that she had a direct connection to Jehovah. I never fully understood all the orthodox Kosher rules that governed there. Out of that kitchen came the ritualistic foods of Passover, and also homemade strudel and Old World treats like *grieben* and *piroshki*.

Since my grandmother could not read English, I read the newspaper to her every day. It was a heady business for a nine-year-old. My friends were probably more interested in Glenn Miller at the time, but my grandmother and I were news buffs and our heroes were people like H.V. Kaltenborn.

My grandmother could see right through Adolph Hitler. She had not read *Mein Kampf,* but she knew. She was not in the least reassured when Chamberlain came back from Munich talking about "peace in our time." She wasn't all that sure about America, either. My family believed very strongly in civil rights for blacks, not only because it was the right thing to do but because we felt that we Jews were next. By this time my father, also an immigrant, had become successful in business. He brought over some Jewish relatives from Germany and helped others to go to Israel. But other relatives chose to stay in Germany. My grandmother and I couldn't understand that; it was so clear to us what was going to happen.

I had a recurrent daydream at that time. In it, a group of dinosaurs sat around talking about the impending ice age. Soon all their escape routes to the south would be cut off. If they didn't move soon, they would freeze to death. But they kept on talking. I always stopped the daydream before the last dinosaur had frozen.

This phenomenon of procrastination, particularly under group influence, has always fascinated me. Sometimes it seems as if we don't see what is going on; other times it seems we see what is happening but don't act on it—as if there were some kind of prohibition on individual action, as if some kind of direction from the group were needed.

Returning now to the parable of Joseph that began this essay, it follows the classic pattern of predicting doom if we do not alter our ways. Today there are many predictions of doom. Intermittent warfare has existed throughout the world, and with it the constant threat of escalation to World War III, a nuclear holocaust. In perhaps less dramatic areas, we are also aware of the ever-increasing pollution of our air, water, and natural scenery. Our teeming, problem-ridden cities and their antiquated educational systems cry out for reform yet remain resistant to change. Every day the media frighten us with stories of crime, violence, and drug abuse. Our young people regard our form of government as meaningless, aware that an undeclared war raged on for too many bitter years. Many of them see this country as a consuming machine, with an increasingly voracious appetite that responds to advertisements of products and services for which we have no real need. There is the threat of worldwide inflation, of terrorists obtaining atomic weapons, and of some kind of irreversible ecological catastrophe.

Until quite recently, I shared this sense of disillusionment. Perhaps I was overly influenced by some of my favorite authors, such as Rachel Carson, Paul Ehrlich, Aldous Huxley, and George Orwell. They painted pictures of a future marked by pollution, population explosion, and a "big brother" totalitarian state with little variety, privacy, or freedom. I was overwhelmed by the complexity of the situations and problems they presented. It seemed that one would have to study for a lifetime to become an expert and to understand even a single problem like inflation, nuclear disarmament, food supply, international trade, or energy needs. I began to distrust the experts. They disagreed among themselves. Furthermore, all these problems were interrelated and there was no overall expert. Gradually I abandoned my search for an expert and turned to myself for a fresh look at these problems

Could an argument be made that these times are no more perilous than in times past? Perhaps we are only more aware of potential disasters and have no readily available succor such as a religion or national purpose. Perhaps our discomfort comes more from the widespread isolation and alienation of modern life than from a realistic appraisal of the dangers ahead. Maybe we are inundated by daily news and have lost a sense of historical perspective. Maybe our pessimism comes from unrealistic impatience to make things better. Perhaps we are discouraged because we feel impotent to do very much and feel that America and ourselves are no longer the center of action. Our discomfort may be more impatience than pessimism.

As I tried to identify what I have called underlying trends, several phenomena began to emerge:

1. The risk of war between major powers diminishes each year and may shortly become extremely unlikely. We have not yet afforded ourselves the **comfort** of the recognition of this probability. It is likely that we will begin to in the next few years—and that this recognition will have far-reaching implications.

2. Our society shows signs of evolving toward fulfillment of real democracy in the broad sense of acceptance of deviancy, of appreciation of differences, along with guaranteed minimum standards of education and health. I am referring here particularly to the various liberation movements which are changing our perceptions so that we now have many models of beauty—whatever a person's color, religion, sex, age, and life style. We have not afforded ourselves the **joy** that there is in this evolution that emphasizes the importance of individual dignity. Similar phenomena seem to be occurring in all the developed countries of the West.

3. There is increasing concern about ecology and further expansion of the industrial state with attendant problems of pollution. The possibility of exhaustion of natural resources, and a potential ecological disaster are forcing a reassessment of our previously unquestioned goals.

4. There is beginning attention to developments in other parts of the world, particularly Communist China, that might have great potential as a model for underdeveloped countries. Recent reports indicate great progress there, and one quarter of the world's population now seems able to provide for itself materially and with apparent cohesion and purpose.

5. There is beginning awareness of the potential for rapid change in basic attitudes and values in society by modern means of communication. Television, particularly, can dis-

seminate information even to those who cannot read or write, and can effectively cross language barriers by emphasizing similarities among people and also emphasizing an appreciation of their differentnesses.

So I have done an about-face; I have begun to see hope for solutions to the problems that seemed overwhelming only a short time ago. An appropriate analogy is the children's game, "Pick-up-Sticks." The sticks are thrown out, often in a pile that looks hopelessly entangled at first glance. The aim of the game is to remove each stick without moving any of the others. Children become very adept at applying pressure on the end of a key stick in just the right amount and direction, and thus extricating it. Of course, with the removal of each successive stick, the solution to the problem becomes increasingly simple. Analogously, with respect to the problems of the world, once the key "pick-up-stick" of fear of war between major powers is removed, the whole situation is simplified. Our society's evolutionary trend toward real democracy will become more manifest. Technological change can be seen as providing solutions rather than merely creating overwhelming new problems. In fact, it seems likely to me that we have entered an era in the history of man when very real progress will be made in the age-old problems of war, starvation, ghettos, persecution, economic depression, and even such major health problems as cancer. We dare to hope.

The Pick-Up-Stick of War

1

My grandmother died just as World War II came to a close. I wish she were alive today so that I could talk to her about the many changes that have taken place since her death.

Her attention would turn immediately, I am sure, to the ongoing Israeli-Arab situation. She would be excited about the establishment of an Israeli state, but fearful that it would be overrun and the Jews would lose their homeland. The threats of Arab leaders to drive the Jews into the sea would seem very familiar to her. I think she would be afraid that a war between Israel and Syria or Egypt could lead to World War III, as the events at Sarajevo led to World War I. Grandmother would be concerned that the possibility of a return of the 1974 oil embargo would bring about a worldwide economic inflation and recession. And she would look for another Hitler or Mussolini in the major countries. She would see that the leaders of Russia and China certainly don't seem like Hitlers; but she would point out that we really don't know very much about them or their successors.

Yet I think that after she had a chance to fully analyze the developments, Grandmother would gradually become optimistic. She would recognize that the old methods of international relations are no longer practiced; that the old expansionist tactics are no longer used on a global scale.

Nearly every country on the face of the globe is now vitally concerned with birth control. This is certainly a far cry from the way things were when I was young. Then we believed that sheer numbers were significant. I can remember counting the population of the Axis and of the Allies, and being worried about the "yellow hordes." Today all developed countries have seen the immense growth of their cities and the development of the giant bureaucracies necessary for mail delivery, sewage disposal, communication, transportation, power supply, housing, health, and education. And they have seen the headaches attendant upon these developments. It seems to me that the leaders of these countries no longer think they have the answer to everything for everyone. Rather, it makes more sense to assume that Russia, China, the United States, France, England, and Japan want to work out their own solutions to their problems— each country doing so in terms of its own history, geography, and national resources.

My grandmother would be impressed by the failure of any major power to intervene militarily in the Middle East in response to the oil embargo. She would understand that this was in part due to the deterrent power of nuclear weapons. I would tell her about President Kennedy's dilemma during the missile crisis in 1962. At that time he thought there was a three-to-one chance of war, and he therefore wanted to warn his wife Jackie to leave New York City. Whether or not to warn her presented a real moral problem for him, which he finally resolved by not urging Jackie to leave. The point I am making here is that the leaders of each country and their families are just as likely to be endangered in an all-out war as is anyone else. In this sense, the atom bomb is a great leveller (pun intended). No longer can a general sit behind a desk and with perfect equanimity "send the boys out to fight." And the generals and their commanders-in-chief know it. Hitler almost succeeded in conquering Europe without Germany even being bombed. That day has passed.

At the end of his life, Einstein said that if he had it to do over again, he would prefer to be a plumber. He said this at a moment when he regretted his participation in the invention of the atom bomb that destroyed Hiroshima and Nagasaki. I disagree with him. I think that history will show that the invention of the atom bomb was a significant contribution to the achievement of peace among modern nations, paradoxical as that may seem. Man has used this ultimate weapon; the stakes are clear. With little to win and everything to lose in a nuclear war, who wants to gamble?

Turning her attention to another area, my grandmother would be impressed with the European Economic Community (EEC), or Common Market. She would be astonished to see those ancient enemies Germany and France bound together economically in the Common Market and heavily associated militarily as well. She probably would not be able to understand our tendency to take the growth of the Common Market for granted. To her, its growth (from the original six countries— France, Germany, Italy, the Netherlands, Belgium, and Luxembourg—to include also the United Kingdom, Eire, and Denmark) would be anything but predictable. I am sure this would look to her like the near-realization of an old dream: the United States of Europe. Yet in many ways the current situation is better than that dream, for each member country in the Common Market has maintained its independence, national culture, and heritage. The EEC is certainly not perfect, and its monetary stability is more a plan than a reality. Yet it does present a model of how modern states can cooperate.

The EEC hopes to have a common unit of EEC currency by 1980. In addition, America and Japan feel a close military and economic allegiance to the British Commonwealth and, via this, to the Common Market. Because of this allegiance, both countries have already established economic conditions that allow control of currency and further unite the economies of all countries. To be sure, it hasn't all been worked out yet. Inflation is still a matter of great concern to all nations and much bickering among them still occurs. Yet when viewed historically, the present situation gives great cause for hope.

My grandmother and I would probably agree that historians may well see the formation of the Common Market as a turning point in the evolution of society. And the forerunner of it was the Marshall Plan, with its great expenditures of monies overseas, which helped in the economic rebuilding of European countries. We should feel proud of our role in that development, as well as of our current strong support for the Common Market. The stability of the world today depends to a large extent on a prosperous, peaceful Germany and Japan. And although I can't quite imagine my grandmother running out and buying a German-made car, I think she would be pleased by Germany and Japan and by our relations with them today.

My grandmother's mind would probably be "boggled" by international trade today. It is a far cry from the Marco Polo kind of expedition she was acquainted with, where caravans carried goods from one country to another. She would see that today's trade among countries with intertwining and interlocking corporations is so complex that it is difficult even to define the basic economic unit. Their degree of complexity is exemplified by International Telephone and Telegraph, not the largest by any means; its world sales of 7.3 billion dollars exceeds the gross national product of Portugal or Chile. Corporations like this one are owned by shareholders who are citizens of many different countries. Thus economic ties not only cross international boundaries, but they recross them again and again in an ever-growing network.

As a result of expanded trade relations, by the end of 1973 the United States was Russia's largest trading partner. In that year alone, the U.S. exported 1.3 billion dollars' worth of goods to the U.S.S.R. Companies such as Occidental Petroleum, Control Data, and Pepsi Cola have signed or are exploring long-range agreements with the Soviet Union—agreements that involve billions of dollars. This trend is rapidly accelerating. The fact that these gigantic investments would be wiped out in the event of nuclear holocaust has to give many sobering second thoughts to individuals in power who might still have occasional thoughts about war.

It seems that as the economies of countries become entwined, economic and political units expand to worldwide dimensions. The European Coal and Steel Community was founded on this basis. Germany, France, Italy, Belgium, Luxembourg, and the Netherlands each put their coal and steel industries under a cooperative controlling organization so that no one country would have the power to wage a war in Europe. The success of this organization is what made the Common Market possible. The ultimate result of such cooperative activity could be a worldwide amalgam of capitalism, socialism, and communism, with economies and resources so integrated and jointly controlled that the possibility of world war becomes remote indeed.

I realize that I have dealt with a truly massive and complex topic in a highly simplified and general manner. My point is simply this: The combination of capacity for nuclear war in all the major powers and the economic ties that supercede geographical and political boundaries has greatly diminished the probability of global war. Small wars will continue, no doubt, such as in Cyprus between Turkey and Greece, and particularly in the underdeveloped countries. The hope is that when the great powers have achieved real understanding, they will be more effective in working out alternatives to war for the smaller countries.

In the next chapter I want to turn to the evolution of society and its relationship to the pick-up-sticks of racism, sexism, divorce, religious prejudice, and related domestic ills.

Domestic Trends 2

The trends underway on the domestic scene would probably please my grandmother as much as the international developments just described. Yet at her first glance the scene would not look very different from what it was at the time of her death. The major social institutions—particularly schools, churches, and jobs—are largely unchanged. The automobile remains the chief means of transportation. The jet airplane would be new to her, but it would not surprise her. Television has become an institution; but, again, this wouldn't surprise her, as TV is merely an extension of the radio, movies, and even home movies which were common in her day. The telephone was the chief means of communication then, as it is now. Little change has occurred in the postal service—in fact, probably not enough change! The whole space program would, of course, be new to her and she would be excited about our having sent men to the moon. She probably would have anticipated the space age, since she was familiar with science fiction and knew that rockets and missiles were used at the end of World War II. The political parties are the same. Newspapers have the same formats. Financial news—whether stocks have gone up or down —is reported now as it was then; and people still look to the gross national product as an indicator of whether or not our country is "getting ahead." Where significant changes *have* taken place is in the realm of interpersonal relations—how people feel about themselves and relate to others.

Let's begin by considering the case of black people. When my grandmother died, there were no "blacks" in St. Louis; nor were there "blacks" in the early 1950s when my wife and I joined CORE—the Committee On Racial Equality. We picketed to open the downtown restaurants and hotels to Negroes. We were careful not to use the term *colored*. *Black* and all it now connotes were yet to come. In those days, the membership of CORE was predominantly white, middle-class, and Jewish. My grandmother might have imagined legislation that prohibited discrimination, enforced desegregation of schools and public facilities, and increased employment opportunities. What she could not have imagined was the "black is beautiful" movement. She would be fascinated by how it came about. I would fill her in on the civil rights marches in Selma, Alabama; the assassination of Martin Luther King, Jr.; the riots in Watts and other cities in the late 1960s; and the then-prevalent expectation of increased violence, if not revolution. I would have to tell her that no one I knew five years ago predicted that Bobby Seale would run for the office of mayor of Oakland, California. I would tell her about the prominent positions blacks enjoy in sports today, and about the changed image of the black as represented on television. Grandmother would want to know why more people aren't aware of these changes and more excited by them. In her time, it seemed that there was just one model of beauty—the white, young, middle-class, Anglo-Saxon. She would see that now there are many standards by which people judge physical beauty, and there are models of beauty with every possible skin color.

My grandmother would be pleased that Jack Kennedy, a Catholic, had been elected president, and that there is relatively little prejudice against Jews and other religions today. Her astonishment and pleasure would continue as I pointed out other important aspects of contemporary life. In her day, divorce was viewed as failure, and a blight was cast on the divorced person that could affect his entire life. The words *creative divorce*, gaining in acceptance today, would have cancelled one another out in her time. She would be surprised, too, by our changed attitudes toward sex; acceptance of premarital sex; sex education in public schools; open discussion on venereal disease, contraception, and abortion; and increasing acceptance of homosexuality as an alternate model of sexual behavior. It would be hard for her to believe that marriage is not necessarily an automatic goal for young people these days. However, she would be both surprised and pleased by the responsibility young people show in limiting the size of their families when they do marry. The women's liberation movement would startle Grandmother, but after grasping its implications, she would be very excited by the number of people whose lives have been and will be significantly bettered by this movement. I know she would be pleased about the changed attitude toward aging and the fact that we seem to be moving away from an exclusively youth-oriented culture. Models of beauty for different ages are beginning to emerge, just as they have emerged for different skin colors. My grandmother would again be startled by our changed attitude toward authority figures (physicians, educators, politicians, and priests are no longer placed on unchallenged pedestals); but once she understood it, she would approve.

My grandmother would want to know how all these changes occurred so fast, and I could give her no easy answer. In a later chapter I will discuss my thoughts on the important role of television in speeding up this process. But primarily I would have to tell Grandmother that the evolution came through struggle—usually against great odds, in the face of which committed people fought on because they felt they had to. They knew they were right, but they also knew there was no guarantee of success. The Loyalists lost in Spain; generations of blacks were subjugated in the American South and the cities. I would have to tell my grandmother that often change was forced on us at great cost to all concerned. For example, our involvement and failure to win in Vietnam taught us a great deal. It was not the peace movement that stopped the war; what finally brought us to our senses was the determination of the Viet Cong and the North Vietnamese to fight on indefinitely at whatever sacrifice. For our progress in race relations, we are indebted to Martin Luther King and countless unknown martyrs. But such progress probably could not have taken place without major riots in Watts and Trenton, and the daily smaller incidents of violence in most cities that raised the consciousness of the minorities. We learned from our mistakes. And it is important to know that sometimes we just "lucked out."

The total picture would suggest to my grandmother a very important, escalating trend. I think she would agree that in a very real sense this trend is a continuation or fulfillment of the picture of America she had when she first came here as an immigrant. America was then the "land of opportunity," which meant that people had a chance to make a living, to practice their religious beliefs, and to have political freedom. I think she would be delighted that this concept of opportunity is now extended so that people are defining the kind of life style they want and how they will relate to one another. Grandmother would be pleased that the system has been sufficiently flexible to allow these major changes to come about. She would understand immediately that it is perfectly all right—in fact, commendable—to feel good about yourself, whatever your skin color, marital state, sexual preference, or religion. Thirty million blacks, other millions of Chicanos and native Americans, one hundred million women, countless millions of divorced people, and still more millions of homosexuals now can begin to feel worthwhile and accepted by the majority in spite of—or perhaps even because of—their differentness.

Knowing my grandmother, I am sure that at this point she would narrow her eyes and ask at whose expense these vast social changes were made. She'd be delighted to learn that no one was really hurt in the process—although many feared they would be. After all, Caucasian beauty is not diminished because there are other models for beauty as well.

I think Grandmother would be particularly pleased by the scope of these social developments, knowing full well the degree of suspicion and resistance we all tend to display toward change of any kind. The fact that even greater advances lay ahead would please her all the more. "If women are freeing themselves from their stereotyped role, why can't men free themselves too?" she might ask. This question would reflect her awareness that men are stuck in limiting roles that keep them from getting in touch with their emotions and particularly from expressing tenderness and intimacy. My guess is that Grandmother would see these changes not as a strictly American product, but rather in a worldwide perspective. She would see them as part of a development which started many centuries ago when kings lost their unique places and democracy emerged as a political system. She would recall that it took a long time for children to get out of the mines, women to get the vote, and labor to become organized. Once these changes occurred, however, an irrevocable step had been taken and there could be no going back. My grandmother would be able to see that these changes did not take place because of a particular theology, political system, or even nationality but through a natural evolution.

Overall, I think what might puzzle my grandmother the most is why we apparently haven't allowed ourselves the natural sense of pride and pleasure in the fact that these social advances have taken place during our lifetime. I could tell her that this is probably because we are too close to the changes to see them clearly. Or perhaps the intensity of the struggle blinds us to the significance of the results. In any event, it is important for us to be aware of the progress that has been made, for this awareness can give us increased confidence, strength, and patience.

There will always be those among us who are apprehensive about the results of great changes. Many people fear some kind of retaliation. We saw Nazi Germany follow the Weimar Republic. We saw Allende overthrown in Chile. Open enmity now exists between people of different races in the cities. Once the white majority felt patronizing condescension toward and superiority over the minorities; now they feel fear and respect, which is much less comfortable. The black man is vastly more aware of his resentment and anger, but now he has a sense of the exhilaration of power. Still, he doesn't know what the attitude of the white man really is when they encounter each other. Of course, this is often different where blacks and whites live together in an intimate situation such as military service, college, or marriage. But considering the total picture, most of us realize that even though the race situation is uncomfortable today, we are on the right track.

My final point is this: It is perhaps all too typical of our society that great attention is paid to our gross national product—an index of business activity with important correlates to unemployment figures. What I would like to see is a similar index for national "people dignity." Perhaps if we had such an index for measuring dignity, we would be more aware of the significance of the changes I have described.

Violence and Human Nature 3

The idea that we are living in a unique time in the evolution of society, a time when warfare may become largely outmoded in this century, always meets with great resistance. People point out that man is capable of a kind of violence unknown elsewhere in nature; that man is virtually the only species that destroys his own kind in mass killings. The general assumption is that this aggressiveness is part of human nature. This brings us to the old dispute over whether man is inherently aggressive, with destructiveness in his genes, or whether aggression is acquired behavior. Conrad Lorenz points to a territorial instinct, genetically controlled. Other writers, such as B.F. Skinner, maintain that man is conditioned to aggressiveness by his environment and by social influences. The Bible postulates original sin. Freud and others have spoken of a death instinct in the unconscious. In his recent book *The Anatomy of Human Destructiveness,* Eric Fromm reaches the conclusion that man is *not* genetically aggressive. He has counted up the major battles throughout history as follows: 238 battles in the 17th century, 631 battles in the 18th century, 651 in the 19th, and 892 in the 20th up to 1940. Since then the number has increased appreciably, but Fromm argues that this increase is not due to man's inherited characteristics as an aggressor but rather to an acquired aggressiveness supported by a new technology.

Most writers begin with the assumption that violence is everywhere. In addition to wars, they point to the assassinations of Jack and Robert Kennedy and Martin Luther King; the danger of muggings in most cities; the senseless killings by a man gone berserk that fill the newspapers from time to time; the occasional occult or "clan" killings; the bombings of a political nature that were prevalent a few years ago; and more recently the much-publicized Zebra and SLA murders in California. I disagree with the initial assumption of these writers. As a matter of fact, I am struck by the relative infrequency of aggression. I haven't seen a good fight in twenty years. I know they happen; but somehow whether it's in a bar, at a ball game, in a psychiatric clinic, in a juvenile hall, or wherever I find myself, I always miss the fight. I've come to the conclusion that there is a great deal more talk about fighting than there is actual fighting. There may be as many as 50,000 people at a given sporting event—many consuming goodly amounts of alcohol and feeling great disappointment or anger when their favorite team loses or is ridiculed. I wonder just how infrequent outbreaks of fighting under such charged circumstances will have to become before we will take note of it!

Fights on city streets, in spite of the very crowded conditions usually present, are really very infrequent, even on New Year's Eve. In suburban grade schools, junior highs, and high schools, fighting is also rare—although when it does occur, it attracts much attention. Youth gang wars in the slums capture the headlines, but do they represent the totality of life in the ghetto? It seems to me that the evidence points to a view opposite to that held by most commentators on our culture. When you think of the size of this country—over 200 million people, most of them living in crowded cities under conditions of great tension and frustration—it is striking how little fighting there is. This is especially remarkable when you consider our high level of consumption of alcohol, amphetamines, marijuana, psychedelics, barbiturates, and other drugs. I realize that only a small percentage of crimes are actually reported. Nevertheless I am even more impressed with the relative absence of violence in the face of the so-called normal tensions of life—conflicts between boss and employee, husband and wife, parents and offspring, and neighbors.

However we look at it, life gets pretty difficult for all of us at one time or another. My own guess is that the majority of our population have considered suicide at some time in their lives. As a psychiatrist, I know how many chronically disturbed people in our society have received or are now receiving psychiatric treatment. An even greater number of equally disturbed people have never sought treatment. With the ready availability of guns and other weapons, it is very easy today for one of these unhappy people to kill a neighbor or public figure. Remember George Metesky, the one-time "mad bomber"? For sixteen years in the 40s and 50s, he terrorized New York City by setting off explosives in theaters, terminals, libraries, and offices. In all, thirty-seven explosions were traced to Metesky. He was eventually arrested; and, when psychiatrists ruled him insane, he was sent to the Manhattan State Hospital for the Criminally Insane. Thus we had one man terrorizing a city of eight million people, with the attendant publicity creating the impression that mad bombers were everywhere. I think this is almost always what happens. When single instances of violence occur, we give them so much publicity that we begin to think that most if not all people are capable of such violence—possibly even including ourselves. To repeat, in view of the misery of so many people's lives and the frustration and anger they feel, I am impressed not by the existence of some violence but rather by its relative infrequency.

I certainly do not dispute the chronic occurence of muggings and other kinds of criminal violence. But is this evidence of innate or irreversibly acquired aggression? I think not. Mugging is a way of life—a vocation, a livelihood—for the mugger. Such behavior is taught and accepted by his peer group and reinforced by reward. Such action is very similar to the pickpocketing that Dickens' Fagan taught to Oliver Twist. And is war an indication of innate or irreversibly acquired aggression? To begin with, let's consider whether or not group behavior on such a large scale tells us anything about the individual. During World War II it was said that for every man in the front lines, there were nine men behind the lines. It seems to me that the typical World War II soldier simply did his job. Whether the circumstances required that he clean the latrine, peel potatoes, march around the post, or kill the enemy, he did his job. In this way the soldier was very much like the mugger. This was his way of life. Killing was seldom if ever done for pleasure. When unnecessary killing did occur, it was usually the result of fear, boredom, or frustration.

Although I might have trouble convincing my grandmother of the truth of my opinion, I want to state here what I feel is a very obvious, yet often overlooked, explanation of war: Given the framework of participant countries and the evolutionary state of society at a given time, almost all wars make sense. We tend to forget that warfare generally is very profitable for the victor. We defeated the American Indians and took over this continent. We defeated Spain and obtained colonies. Communist China drove out Nationalist China. India defeated Pakistan and liberated Bangladesh. Israel preserved her homeland by defeating the Arabs in two wars. Victors in warfare consider themselves to be chosen people and thus entitled to the territory or population in dispute. In a religious or political war, the conqueror feels that his religion or political belief is vindicated by his victory, and thus he feels little or no guilt over conquering the "enemy." In the winner's mind, the victory itself is sufficient evidence of a superior moral position. I see no point in calling such adaptive and rewarding behavior a sign of innate or irreversibly acquired aggression. We have seen that it has taken time for other changes to take place. It makes sense to me that it also is taking time for war to become outmoded.

Let's look for a moment at a man's use of the automobile. Nearly 40,000 people are killed in automobile crashes every year. Does this indicate something about human nature? Does the fact that smoking continues in spite of evidence that cigarettes cause cancer tell us something about human nature? I think not. These are acquired behaviors that make very good sense when one looks at the context in which they were learned. The automobile is a fascinating gadget. We take it for granted, but it is amazing that almost every adult can learn to master such a powerful mechanism and can zip around at sixty to eighty miles per hour. It also makes sense that the use of the automobile is overdone, particularly since automotive pollution is a relatively recent concern. If smoking is enjoyable, it again makes sense that people will continue to smoke regardless of the known risk of cancer. In both these cases, an acquired, pleasurable habit becomes part of our way of life and is very difficult for us to change. However, we *do* use safety belts, set more sensible speed limits and more stringent requirements for drivers' licenses and insurance, and take steps to reduce smog from exhaust fumes. Ralph Nader is a relatively new but powerful "institution." Similarly, attempts *are* being made to help people stop smoking, and research in this area will continue. The point is that underneath all of this is a growing trend toward appreciation and preservation of life—and this trend is what makes the long-range forecast favorable.

In his perceptive book *The Crime of Punishment,* Dr Karl Menninger concludes that our failure to modify our penal system indicates that in some way society needs this penal system.

Since we like to read about crime, arrests, trials, and punishments, we must in this way be vicariously fulfilling some repressed need. I think it is unnecessary, however, to postulate such a need in society or in the individual. I believe that, given the state of evolution of our society, our penal system as bad as it is in many respects correlates well with the total picture of society. In the past our energies have gone toward winning wars and industrializing the nation. Only lately have we turned toward creating real equality among citizens by means of, for example, the "black is beautiful" and women's liberation movements. It seems to me that changes in the penal system will occur only after our more basic needs are met. It is sensible for us to first put our energies into rejuvenating the cities and other social problems. Unfortunately, books such as Menninger's, Lorenz's, and Fromm's leave us with the feeling that, either because of inherited or acquired characteristics, change in our society will be very, very slow if not altogether impossible. My argument is exactly the opposite.

Catastrophic Expectations 4

In 1968 a book entitled *Population Bomb* scared the daylights out of a lot of people. Paul Ehrlich, Professor of Biology and Director of Graduate study of the Department of Biological Sciences, Stanford University, asserted that medical advances have upset the natural balance which occurs between the birth rate and the death rate and that we are presently offered the choice of *population control or a race to oblivion* (the subtitle of Ehrlich's book). At one time there was a very high mortality rate among the young of underdeveloped countries. The introduction of DDT in 1947 and progress in controlling such diseases as malaria, yellow fever, smallpox, and cholera resulted in a great decrease in the death rate in most of these countries. Such medical advances as discovery of antibiotics and blood transfusions have increased women's reproductive years and have generally increased life expectancies all over the world. Ehrlich's position is that all of these facts will inevitably lead to war, famine, pestilence, and eventual destruction of both developed and underdeveloped countries.

The second chapter of Ehrlich's book, entitled "The Ends of the Road," consists of a series of scenarios in which these kinds of disasters occur as mankind slips into the "famine decade." Scenario One begins in 1972 with catastrophic floods in China, breakdowns in communications, massive famines, and riots in China, India, and Brazil. China blames the United States for political intervention in Canada's decisions not to sell more wheat to China; Russia also wants Canada's dwindling wheat reserves; war develops between China and the U.S. in Southeast Asia. Finally, the United States uses nuclear bombs against China, and China succeeds in delivering five dirty thermonuclear devices that cause the death of 100 million Americans due to fallout.

Well, the year 1972 has come and gone without these events actually occurring, and yet the fear remains. Dr. Ehrlich's book and others of its genre have had an unexpected effect on many people. Castigating the readers, these books point out that America comprises only 15% of the world's population but uses 70% of its natural resources. Instead of making people want to mobilize for action, these books leave many readers depressed and bewildered. We are led to believe that the invention and dissemination of antibiotics was irresponsible. And further, it is implied that because we are Americans and enjoy a high standard of living, we are responsible for the deaths of others.

The world has changed since Dr. Ehrlich wrote his book. China has been able to feed itself and conduct a highly successful program of birth control, apparently approaching a stable population. One hears conflicting reports about India—apparently gains in food production have been offset by the population increase there. The situation has been further complicated by the increased cost of oil for underdeveloped countries such as India, and this may impede agricultural progress. I am not a demographer or an expert on population statistics, but I do not regret the invention and use of DDT, antibiotics, blood transfusions, and the like. I know they have played an important role in increasing the population of the world, particularly in the underdeveloped countries. But these developments are all part of the increased scientific knowledge which has also given us very promising means of contraception; and has resulted in modern communications that can spread information of these means and thus ultimately help to stabilize population.

China's success with its population problem should be studied by the underdeveloped countries, as it suggests a way that may be practical for them to emulate. Somehow the Chinese were able to mobilize their country and, without great emphasis on modern means of contraception or abortion, have been able to control their population increase. In any event, Ehrlich's analogy of population explosion to nuclear holocaust seems inappropriate to me. There has been widespread malnutrition in the underdeveloped countries for centuries. If it increases, it will be tragic; but mass starvation will not occur all at once like a holocaust. And it would certainly be preceded by gradual depletion of the resources of the underdeveloped countries, which would render them militarily weak and would decrease—not increase—the likelihood of their instigating a global war.

America has reduced its own birth rate and may now be more successful in persuading other countries of the necessity to do the same. A major point of this essay is that "human nature" is much more flexible than we have believed. The general attitude was that we could go to the moon and build bridges and dams but that to change basic attitudes was impossible. Events have proved otherwise.

Huxley's *Brave New World* and Orwell's *1984* are two other books that have influenced many Americans. They portray a "big brother" kind of state in which the average citizen enjoys little privacy because his life is controlled by automation and electronic surveillance. This is a real threat and we are indebted to the authors of these books not only for providing us with exciting fiction, but also for pointing up a real potential danger. However, I think many of us will be frightened by *1984* long after the actual year has come and gone, just as has been the case with Dr. Ehrlich's dire predictions. Once a fear has been implanted, it is very hard to dislodge.

Probably most Americans were fascinated by the Watergate hearings. Some see the hearings as an indication that 1984 is coming faster than predicted. I disagree. What better example of exciting education could there be than a real-life drama like this available in one's own living room every day? We were witnesses to the misuse of the technology of microfilm and magnetic tape and electronic surveillance. However, I do not believe that it follows logically that we will allow such misuses to happen indiscriminately. I think it is more likely that electronic technology will be used to prevent encroachment on our civil liberties. Legislation is now being considered that would regulate the use of money and television time for political campaigns. The very technology that could enslave us can also be used to regulate and supervise government agencies, large corporations, and political parties that might encroach on our liberties.

Again we have the paradox. Instead of feeling good about our awareness of potential problems and our abilities to deal with them, we remain frightened and insecure and all too willing to see ourselves as progressing steadily toward our doom. We seem to take a potential danger, project it into the future as fact, and enlarge it logarithmically. We simply do not take into account that if we don't want this projected future to happen, we can develop ways to achieve a different kind of future.

The Cities

5

I recently returned from a trip to New York City with my seventeen-year-old son Dan. It was a business trip for me and a chance for Dan to look over some eastern colleges for next year. He was brought up in a suburban part of Palo Alto, California, and—like many of his friends—was curious about life in the East. He had heard stories from both my wife and me about "the good old days" in Greenwich Village and Boston, where each of us had lived before we married and during my psychiatric residency. Dan had also heard his share of stories about violence in the eastern cities in recent years. A good friend of his had worked in New York City during the previous summer. One lunch period, this gregarious, innocent California youth walked through Harlem and was mugged after only three blocks.

Dan and I had lunch with a business associate of mine, a woman who lives in New York. After she and I had taken care of business, I asked what it was like to live in New York City. I hoped that her answer would help Dan to become more familiar with life there and to feel less apprehensive. It didn't go that way. My associate described how her husband, an artist, had his apartment broken into while he was working there, and how he was robbed by the two drug addicts who broke in. One of the addicts wanted to kill him for no apparent reason, but compromised and "only" stabbed him twice. One such story followed another, culminating in Dan's asking how people lived under such a constant threat of violence. My associate then described the fears of her colleagues and their mass exodus to the suburbs at night, adding that they were very concerned lest this solution become impossible in the event of gas rationing. I don't know to what extent the fears of these people are based on fact or fiction; but it is a fact that fear is pervasive in New York —greater in certain areas, greater at night, but present at some level at all times. The New Yorkers I talked to seemed to think it was getting worse, with the middle class fleeing to the suburbs and taking with them the tax base on which the schools and other public facilities depend.

This brings us to the next pick-up-stick—the plight of the cities today. What is the long-term trend for the cities?

My grandmother might approach this subject from a historical point of view, looking for underlying trends. Population shifts stand out from this perspective. In the first few decades of this century, a million immigrants came here each year from Europe and were assimilated in the cities. Like my grandmother and my father, these people needed to learn a new language, new ways, and often a new trade. At that time, 70% of the population of the U.S. lived in rural areas. Now the farm population is only 7% of our total population. This century has seen a great increase in black population, and increasingly in the last three or four decades, blacks have moved from the rural South to northern cities. A big influx of population from Puerto Rico, the Phillipines, and Mexico has occurred. In a sense these large population shifts are over and done with now. Less disruptive shifts are occurrring—shifts in which both the urban and rural populations are moving to the suburbs and small towns. Immigration from foreign countries has been virtually cut off, and the farm population can hardly decrease further. These vast migrations of populations are, however, only part of the story. It is important to take a look at what else has been going on in America during the last sixty years.

For decades we have talked about revitalizing the cities, but our energies have gone elsewhere. Vast industrialization of the whole country has taken place, with sudden spurts in World Wars I and II and the Korean war. This again caused population shifts. For the past thirty years, our country has been virtually in a continual state of war, with vast resources going into armaments and the space program. Our attention has gone to providing automobiles, radios, television sets, and refrigerators— all kinds of appliances and provisions for the so-called good life —to the vast middle class. Until recently no one challenged the idea that such material aids were essential for personal fulfillment.

So, should we be discouraged about the present plight of the cities? I think that, under the circumstances I have just described, the situation is just about as good as we can expect. I think if we look at the picture a little closer, we will see that necessary, very difficult, first steps have been taken. Countless well-intentioned attempts to rejuvenate the "inner city" have been made in many U.S. cities throughout the past several decades.

The Pruitt-Igoe Housing Development in St. Louis comes to mind. It was designed for blacks by whites who were doing their best to save money in order to build more housing units. One example of the kind of cost-cutting they did is having elevators stop at every other floor. Although the bu'ldings in the development were called "apartment houses," they looked like concrete, vertical barracks. Naturally, blacks resented this and nearly every other aspect of the development. In retrospect it is easy to see why. Eventually this project was condemned and torn down. If such a housing development were to be designed today, it would probably be done with input from the people who were going to live there and were aware of the needs they as tenants would have. We learn from mistakes. They are our best teachers.

In mid-1973 the *Christian Science Monitor* ran a series of four articles on the "Revival of the Neighborhood." Dr. Norman E. Long, a St. Louis urbanologist, was quoted as saying, "People are beginning to discover the values of community. Neighborhoods in which people care about their kids, their houses, and each other make the difference in a city between delinquency, blight, and decay and the vitality of processes of renewal that make an aging city an attractive place to live."

The *Monitor* contacted many experts for its series and reported a "surge of grass-roots activity across America. . . . There seems little doubt that a renaissance in neighborhoods is taking place. . . . Most major cities have seen an explosion of neighborhood groups. Chicago, for example, has more than 500 community associations, home-improvement groups, block clubs and single purpose, citizen-action organizations. Some 42 of the neighborhood organizations have an office and full time staff personnel—and many of the roots go back 10, 20, 40 years. New York City has more than 5,000 block associations. In San Francisco more than 75 neighborhood groups are saving Victorian houses, keeping pinball machines away, and fighting other battles. Sometimes neighborhoods can be revived by federal programs such as urban renewal or model cities. Officials at the Housing and Urban Development Department (HUD) in Washington point to New

Haven, Conn., Fresno, California, and Pittsburg as examples of good urban renewal in inner city areas. Citing a federal flow of dollars of more than $1.4 billion a year into neighborhoods, HUD officials also say that the much-criticized "bulldozer" approach to slums is being phased out in favor of rehabilitating existing older communities. Instead of tearing down old buildings, the officials say, the policy is now to provide inexpensive loans to property owners for refurbishing. In some cases, grants of up to $3,000 are made to those who can't afford a loan. Future federal aid would come in the form of revenue-sharing grants to cities and states, under legislation now pending in Congress."

My grandmother and I never discussed cities, but I am sure she would be the first to recognize that before any significant change can take place in the rejuvenation of the cities, we have to change our motivation and attitudes. The desire to do good for others is simply not enough. The potency of "black is beautiful" with all it involves must precede real change. We must also have the conviction of ultimate success. We should acknowledge that rejuvenation of the cities has a top priority, and that the resources that went to industrialize our country and fight wars should be made increasingly available for this undertaking. Widespread concern about the plight of the cities, ecology, and pollution of our environment are relatively new. We must realize that it takes time for such concern to grow, particularly at the beginning.

For example, in 1966 the Mount Sinai Hospital in Cleveland faced a decision that required much soul-searching. The hospital was located in downtown Cleveland, in a changing neighborhood; and it needed expansion and modernization. The outpatient clinic had traditionally served a predominantly white clientele but then the hospital found itself a part of a black neighborhood, with a predominantly minority clientele. Vandalism and other crime had become very significant problems. Mt. Sinai was a private institution and was in no way obliged to remain in downtown Cleveland. An important segment of the board of directors recommended moving to the suburbs as other private hospitals were doing. To stay in its present location would require a great expenditure of money for security of both personnel and property. The board eventually made the decision to stay, feeling a moral obligation that could not be sidestepped. Board members recognized that they were endangering the future of the hospital by bucking the prevailing trend toward abandonment of the city. Their decision would have been much easier if there had been a stated, fully accepted, national decision to revitalize the cities. What is needed in making this kind of stand is the kind of commitment that England had during World War II, when the decision was made to fight on to victory even though 2 million casualties from bombing were fully expected. This kind of commitment to do whatever needs to be done will be a large factor in the battles of urban renewal.

The trials and tribulations of the board of directors at Mt. Sinai Hospital continued for several years. That was a time of much talk about burning cities, in the wake of the riots in Watts, Trenton, and elsewhere. Mt. Sinai personnel had many meetings with the community. At first they were confronted with angry, militant spokesmen for minorities who found it difficult to trust the hospital's good intentions. As time passed, a basis of understanding developed. The militant, negativistic leadership of the neighborhood mellowed. Eventually real cooperation developed in making practical decisions about how the hospital should operate within the limits of its resources. Mt. Sinai Hospital deserves great credit as a pioneer, not only for its decision to stay in the city but also for having the wisdom and foresight to allow responsible leadership to emerge from the community. Mt. Sinai is a good example of the fact that time, patience, and positive expectations are necessary if these kinds of developments are to take place.

The *Christian Science Monitor* lists several extremely practical ways for individuals to help with urban problems:

What you can do

If you live in a big, or little, city and can see that things need to be done in your neighborhood, here are some suggestions, guidelines, and quotes, gleaned from neighborhood activists around the United States:

- Don't look for someone else to start the ball rolling. And don't be concerned about not being representative by appointing yourself a committee of one and calling the first meeting (after publicizing it).

- Most important: What you are tackling has to be a real issue affecting the neighborhood or community, not necessarily one person. A little research (library, newspapers, other people) may be in order. Begin to develop a mailing and phone list. Be prepared for long hours away from home in the evenings.

● Stick with the issue. If your initial efforts are successful and you begin to get help and attention, resist the temptation to broaden your effort. If you don't have any money, plan some fund-raising events: block parties, garage sales, entertainment, etc. Try for grants. (For complete information on how to get grants write Grantmanship Center, 7815 South Vermont, Los Angeles, CA 90044.)

● Even more important than money is knowledge. Know how political decisions are made by local government which affect your neighborhood. Get to know statutes and zoning laws. Never underestimate the power of a bureaucracy not to return your phone call again and again. Keep people notified. A phone call is only as good as the follow-up. Always list two phone numbers on flyers or announcements.

● Try for broad support once you get rolling: businessmen, teenagers, senior citizens, etc. Delegate authority to people who come to meetings all the time. Avoid dead-end strategies like wanting to "control" an issue or "administer" a program.

Cultivate the support or interest of politicians and key city employees. (After a minor victory by a neighborhood group in the East, it "awarded" a helpful city official a plaque. He was overwhelmed, and forever after became an ally.)

● If you get promises from agencies, be persistent so that you get what you want on the date agreed to. (A California neighborhood group publicized a celebration and dedication to be held on the date the city promised new stop signs would be in place: "We gently put a little pressure on them." All seven stop signs were placed on the date agreed.)

● If the issue is "visual" take some photographs. Prepare a presentation. Have good speakers on hand to tell other groups about the issue. Offer guided tours for the press if the issue is at a location or could be considered news. Keep remarks at hearings or before boards short, clear, and to the point. Pack the audience if you can with orderly supporters who know when to cheer and when to keep quiet.

● Try not to be discouraged if you fail the first time. (One group in the Midwest created a "no fail" organization. Volunteers commit themselves for a certain number of hours a month to be on hand at a phone number, to respond to requests for help like shopping, repairs, information, etc.)

● You don't have to start your own group. Join one already on its way. People come and go. Don't expect any more of them than you would of yourself, and perhaps less. Have fun. The experience should make you grow.

Now that colleges have increased their enrollments of minority students, a widespread belief exists that educated blacks will join the middle class and move to the suburbs, turning their backs on their brothers in the cities. I think this is not going to be the case. I believe we will see blacks and Chicanos returning to the ghettos and changing the educational and social systems in imaginative ways that would be impossible for even the most well-intentioned white "do-gooder." Another rapidly escalating trend is that of blacks holding public office. First we saw a black mayor in Cleveland, and then in Atlanta, Detroit, and Los Angeles. Most major cities will have close to a black majority in population by 1980, and it is likely that many of these cities will also have black mayors. This trend is not a token advance, since the image and lives of all members of the black population will be affected. A similar shift of political and economic power was seen when the previously downtrodden Irish, Jews, and other waves of immigrants came into their own politically and economically. In the future, as cities need workers to build new systems of rapid transit, many jobs will go to members of minority groups as a result of their newfound political "voices"; and there will be other equally important consequences of minority political power.

The problems of the cities involve much more than the minorities. The disadvantaged, the discouraged, the "losers" tend to gravitate to the anonymous inner belts. We are just beginning to address ourselves to such problems as alcoholism and drug addiction. The alcoholic has been treated largely by the penal system in the past. Only recently have mental health clinics been widely established and encouraged to treat alcoholism. Methadone clinics and other ways of treating heroin addiction are new. I believe that much progress will be made in the treatment of these and other problems, which are a reflection of our way of life and our educational system. Breakthroughs will take place in many unexpected areas. For example, we are just beginning to learn about dyslexia and other learning problems. Many non-readers label themselves "dummies" and misfits in their early years of elementary school. Many forms of learning disorders exist, some of which would respond to new teaching techniques. And simply knowing the causes of particular difficulties will help many children and their families to cope with their school problems.

I think it is safe to say that the problems of the cities are magnifications of our individual problems. When we are fright-

ened and insecure, it is all we can do to take care of ourselves
and our families. When we feel secure about ourselves, then we
can set about thinking of our community and building community centers, better schools, and effective health care facilities.
People are beginning to recognize a need for new neighborhood institutions. We are basically an ingenious people.
When we allow ourselves to see needs and problems and realize
that we have the ability and resources to fulfill and solve them,
we can do it. In other words, I think it is just a matter of time until
we recognize the need for new kinds of community centers and
then set about creating them.

Even though the problems of alcoholism, crime, and drug
abuse are an integral part of our widespread alienation and lack
of purpose—and of the hopelessness that permeates much of
our contemporary life and to which a great deal of publicity is
given—the picture is not all bad. The work of family therapist
Virginia Satir is an excellent example of the reasons I have enormous hope for the future. In her book *Peoplemaking*, starting
with the concept of self-worth and recognizing that far too many
of us have very low opinions of ourselves, Mrs. Satir has put together new ideas to form a fresh way of looking at the family as a
communication system—a system that can be understood by
almost everyone. She has devised ways for an individual to recognize what his own feeling of self-worth is; and, once having
grasped that, he can begin to grow and lead a fuller life with his
family and friends. When people can begin to understand the
human problems that are inherent in social systems, hope for
change may enter. Other authors, such as the late Chaim Ginott
(*Between Parent and Child*) and Thomas Harris (*I'm Okay,
You're Okay*) are helping to popularize ideas about building up
self-worth, particularly in the middle class levels of society.
Again, it is probably just a matter of time until all levels of society
are exposed to these kinds of ideas.

In fact, the people whose works are included with mine in
this book exemplify—each in his own way—the trends toward
paying more and more attention to man's internal life. They
speak much better for themselves than I can speak for them.

The late Fritz Perls was an extremely powerful person and
the originator of Gestalt therapy. The dissemination of his
insights has helped many people to experience life differently
and to develop new value systems. Sheldon Kopp's writings
approach this problem from a different vantage point, but are
also very effective in helping people to assess their lives and

form new values. The particular insights of Fritz and Shelly will be elaborated upon later in my introductions to their respective sections of this anthology.

Raven Lang's *The Birth Book* shows us another direction. It is a reflection of a movement that recognizes the beauty and importance of the birth process as a growth experience for the mother, father, and—potentially—the rest of the family and its friends. Natural childbirth, particularly home birth, can be an extraordinarily humanizing experience. And on the opposite end of the spectrum of experience, paradoxically enough, even death will one day be recognized as an important growth experience.

I want to make the final point that a slum or ghetto is a state of mind to an extent that has not been really appreciated—it is an embodiment of absence of hope and purpose and dignity. Heretofore we have been discouraged because it was assumed that the human being was so hard to change. We are extremely knowledgeable, technologically speaking, but we know little about inspiring hope and confidence. Changes in attitudes—as exemplified by the recently-born liberation movements—show us that humans are remarkably flexible. Is this flexibility going to continue to evidence itself? I believe it is. And I believe that one of the ways it will show itself is in the growing realization that among the greatest gifts we can give ourselves and our children is the creation of safe cities. How will this creation be achieved? Well, I have spoken only in general terms because—quite frankly—I don't know the precise answer to this question. Nor do I think it is possible to predict the actual breakthroughs that will occur any more than it was possible to predict the specific battles of World War II. But there was a point in that war, even before the Normandy invasion, when the outcome of the war was evident. With respect to the battle for our cities, too, the details will unfold as we proceed; but I think the final outcome is already clear. As we find out more, it is likely we will discover that social engineering is not so different from general engineering. Of course, many, many specific problems must be worked out, often by trial and error. Confidence to work them out will come when we acknowledge how far we have already come; and when we truly recognize the importance of the kind of individual dignity that comes from movements such as "black is beautiful." These movements are the first and vital steps in the direction that will bring us ultimately to our goal—restoration of our cities as humane places for humans to live.

Society and Human Nature　　　6

I would like to return briefly to a consideration of the liberating trends with regard to women, minorities, and changed sexual attitudes. What has happened to allow changes in areas that for so many years were thought to be governed by fixed patterns, basic to human nature? Popularizations of Freudian psychology have told us that attitudes toward skin color have profound meaning rooted in the anal (bowel-training) period of psychosexual development and are most difficult to change. It has also been a popular belief that the black man represents increased sexuality and is threatening to the Caucasian at the phallic level of psychosexual development. Other theories have stressed the importance of a rigid class structure to protect the white "blue collar" worker from economic competition with the black man. It has been thought that the attitudinal changes inherent in changed sexual mores and women's liberation would undermine the family as the basic institution of our society. All of these are examples of what seemed to be firmly-rooted attitudes. In the face of these, we must marvel that change has taken place at all, let alone that it has occurred so rapidly. How *has* it happened?

On one level the answer seems fairly simple. There is a raising of consciousness within the oppressed minority groups whereby a new identity emerges. This process is often spearheaded by leaders who will make any needed sacrifice—from risking public ridicule to death—to force the so-called establishment to relate to this new identity. A moving description of this process is found in Huey Newton's book *Revolutionary Suicide*. It seems that almost all significant social advances are the results of long struggle, from getting children out of the mines to giving women the vote. On another level, there is a complementary change going on within the establishment. It often has the power to enforce the old ways but has lost the determination to do so. It is of interest that the changes that have taken place are not necessarily legal ones. No law can change our perceptions. There was no vote that I know of that called for increased acceptance of divorce, premarital sex, homosexuality, etc. In this chapter, I shall discuss some factors that affect the consciousness of the community.

I am sure television has contributed a great deal to the creation of "black is beautiful." Branch Rickey played a pivotal role in seeking racial equality when he put Jackie Robinson on his Brooklyn Dodgers baseball team in the mid-forties. Robinson was the first black man to be allowed in the Major Leagues. Since then, of course, blacks have become extremely important in professional athletics. Sports have been very important to television, and television has been very important to sports. When we watch TV or a movie, we often enter a unique state of consciousness: We become unaware of time and place, although we can shift back and forth at will. If it is an absorbing movie, it is an hour out of our lives—that is, our "egos" cease to exist for an hour and we "become" the movie. We identify with one or more characters; and the movie is our total experience, as in a dream. We largely stop having thoughts of our own; we "speak" the dialogue of the various actors and experience their feelings while responding to the music and the visual effects.

This altered state of consciousness, of getting out of oneself and "being" the dramatization, has been studied very little in depth. Perhaps something similar happens if we play a musical instrument or get caught up in a book. This power, this ability to identify and the enjoyment of the process, may be related to the ability of children to learn so rapidly in infancy and childhood, and to learn language by using adult behavior as a model. In any event, when we're caught up in a football game on television, we "become" the player who crosses the goal line. If he's black and it's his team we're rooting for, then at that moment we *are* that man, whether we are white, yellow, red, brown, or—like him—black. This is certainly true when we follow a story on TV in which there are sympathetic black characters. It is as if we become these people. And laughter seems to help this identification take place. I think that even the quality of our laughter has matured and become more empathetic. "Stepin Fetchit" and Fred Sanford are not even in the same category; one is a caricature and a demeaning one at that, and the other is a real and believable character who just happens to be pretty damned funny. But I am digressing.

Returning to the group experience, it may just be that at moments when people are experiencing similar emotions, contact can be made and group identification can be formed. For example, when we go to a gripping movie, we enter the theater as strangers. At the end of the film if there are tears in our eyes, we usually wipe them away in an embarrassed manner and leave as strangers still. Yet at that moment and for some time after, the people to the right and left of us are undergoing intense feelings that very likely parallel our own. It is a moment when, with permission, we could reach out and make contact with these other people and acknowledge what we are all sharing. I think we also experience this kind of moment when we are in a group of people laughing at a comedian together. It is not an interaction involving just the comedian and each laughing individual. Actually we are all participating in the laughter in a communal way, even though not really acknowledging this to ourselves. We know surprisingly little about psychological phenomena at this level of interaction. It seems to me that this is an extremely important area, but one that we are only beginning to study.

I'm sure we are all aware of how suddenly our tastes in music and food seem to change. Certain colors, too, seem to become popular and then suddenly to lose their appeal for us. We sometimes ask ourselves, "Are we men or are we sheep?" A sheep is supposedly cowardly, very much influenced by other sheep, and easily intimidated if the rest of his group is frightened; a man is supposed to make independent judgments. The problem is that our perceptions or emotional reactions to what we see are very much influenced by others. In the daydream I mentioned at the beginning of this book, the dinosaurs see that the ice is increasing and their escape route is being narrowed. Somehow there is a communication among the group that this is a phenomenon to be talked about and analyzed. It does not have the meaning to them that they should get up and do something.

We know little about the influence of large group phenomena on perception. I once heard Gregory Bateson make some interesting observations about this. He spoke of a dog that hears a sound and turns its ear to hear better. Other dogs and animals see the ear turning. This is a communication to them that one animal in the group has a startled reaction. The direction of the ear's turn can even tell them where the sound is coming from, and then they will also listen and hear it. Their behavior in turn affects the first dog. Bateson also cited the similar example of a flock of birds flying when suddenly one becomes frightened and veers off. The rest of the birds will follow this one. And if the first bird happens to be extra-sensitive because of some experience of its own or there is some other reason for its being slightly "paranoid," it may become the recognized leader of the flock.

I think that the distinction between being a sheep or a man is grossly oversimplified. Man grows up in a family and has a long period of dependence for his survival on his parents. He learns to learn by identifying with others and takes on their styles of perceiving and thinking. Our brains are indescribably complex. For example, we have to distinguish between dreaming and being awake, and we have to make some kind of sense out of everything that happens in the complicated lives we live.

Suppose you were walking and came to an intersection. A crowd of people was waiting for the light to change. Suddenly the light flashed "Walk," but nobody walked. What would you do? On one level your reasoning would tell you that since the light had changed, it was okay to walk. But on another level you would know that the other people also wanted to walk, and you would think that there was some reason why they didn't move. Eventually you might look up and down the street and make your own judgment about whether or not it was safe to walk. But, most likely, you would be quite uncomfortable until you could explain to yourself why the other people didn't walk. However, you would take all this in immediately and put it together without using words as thoughts. You would have the instant perception that something was not right when the other people didn't move.

It is often said, "I don't know anything about art, but I know what I like." We pride ourselves on being men and not sheep, and on making our own judgments. Yet we know little about what determines what we like, in art and in many other areas as well. It is likely that for most of us what we like in music, art, and all kinds of things is influenced by a group of which we are not aware.

The saying of the oracle at Delphi, "Know thyself," is usually interpreted as referring to being in touch with one's karma or fate; or finding out that one is—in a Freudian sense—in love with one's mother, or is in some way a villain, or feels guilty about some sin one has committed. Another application of the dictum "Know thyself" would be to study one's self. Few of us have stopped to determine how we like to spend our time —how much time we would like to spend by ourselves, how much with other people, or in what way and with how many others. We may not know the techniques for making time for ourselves, or for getting together with others or getting away from them. Few of us have studied ourselves to find out how we relate to objects. Do we like working with wood? Fixing cars? Cooking? What is it about these activities that we like? How can we bring more of them into our lives? All of these are very tricky matters because it is easy to satiate ourselves with a particular activity instead of permitting ourselves to realize that variety might be better—at least for some of us. All too few of us are aware of our mood swings, what causes them, and how to cope with life depending on what mood we are in at a given moment. In addition, few of us know much about how we are affected by large groups or societal influences.

The traditional attitude in this country has been a *laissez faire* attitude. We seem to simply hope that what is good for most people will somehow emerge. But I think we do not address ourselves sufficiently to the question of how groups are influenced and, in turn, influence individuals. Television is a compelling influencer, and I think we simply swallow a lot of what it spews out without questioning it. TV tells us that life in the suburbs is happy and desirable. But do people in the cities ask themselves if they really would be happy in suburbia? My guess is that there are plenty of people in the so-called ghettos who would hate the commuting life, the white collar job, the keeping up with the neighbors, and the isolation of the typical suburban home. Is all of this really fun? Who laughs more, the urbanite or the suburbanite? Who has the more satisfying sex life? Who hears or plays more music? Who is more spontaneous? Who says what is on his mind and has more variety in his life? Who enjoys his body more? Who even asks these kinds of questions, let alone tries to answer them?

Let's consider for a moment the sudden blossoming of great creativity in architecture, painting, theater, and democratic processes that occurred in Athens during the classical period of ancient Greece. All this creativity was produced by a small population, many of whom were slaves or women who had no vote and apparently did not officially participate in the arts or government. I doubt that any sudden increase in the birth of geniuses took place. Somehow, some kind of feedback system became established, with positive, reverberating feedback that caused or allowed the Golden Age to come about. My own hunch is that it had something to do with the theater. We know the theater was part of the Greeks' religion; and that all or a goodly portion of the population watched the Greek tragedies and comedies and probably participated as the chorus. I suspect that intense emotional states occurred in the audiences as well as in the actors, and that these states persisted afterward when the people went home. Such theater, with its pageantry and religious import, allows identification with other people in the community and stimulates creativity.

My hope is that we will gradually learn a great deal about group influence—once we allow ourselves to recognize its power—and that we will then carefully study the ways we are affected by it. We could then use it to gain more control over becoming the kind of people we want to be and creating the kind of society we want. Synanon provides us with a fine example of how a group or sub-society can influence individuals. Traditional methods of curing drug addiction had been largely ineffective, so Charles Dederich formed Synanon to use group influence to help individual "dope fiends," as Synanon members called them. A person joins Synanon, participates in its form of group therapy, and shares its other rituals in close, communal life. He identifies with the group and usually realizes that he can live without drugs. Then he begins to perceive life experiences as others in the group do, and finds this far different from the way he saw life experiences when he was addicted. Synanon started out as a very small organization, housed in an abandoned store in Santa Monica, California. It has now grown huge, with branches in Oakland and Bolinas, forming a new communal life style and educational system for former addicts and for many "straight" people as well.

On a much larger scale, I think we would learn much by the study of China. Even apart from the fact that China possesses one quarter of the world's population, it deserves study because the Chinese are at least attempting to address themselves directly to the subject of group and individual influences. A Chinese official is reported to have said that America was the first country to send a man to the moon, but China would be the first country to make a man. I question whether or not at this point the Chinese know much more than we do about "making a man"; but at least they are talking and doing something about it.

In only twenty or thirty years, China has been able to stabilize its population, feed its people, develop nuclear weapons, and become a powerful and increasingly modern state. In my view the Chinese are fortunate that they have no more automobiles than they did in 1950 and have thus avoided many of our air pollution problems. Similarly, they don't have advertisements blaring out at them constantly as we do. At one time they had the worst drug problem in the world. Now they are virtually rid of it. It has been reported that gonorrhea and syphilis have been stamped out in China. A psychiatrist who visited there reported that neurosis seemed absent. It may be that the people are suffering from anxiety, depression, or neurotic fears and do not complain due to the threat of imprisonment; but I think it is more likely that the neurotic problems so common in our society are much less prevalent, and perhaps even virtually unknown, in China. They do have some psychosis (which involves a distortion of reality and often has an important organic component) but probably little neuroses (which generally is a product of fear, conflict, withdrawal and confusion)

In China, all jobs have dignity and are considered equally worthwhile. In fact, jobs are rotated and a plant manager will work in the field at harvest time. Twice a day everyone participates in group calisthenics. It is reported that marital and other such problems are handled at the local level by having concerned neighbors or village elders talk to the troubled individuals. Each person feels he is making an important contribution, that he is carrying on the traditions of his parents, and that his own children will follow in like manner. He feels a sense of continuity and purpose in his life. And he feels physically good. He has a lot of contact with other people, and his activities increase identification rather than competition, which would tend toward isolation. I am not naive enough to think that there are no areas of conflict between old and young, rural and urban residents, and religious and political leaders—especially in the light of how rapidly China has become modernized. But I do think that in many areas they are making a kind of progress that we are not.

I don't know how much, if any, of what China has hit upon could be adapted to America. We are studying acupuncture, and it is surprising how fast it is being applied as a method of anesthesia and explored as a treatment modality. It is possible that we will become sufficiently interested in how the Chinese have overcome their drug problems and other related social ills so that we will study and perhaps adapt their methods in these areas too. It is good to know that 800 million people have discovered ways different from our ways of solving problems; and that their ways work so well for them.

Although many of us might agree with the explicit aim of Communist China—to make a better man—we might not agree with their method of going about it. At present, their ideals seem to be dictated by one man, Mao Tse Tung, who is eighty years old and may have lost touch with young people. On the other hand—and to be fair—even though we have not specifically addressed ourselves to "making a man," we are not in so bad a position as might be the case.

Returning to television for a moment, hucksters may berate us on such uplifting topics as armpits, halitosis, and hangovers but there have been significant beneficial effects of TV as well. My complaint is simply that TV and films could do much more. I believe that it would be helpful if television and films presented more examples of different life styles. For example, several years ago two friends started a business to build geodesic domes with fiberglass exteriors and styrofoam interiors. They asked a third friend, who had an extensive background in design and a long-lived interest in low-cost housing, to join them. He said he would be delighted to participate and go over all the designs and share his ideas with them; however, he insisted that he should get no power or money for his participation. Thoreau was this man's model; and with his background in art, he considers his own life an art form that he is continually developing. He sees power and money as influences that might corrupt his life. If this kind of person could be presented in a real way on television or in films, he might become a model that would have meaning for many young people. Some programs in the last few years have shown a trend in this direction. They have presented people with atypical value systems—for example, Ralph Nader, who rejects wealth and power and pursues an almost monastic life style. For many years Stanley Kramer was a pioneer in producing such movies as *The Defiant Ones* and *The Man Who Came To Dinner*, both of which explored race relations while providing good entertainment. Norman Lear has given us both of the popular TV series "Maude" and "All in the Family." Archie Bunker, of the latter series, has developed into an important national figure who helps us to laugh at and with that part of society and of ourselves that seems resistant to change.

It seems to me that in the developed countries, the media —particularly television—play a dominant role in inducing changes in attitude. In times of war we become very concerned with the morale of the general public and attempt to create a sense of participation and purpose. In peacetime we tend to ignore this issue, perhaps rightly feeling that the dangers of governmental propagandizing are too great. But there are real dangers in our present system. I think we are unduly inundated with frightening news stories that shock us but that also make it even more likely that we will listen to the next newscast or buy the same newspaper the next day. The media compete for the latest exposes of crime and corruption. We tend to read newspapers, listen to radio, and watch television by ourselves or with our immediate families. In a sense, the communication circuit is not complete, as we do not usually respond to the source of our information or even talk much with one another. We are passive recipients, often flooded with more than we can absorb. We do not have the equivalent of the Greek theater or town hall meetings or community centers that really encourage sharing and integration of experience. Life in the city is anonymous and alienated.

As one solution to these problems, I am particularly interested in the possibility of establishing inexpensive neighborhood TV centers where video tape recorders would provide good entertainment and opportunities would be afforded for short discussions of the emotional and social issues involved. The necessary equipment is now fairly inexpensive, and soon there will be accessible libraries of good video tapes. I picture these small centers located in informal home atmospheres, which would facilitate people's making connections with one another. In his book *Future Shock*, Alvin Toffler describes a new, complex syndrome of psychological and physiological symptoms which he attributes to the rapid and unpredictable changes of our society. I think the problem is not the occurence of changes per se. I see the problem as more related to our failure to understand and integrate the positive trends that underlie the changes. Such understanding and integration could, I believe, be achieved in neighborhood centers which would facilitate person-to-person contact and combat alienation.

Double-Digit Fears

7

There remains the pick-up-stick of economic insecurity: fear of inflation, and fear of depression. These fears are probably with us more than other fears. Newspapers "talk" of double-digit inflation in major European countries and Japan, and of the danger of depression and economic collapse in the U.S., should our inflation approach theirs. Almost every time we buy something, we are struck by the high costs and we have to reach deeper into our pockets. What will happen to our savings? How will we manage to pay for the unpredictable "catastrophes" of life, much less the predictable ones such as old age?

A slight panic sets in when most of us think about these matters. This panic reaction is an interesting phenomenon that is helpful to examine, even apart from reality considerations. Most of us today consider our income a reflection of our status in the community. And, more importantly, we use it as a measure of our self-esteem. In the next chapter I shall describe how I think this will begin to change markedly in the next decade. But we are living now, not some time in the future. Money is associated with authority figures. We asked our parents for our allowance; we ask our boss for a raise. How do we justify a raise when many of us are keenly aware of our failings, of how we could have done more or made fewer mistakes? Accountants, lawyers, bankers, all have their own jargon—a secret body of knowledge that is continually changing. Bankers even dress distinctively and, at least in my mind, are associated with morticians, school principals, and judges. There is a great mystique about money and economics. We feel that it is something we should understand, yet the basic principles evade our comprehension. Our first—and often last—reaction is to conclude that it is too difficult for the likes of us ordinary people to master; and, besides, what could we do if we did understand? It's better to leave it to the experts.

In the beginning of this essay, I described how hope entered for me when I turned away from reliance on experts and toward trust in myself. Thus I wondered, "How far can I pursue the subject of economics if I stick with my own observations and common sense, looking for underlying trends that could help me predict the future?" A first step was to question what is so bad or frightening about inflation. If many apparently prosperous countries—France, England, West Germany, and Japan—have for many years had annual rates of inflation in the double-digit (10%—20%) range, why is it so bad? Isn't it likely that if this happened in America, we could learn to play the game too? Prices increase, but wages increase too. Undoubtedly some people are hurt—those on fixed incomes—but more and more these injustices are diminished by cost-of-living clauses. Social security and old age welfare payments are increased. The trend, as I have seen it in my lifetime, is for better protection of the handicapped, impoverished, and aged. Short of some national catastrophe, I expect this trend to continue, particularly as expenditures on armaments decrease and social consciousness increases. The panic subsides for a moment as we reflect on this, but it rapidly comes back. Why?

Secondly, I turned my attention to an observation frequently made but often forgotten—namely, that a regulated economy now exists on a scale unknown in the past. Savings accounts are insured and widespread bank failures will not occur. The Securities and Exchange Commission (SEC) protects us against a stock market collapse. Interest rates control business activities, and industries such as construction are very sensitive to this input. The local, state, and federal governments employ 20%—25% of the working force. It is all very mysterious, and we are frightened when the SEC discovers fraud in a reputable stock brokerage firm. But in reality I think this kind of thing is evidence that the system is working. Perhaps the most convincing evidence of this comes when we review what has happened in the forty-five years since the Great Depression. We have had steady economic growth in spite of World War II, the Korean war, Vietnam, the space programs, and extensive aid to foreign countries.

As I mentioned earlier, when the economies of all major countries become interrelated, the result is a worldwide structure that can give more security than any individual country can have in an uncertain, warring world. I think this is in part due to the arbitrariness of any economic system. As children we are delighted to be given a dime, and a dollar bill seems to have great intrinsic value. It is hard to understand that money is symbolic—an agreed-upon unit in a system of barter. A dollar is worth so much gold or silver, we are told. But what is so important about gold, or silver, or diamonds for that matter? I can understand basing a monetary system on salt when salt is an important item and available in limited amount. But what about when more salt or new ways to preserve or season foods are discovered? In summary, our monetary system, which seems sensible and solid as bedrock when we are young, turns out to be arbitrary and unpredictable as quicksand. For money can become worthless, as it did during the inflation in the Weimar Republic; and we can be conscientious and hard-working yet still unable to get employment, as was the case during the Depression.

Franklin Roosevelt made one of the most cogent observations of all time when he said, regarding the Depression, "All we have to fear is fear itself." I think he meant by this that any economic system is arbitrary, based on complicated—sometimes implicit—agreements and understandings. And that the danger is in losing faith and in threatening to quit the game and take one's marbles home. Today, economic power is controlled not only by the federal, state, and local governments but also by large corporations, foundations, and various power blocks—all of which are irrevocably committed to playing the game. The oil-producing countries with their rapidly accumulating fantastic wealth are fine examples of this. I think Saudi Arabia, Iran, Kuwait, etc. will hire the best economic advisors available. I think the advice will be to lend money to England, France, Japan, and Italy. These are some of their chief customers and good business practice will mean keeping them functioning, thus consuming oil and continuing to be good customers. The more wealth the Arab countries accumulate, the more they stand to gain by a prosperous oil-burning world economy. It will not be hard for them to see that they have a great deal to lose by an economic collapse of a European country with its potential domino effect on other economies and resultant political turmoil which could conceivably lead to war. It is in this sense that the pick-up-stick of economic insecurity will become much less of a problem once it is realized that the pick-up-stick of war between major powers has been removed.

A Return to the Parable

8

I would like to return to the story of Joseph. The theme of "chosen people" is prominent in the Old Testament. There is a blessing that is passed on from father to son, often at the death bed of the father. This blessing gives the son a special relationship to God. It is expected that the blessing will be passed on to the oldest son. Of course, this was not the case for Joseph's father, Jacob, who received the blessing in preference to his twin brother Esau, who was born before him.

These myths have had great meaning for Western civilization. They teach us about family relationships and inculcate a system of values.

The belief in being chosen people gives great strength in uniting a family, a clan or a nation. It is comforting in times of stress and a powerful binding force in times of warfare.

When I was a boy it seemed to me that America was the chosen nation. We had special gifts, Yankee ingenuity, natural resources, but in particular we had a political system which was the special blessing we had inherited. It is interesting that this theme of chosen people, which has its modern counterpart in nationalism, continued even though there was acceptance of the Copernican theory that the Earth orbited around the sun, and continued even when there was acceptance of Darwin's theory of evolution. The Earth had lost its special place, and even man had lost his special place. We could see the inconsistencies of Hitler's version of the chosen people, that of Aryan superiority. Somehow our own version of nationalism, "in God we trust," continued almost unchallenged.

The story of Joseph tells the famous story of the maturation of a talented person. Joseph was the first child of Rebecca, the favorite of Jacob's four wives. The Bible describes how Joseph's older brothers resented his father's gift to him of the multi-colored robe. His brothers were infuriated when Joseph persisted in recounting to them his dreams, which he interpreted as meaning that they should bow down to him and accept him as their leader. The arrogance of this naive youth caused his jealous brothers to exile him by selling him to a passing caravan. This period of exile and imprisonment produces a changed Joseph. He no longer interprets his own dreams. As we see in the story, he credits Pharaoh with having been chosen by God to receive the dream. Joseph becomes a *facilitator* so that Pharoah can make use of God's warning, and help the land of Egypt.

On another level, Joseph was giving very sound, practical advice to Pharaoh—essentially, save in a time of plenty in case there comes a time of need.

I think the story of Joseph can be applied to America. We have gone through our period of being the beloved favorite, of being chosen. We are now in a period of concern over pollution, the ghettos, Vietnam, energy shortage, mistrust of public officials, and worldwide inflation and recession. It seems to many of us that we have betrayed our heritage. There is fear and confusion as well as self-hatred. Part of our self-hatred is due to idealizing the past and criticizing the present. It will be of particular interest to see how we celebrate the Bicentennial Anniversary of the Constitution. We often talk about our constitutional rights, as if they were a political Garden of Eden established 200 years ago. If we do not need to romanticize the past, we can still appreciate the fact that our Constitution, created 200 years ago, was an advance for the time. But we should not overlook the fact that the Constitutional fathers accepted slavery. Women did not have the vote. The Constitution did not prevent a Civil War. My hope is that the Bicentennial celebration will allow us to get in touch with the very significant social advances of the very recent past. We should also see the progress that is being made elsewhere, such as the European Economic Community, a prosperous, peaceful Japan, and particularly the promising social advances in Russia and China. It may be that China has something unique to offer to the underdeveloped countries. Perhaps the most significant contribution we can make to ourselves and to others at this time is to continue to get our own house in order; to recognize and further our progress in race relations and sex relations; and to be a facilitator of the drama of other countries rather than to impose our way. It is difficult to give up the concept of being chosen. A state of uncertainty and confusion emerges for a time. This can give way to the goal of enjoying and appreciating ourselves and our environment, with confidence in our ability to cope with problems that lie ahead, learning from our mistakes as well as our successes.

Addendum

In the first chapter of this essay I described five trends which I think form the basis for considerable hope, and which I think have not received sufficient attention. To recapitulate, these are 1) the increasing unlikelihood of war between major powers, with emerging cooperation—economically and politically—between Russia and America, 2) the trend in America and other western countries toward acceptance of differentness, and implementation of the recognition of the value of individual dignity, 3) the emergence of Communist China as a potential model for underdeveloped countries (and even for economically-developed countries), as another model of a political/economic system that seems to give a good life for most of its citizens, 4) recognition of the importance of ecology and the worldwide exhaustion of many natural resources that is causing an increasing change in our value systems, and 5) a recognition of the rapid rate in which basic attitudes and mores of societies can change, particularly through the influence of television and other rapid means of communication.

The deepening economic depression, and the threat of another war in the Middle East, could affect the rate of change that the above trends are likely to show. We are all aware of the threat that a severe economic depression could cause large-scale, long-term unemployment, and although this could lead to unification within the various countries and increased cooperation between countries, as in certain disasters, it could also lead to a temporary reversal of gains that various minority groups have made. Similarly, many of us fear that the situation in the Middle East could explode and lead to a holocaust between Russia and America. These dangers are very real, but, again, I think there has not been sufficient attention paid to positive trends that I believe are equally real.

America currently is going through an economic recession, with great unemployment,—particularly in the automobile and related industries. We are used to cycles in the economy, with periods of prosperity followed by periods of recession. As I mentioned earlier, controls have been reasonably effective in limiting the range of such swings by regulating interest rates, and the like. We have handled major changes in the economy, such as the shift from war time to peace time, or other dislocations pretty effectively. Usually we have been able to foresee these changes somewhat in advance and plan over a period of many months or years. However, the oil embargo imposed in the winter of 1974 presented an entirely new element. There was little warning. Suddenly, as we all remember, there was a major shortage of oil and gasoline, then a marked increase in price. This has made it difficult for the individual to make a decision about buying a new car, and has in turn made it difficult for Detroit to plan production schedules, with resultant layoffs and economic recession.

Everyone knows that in the event of another war in the Middle East there is the threat, again, of the imposition of an oil embargo, and the possible return of gasoline shortages and potential marked increase in prices. We are now confronted with a situation where it is very difficult for the leaders of industry to make plans of any long-range significance. So what I am saying is that the pre-existing problems of the economy that were only partially understood and were causing recurrent periods of prosperity and recession (which were manageable) have been complicated by an uncertainty that strikes at the center of the ability to make long-range plans. This suggests to me that if a stable political situation developed in the Middle East, whereby we could count on a flow of oil, even at its current great cost, economic plans could be made and the economic situation would level itself off quite rapidly. It also suggests that even if the oil embargo were again imposed, this time we would not be so unprepared.

At this moment in time (February, 1975) many political forecasters are predicting a 50-50 change of recurrence of war in the Middle East in the next six months. There is no question but that this remains a very dangerous situation, however, it seems to me, the chances of a long term political settlement in the

Middle East are now more favorable than at any time in the past. And if such a settlement were achieved, it would likely be of long duration. It may even offer a precedent for how international conflicts can be settled in the future. In fact, some of the various elements that are new in the situation that strike many forecasters as dangerous seem to me to be factors that give a greater likelihood of peace than before. The foremost of these is the Yom Kippur war of November, 1973, in which Egypt and Syria demonstrated their ability to launch a successful secret attack, and in which they did reasonably well militarily. For internal propaganda purposes they have portrayed the war mutually as a military success. Psychologically, I think this is of great importance and analogous to the acceptance of "black is beautiful," in the sense that it may be that the Yom Kippur war has given the Arab world a sense of dignity and self-esteem that could not be obtained in other ways.

In a similar way, the oil embargo imposed by Saudi Arabia, Iran, and the other oil producing countries has also greatly increased Arab self-esteem, both economically and psychologically, and undoubtedly has given them confidence in themselves and in their future. A third factor is the demonstrable economic vulnerability of America and the European community, the Common Market nations, to the oil embargo and the potential economic and political weaknesses of these countries, which paradoxically has to be threatening to the oil-producing countries once the full import is recognized.

Essentially it seems to me that each of the countries involved in the Middle East situation have a great deal to gain by almost any kind of equitable long-term settlement, and they have a great deal to lose in the event of war, with little likelihood that any of the parties would gain and quite possibly could lose by such a war. It also seems to me that each of the parties involved has much more to be gained by continuing the present state, even if no lasting settlement is achieved.

The sums of money now available to the oil-producing countries make all kinds of projects possible that just a short time ago would have been considered far-out daydreams. It's estimated the the oil-producing countries will have 60 billion dollars accumulated in 1975 that they will be unable to spend. Heretofore the Palestinian refugee problem seemed unsolvable; there are two or three million Palestinian refugees. If the 60 billion were distributed to them it would come to 30 thousand dollars per person. America and Japan and the Western developed countries should be willing to contribute many billions to any solution that would provide stability in the Middle East, and guarantee a predicatble supply of oil.

Israel is paying 40% to 60% of its budget for military purposes. Russia has undoubtedly spent billions to rearm Egypt and Syria. Everyone knows the above facts. Difficult negotiations and bargaining will be necessary before the appropriate share of the cost of maintaining peace can be determined and deemed satisfactory by each nation. All of this will take time, but undoubtedly some of the best minds in the world will be working on these kinds of solutions over the next few years. In fact, it's likely that such solutions have been worked on for a considerable time and what is probably needed is an opportune moment for such apparent grandiose propositions to be presented in a favorable environment.

It might be helpful to take the indidvidual countries and see how the leaders of these countries might see what they have to win and lose in the event of war. Let us begin with Israel. Israel must have learned in the November, 1973, Yom Kippur war that it is unlikely that she will be allowed to enjoy the fruits of victory, even if she were to win a war. In that war, Israel had 20,000 Egyptian troops surrounded, but because of the threat of Russian intervention she was forced by America to make peace. Now this paradox applies to both Egypt and Syria, as well as Israel. That is, if they were to be successful militarily it is likely that before a complete victory were accomplished either Russia or America would intervene and, likewise, the intervention of one major power would likely necessitate the intervention of the other with unpredictable results. Israel has the further problem that if she were successful in defeating Egypt and Syria militarily, without the intervention of Russia, it is possible that in such a preventive war she would lose the future support of America and be further isolated. Israel has to look beyond winning any particular battle or war and must plan for a long-range future. A victory which would antagonize America would leave Israel in an impossible position.

Egypt has many of the same considerations. If she were able to defeat Israel militarily, it is likely that before reaping the rewards of such a military triumph America would intervene with unpredictable results. On the other hand, in the event of a difficult war, whether Egypt were successful or unsuccessful, it is likely that the Suez Canal (soon to be reopened and to bring in close to a billion dollars in revenue a year) would be again closed. It is quite possible that the Aswan Dam would be destroyed. There is speculation that Israel already has tactical atomic weapons, and there is the real probability that if Israel felt she were about to be destroyed that she would, in desperation, use such ultimate weapons. On the other hand, it should be apparent to Egypt that a negotiated peace is likely to produce a share of money from the oil-producing countries and financial and technological help form the Western countries. Also a negotiated peace with Israel is likely to give Egypt a large part of the Sinai Peninsula, including oil fields—fields that produce a half billion dollars worth of oil a year.

The pros and cons of war as it may appear to the leaders of Syria are harder for me to evaluate. It appears that the present regime in Syria may have a greater need for war tension (and for Israel as a scapegoat) in order to maintain internal unity than has Egypt. Syria currently is enjoying a relationship with Russia whereby it is receiving considerable military and economic help. On the other hand, Syria knows that in the event of war, Damascus could be captured by the Israelis and might be destroyed by its nuclear and/or conventional armaments. Syria also might see that as Egypt negotiates with Israel for peace, that she will become increasingly isolated and perhaps lose her bargaining power.

The Palestinian refugee problem always has been the major stumbling block to peace in the Middle East. The emergence of Arafat and his recognition by the United Nations appears promising to me. I think we should not be misled by photographs of his appearing at the United Nations with a weapon. Any leader of the Palestinian Liberation Movement would be a militant, and must maintain that position for internal leadership. The important trend is the ability of one person or organization to represent this movement, and then to be able to negotiate effectively with the West, Israel, and the oil-producing countries in order to work out a plan whereby Palestinians can achieve a viable economic and political settlement.

Undoubtedly many months and perhaps years will be necessary before such a complicated peace settlement can be negotiated. During this time, terrorist activity and retaliation by Israel against the Palestinian refugees and countries that harbor them, such as Lebanon, will continue. Terrorist activities have been common for a number of years, including the massacre of the Israeli Olympic team in Munich, killings of Israeli school children, hijacking of airplanes, and on the other side, related retaliation, all of which were brutal and provocative. What is important to me at this point is that all the parties are accustomed to this strange ritual of terrorism and retaliation, and somehow have worked out a very primitive barter system whereby all parties can live with it. I suppose there is no end to men's ability to be creative in his brutality to his fellow man, but it would appear that the past few years have provided a period of desensitization and, if not toleration, at least expectation of such peculiar exchanges.

Many paradoxes and intrigues exist in the Middle East situation. To me the most encouraging paradox is that Saudi Arabia, Iran, and other oil-producing countries require both a strong Russia and a strong America in order to be safe from intervention by either side. Russia is a threat because of her physical proximity, military strength, and basic philosophical, economic, and political disagreement with the basically capitalistic structure of the Arab sheikdoms and kingdoms.

My hope is that the current economic depression in America and the Western countries will be seen as a threat to the leaders of Saudi Arabia and Iran. It is important for the security of these countries that America remain strong and confident in her ability to confront effectively Russian expansion of its political and economic power. The paradoxes are further compounded by the realization that it is important for America that Russia be reasonably successful in its international and certainly its domestic, economic, and political affairs. On the other hand, it is important for Russia that America remain strong economically, and politically, domestically, and internationally.

I have presented the above arguments to a number of people who generally agree with me. Even though they agree with me they feel that I have not paid sufficient attention to irrational, impulsive motivations in human behavior. It may come down to a matter of timing. It seems to me that all of the major participants: Saudi Arabia, Iran, Egypt, Syria, Israel, America, Russia, Jordan, the Western countries, other oil producing countries, will have time to evaluate the pros and cons of these major decisions and decide that peace and even prosperity for the enemy is in their own best interest.

And finally, I think an outgrowth of the energy crisis will be increased awareness of the importance of ecology, with a recognition of the ability of various countries to reach political compromises and cooperation. This, in turn, should cause greater awareness of problems of over-population and hunger and lead to innovative programs to modify distribution and production of food.

Part II

- Excerpts from **Peoplemaking**

- **When I Meet a Person**

by
Virginia Satir

Virginia Satir

The family is the basic unit in all cultures that have been observed; but it is only recently that we have begun to study the family as an institution. And it remains a very basic institution although much of life is changing rapidly throughout the world. Today we live longer. We expect more from life. We have ever-increasing mobility. Many choices are open to people in today's world. For example, not long ago in Japan almost all marriages were arranged. It was enough to work hard, survive, and respect the traditions of the country. Today there is an increasing expectation of romantic love and personal growth within the love relationship and family, with the resultant turmoil that always accompanies a challenge to tradition.

It does not follow that because we fall in love, we know much about living with another person for an extended period of time. It certainly does not follow that because we have the biological capacity to procreate, we know much about being parents. Many of us believe that such knowledge is natural or easy to learn. It is neither.

There are many widely publicized alternatives to traditional marriage, from communal marriage to agreed-upon transient relationships. Some observers question whether the family will survive. But I am not doubtful that it will, and neither is Virginia Satir. Both of us believe that today's sometimes tumultuous reexamination of traditional marriage is not only the logical consequence of the new alternatives but is a healthy phenomenon. And we are gratified to see that today the emphasis is on the quality of each relationship rather than on its legal or religious label.

I first met Virginia Satir eleven years ago, when she was teaching conjoint family therapy at the Mental Research Institute (M.R.I.) in Palo Alto, California. She was (and still is) a large, good-looking, blonde, who exudes warmth and vitality. The program at M.R.I. was the first family therapy training program in the country. My psychiatric training was orthodox Freudian, and Virginia's innovative ideas had such an impact on me that I joined her and Don Jackson at the Institute. In my position as administrative director of the program, I had the opportunity to see the effectiveness of Virginia's techniques. She used one-way mirrors and audio and video tapes; she developed games and exercises, and exposed and involved herself in demonstrations and simulated family interviews. These techniques have become so widely accepted today that it is easy to lose sight of the creativity that produced them. Virginia Satir has probably contributed more than anyone else in the field to the conceptualization of what goes on in a family and to teaching professionals. Her textbook, *Conjoint Family Therapy,* has become the bible for students everywhere.

The first of Virginia Satir's articles included here is a composite of selections from her book *Peoplemaking.* This article constitutes an introduction to her basic ideas. Of particular importance are the widely popularized communication stances which she has developed into a variety of exercises. These stances and exercises give people the language and tools they need to understand their behavior and even to change their lives.

Introduction to *Peoplemaking*

In my years as a family therapist, I have found that four aspects of family life keep popping up in the troubled families who come to me for help. They are—

> the feelings and ideas one has about himself, which I call *self-worth;*

> the ways people work out to make meaning with one another, which I call *communication;*

> the *rules* people use for how they should feel and act, which eventually develop into what I call the family system; and

> the way people relate to other people and institutions outside the family, which I call the *link to society.*

No matter what kind of problem first led a family into my office—whether a nagging wife or an unfaithful husband, a delinquent son or a schizophrenic daughter—I soon found that the prescription was the same. To relieve their family pain, some way had to be found to change those four key factors. In all of these troubled families I noticed that—

> self-worth was low;

> communication was indirect, vague, and not really honest;

> rules were rigid, inhuman, nonnegotiable, and everlasting; and

> the linking to society was fearful, placating, and blaming.

Fortunately, I have also had the joy of knowing some untroubled and nurturing families—especially in my more recent workshops to help families develop more fully their potential as human beings. In these vital and nurturing families, I consistently see a different pattern—

self-worth is high;

communication is direct, clear, specific, and honest;

rules are flexible, human, appropriate, and subject
to change; and

the linking to society is open and hopeful.

No matter where a surgeon studies medicine, he is prepared to operate on human beings anywhere in the world, because the internal organs and the limbs will be the same. Through my work with families, troubled and nurturing, in the United States, Mexico, and Europe, I have learned that families everywhere have certain working parts in common, too. In all families—

*every person has a feeling of worth, positive or
negative;* the question is,

Which is it?

every person communicates; the question is,

How, and what happens as a result?

every person follows rules; the question is,

What kind, and how well do they work
for him?

every person is linked to society; the question is,

How, and what are the results?

These things are true whether the family is a *natural* one, where the man and woman who sired and conceived the child continue to care for him until he is grown; a *one-parent* one, where one parent leaves the family by death, divorce, or desertion, and all of the parenting is done by the remaining parent; a *blended* one, where the children are parented by step-, adoptive, or foster parents, not by the persons who brought them into the world; or an *institutional* one, where groups of adults rear groups of children, as in institutions or the modern day commune.

Each of these forms of family has its own special problems in living, and we will return to them later. But bascially, the same forces will be at work in all of them; *self-worth, communication, rules, and linking to society.*

In this book I will talk more about each of these crucial factors, to help you discover how they are operating in your own family and how they can be changed to reduce problems and increase the vitality and joy you can find with one another. Think of my words not as the voice of a so-called expert, but as the accumulated experience of someone who has shared the happiness and sorrow, the hurt and anger and love, of many families.

I am not going to scold anyone in this book. As a matter of fact, I should probably pin medals on many of you for doing the best you know how with a difficult situation; the very fact that you are reading a book like this tells me that you really care about the well-being of your family. It is my hope, however, that I can give you something more valuable than medals: namely, some new ways to find a better life together as a family.

The relationships in a family are extremely complex. To make them a little easier to understand, I will use many *as ifs*. These won't add up to the kind of sophisticated model the scholar constructs, but rather they will offer you a variety of ways of looking at your family system, in the hope that you'll find some that have real meaning for you.

As you read, you will come upon suggested experiments or exercises. I hope you will do each one as you come to it, even if at first it seems simple or foolish. Knowing *about* the family system won't change anything. You must learn *how* to make that system work vitally yourself. These experiments are positive, concrete steps your family can take to become less troubled and more nurturing. The more members of your family who take part in them, the more effective they will be. You will begin to *feel* your system working and sense whether it is leading to trouble or growth.

Perhaps you might wonder how to get the rest of your family members to participate in these exercises with you. This might be especially true if ruptures are already occurring in your family.

My suggestion is that you become thoroughly familiar with what you are asking so you will be able to more clearly present your request. If you feel enthusiastic and hopeful about what you think might happen, you will probably communicate a sense of excitement, which will make the invitation attractive and make your family members want to try along with you. By setting your request in a simple straightforward question—Will you participate with me in an experiment that I think might be useful to us?—you maximize the opportunity for a positive response.

The problem most people encounter is that they try to badger or demand or nag their family members to go along with them. This turns the transaction into a power struggle, which usually works in the opposite direction.

It is possible that at this point in time, things are so ruptured nothing can be done. The chances are pretty good that if your family members live under the same roof, they will be willing to at least try.

I have seen much pain in families. Each one has moved me deeply. Through this book I hope to ease that pain in families whom I may never have a chance to meet personally. In doing so, I hope also to prevent the pain from continuing into the families their children will form. Some human pain is unavoidable, of course. But as a people, we don't always put our efforts in the right place, to change what we can and to work out creative ways to live with what we can't change.

There is some possibility that just reading this book may evoke a little pain for you. After all, facing ourselves has its painful moments. But if you think there may be a better way of living together as a family than the way you are living now, I think you'll find this book rewarding.

What's *Your* Family Like?

Rearing a family is probably the most difficult job in the world. It resembles a merger of two business firms, putting their respective resources together to make a single product. All the potential headaches of that operation are present when an adult male and an adult female join to steer a child from infancy to adulthood. The parents in a nurturing family realize that problems will come along, simply because life offers them, but they will be alert to creative solutions for each new problem as it appears. Troubled families, on the other hand, put all their energies into the hopeless attempt to keep problems from happening; when they do happen—and, of course, they always do—these people have no resources left for solving them.

Perhaps one of the distinguishing features of nurturing parents is that they realize that change is inevitable: children change quickly from one stage to another, nurturing adults never stop growing and changing; and the world around us never stands still. They accept change as an unavoidable part of being alive and try to use it creatively to make their families still more nurturing.

Can you think of a family that you would call nurturing at least part of the time? Can you remember a time recently when your own family could be described as nurturing? Try to remember how it felt to be in your family then. Do these times happen often?

Some people may scoff at my picture of the nurturing family and say it isn't possible for any family to live that way. To them I would say, I have had the good fortune to know a number of these kinds of families intimately, and *it is possible*. Alas, only four families in perhaps a hundred know how to do it.

Others may protest that with all the pressures of daily living there just isn't time for most people to overhaul their family lives. To them I would say, we had better find the time; *it is a matter of survival.* I consider this our first priority. Troubled families make troubled people and thus contribute to crime, mental illness, alcoholism, drug abuse, poverty, alienated youth, political extremism, and many other social problems. If we don't give our best efforts to developing the family and making people who are more truly human, I see our present social problems growing worse and worse, perhaps ending in extinction for us all.

But if the price of failure is high, so is the reward if we succeed. Everyone who holds a position of power or influence in the world was once an infant. How he uses his power or influence depends a good deal on what he learned in the family as he was growing up. If only we can help troubled families become nurturing—and nurturing ones even more nurturing—the impact of their increased human-ity will filter out into government, education, business, religion, all the fields that determine the quality of our lives.

I am convinced that any troubled family can become a nurturing one. Most of the things that cause families to be troubled are learned after birth. Since they are learned, they can be unlearned; and new things can be learned in their place. The question is, how?

First, you need to recognize that your family *is* a troubled family.

Second, you need to have some hope that things can be different.

Third, you need to take some action to start the changing process.

As you begin to see the troubles in your family more clearly, it will help you to realize that, whatever may have happened in the past, it represented the best you knew how to do at the time. There is no reason for anyone to feel guilty himself or to blame others in the family. The chances are that the causes of your family pain have been invisible to all of you—not because you don't want to see them but because either you don't know where to look for them or you have been taught to view life through mental "glasses" that keep you from seeing certain things.

In this book you will begin to take off those glasses and look directly at the things that cause joy or pain in family life. The first is *self-worth*.

Self-Worth: The Pot That Nobody Watches

When I was a little girl, I lived on a farm in Wisconsin. On our back porch was a huge black iron pot, which had lovely rounded sides and stood on three legs. My mother made her own soap, so for part of the year the pot was filled with soap. When threshing crews came through in the summer, we filled the pot with stew. At other times my father used it to store manure for my mother's flower beds. We all came to call it the "3-S pot." Whenever anyone wanted to use the pot, he was faced with two questions: What is the pot now full of, and how full is it?

Long afterward, when people would tell me of their feelings of self-worth—whether they felt full or empty, dirty, or even "cracked"—I would think of that old pot. One day several years ago, a family was sitting in my office, and its members were trying to explain to one another how they felt about themselves. I remembered the black pot and told them the story. Soon the members of the family were talking about their own individual "pots," whether they contained feelings of worth or of guilt, shame, or uselessness.

Before long this simple shorthand word was helping many of my families express feelings that had been difficult to talk about before. A father might say, "My pot is high today," and the rest of the family would know that he felt on top of things, full of energy and good spirits, secure in the knowledge that he really mattered. Or a son might say, "I feel low-pot." This told everyone that he felt that he did not matter, that he felt tired or bored or bruised, not particularly lovable. It might even mean that he had always felt he was no good; that he had to take what was handed to him and could not complain.

Pot is a plain word, in this use almost a nonsense word. Incidentally, I had this word long before marijuana became popular, so I lay first claims to it. So many of the words professional people use to talk about human beings sound sterile and lack life-and-breath images. Families seem to find it easier to express themselves in "pot" terms and to understand when other people express themselves that way. They seem suddenly more comfortable, released from our culture's foolish taboo against talking about one's feelings. A wife, who would hesitate to tell her husband that she feels inadequate, depressed, worthless, can say frankly, "Don't bother me now—my pot is dragging!"

So, in this book when I say "pot," I mean *self-worth* or *self-esteem*. And pot is what we are going to talk about in this chapter.

In my many years of teaching young children, treating families of all economic and social levels, training people from all walks of life—from all the day-to-day experiences of my professional and personal living, I am convinced that the crucial factor in what happens both *inside* people and *between* people is the picture of individual worth that each person carries around with him—his *pot.*

Integrity, honesty, responsibility, compassion, love —all flow easily from the person whose pot is high. He feels that he matters, that the world is a better place because he is here. He has faith in his own competence. He is able to ask others for help, but he believes he can make his own decisions and is his own best resource. Appreciating his own worth, he is ready to see and respect the worth of others. He radiates trust and hope. He doesn't have rules against anything he feels. He accepts all of himself as human.

Vital people feel high-pot most of the time. True, everyone experiences times when he would just as soon chuck it all; when fatigue overwhelms him and the world has dealt him too many disappointments too quickly; when the problems of life suddenly seem more than he can manage. But the vital person treats these temporary low-pot feelings as just what they are—a crisis of the moment from which he can emerge whole and something he can feel uncomfortable about but does not have to hide.

Other people, however, spend most of their lives in a low-pot condition. Because they feel they have little worth, they expect to be cheated, stepped on, deprecated by others. Expecting the worst, they invite it and usually get it. To defend themselves, they hide behind a wall of distrust and sink into the terrible human state of loneliness and isolation. Thus separated from other people, they become apathetic, indifferent toward themselves and those around them. It is hard for them to see, hear, or think clearly, and therefore they are more prone to step on and deprecate others.

Fear is a natural consequence of this distrust and isolation. Fear constricts and blinds you; it keeps you from risking new ways of solving your problems and so gives rise to still more self-defeating behavior. (Fear, incidentally, is always fear of some *future* thing. I have observed that as soon as a person confronts or challenges whatever he is afraid of, the fear vanishes.)

When the perennially low-pot person experiences defeats—the kinds that would make even a vital person feel low-pot for a while—he feels desperate. How can such a worthless person as he cope with such troubles? he asks himself. It is not surprising that occasionally a low-pot person under overwhelming pressure will resort to drugs or suicide or murder. I truly believe that most of the pain, problems, ugliness in life—even wars—are the result of someone's low pot, which he really can't talk straight about.

Can you remember some time recently when your spirits were up? Perhaps the boss had just told you that you had been promoted; or you wore a becoming new dress and received several compliments; or you handled a difficult problem with one of the children and everything turned out happily. Try to go back now and feel again the feelings you had that day. That is what it is like to feel high pot.

Can you remember another occasion, when you made an embarrassing slip, or a costly error; or you were scolded angrily by your boss or your spouse; or you felt helpless in handling a problem with the children? Again, go back and relive the feelings you had, even though it is painful. That is what it is like to feel low pot.

Feeling low is not really the same as low pot. Low pot essentially means that you are experiencing undesirable feelings at the moment and are trying to behave as though those feelings did not exist. It takes a lot of trust to express your low self-esteem feelings. Low pot is a form of lying to yourself and others.

Now relax for a moment, then feel the state of your pot today. Is it high or low? Has something special happened to give you this feeling, or do you feel this way most of the time?

I hope that several members of your family will try this experiment together. Tell one another your feelings. Compare the things that make you feel low pot or high pot. You may find new dimensions to the people you've been living with all these years, and feel closer to one another as a result.

I am convinced that there are no genes to carry the feeling of worth. *It is learned.* And the family is where it is learned. You learned to feel high pot or low pot in the family your parents created. And your children are learning it in your family right now.

An infant coming into the world has no past, no experience in handling himself, no scale on which to judge his own worth. He must rely on the experiences he has with the people around him and the messages they give him about his worth as a person. For the first five or six years, the child's pot is formed by the family almost exclusively. After he starts school, other influences come into play, but the family remains important all through his adolescence. Outside forces tend to reinforce the feelings of worth or worthlessness that he has learned at home: the high-pot child can weather many failures in school or among peers; the low-pot child can experience many successes yet feel a gnawing doubt about his own value.

Every word, facial expression, gesture, or action on the part of the parent gives the child some message about his worth. It is sad that so many parents don't realize the effect these messages have on the child, and often don't even realize what messages they are sending. A mother may accept the bouquet clutched in her three-year-old's hand and say, "Where did you pick these?"—her voice and smile implying "How sweet of you to bring me these! Where do such lovely flowers grow?" This message would strengthen the child's feelings of worth. Or she might say, "How pretty!" but add, "did you pick these in Mrs. Randall's garden?"—implying that the child was bad to steal them. This message would make him feel wicked and worthless. Or she might say, "How pretty! Where did you pick them?" but wear a worried, accusing expression that added, "Did you steal them from Mrs. Randall's garden?" In this case, she is building low pot but probably does not realize it.

What kind of self-worth is your family building? You can begin to find out with this little experiment.

Tonight, when the family has settled around the table for dinner, try to feel what is happening to your pot each time another member speaks to you. There will be some remarks that have no "pot-content," of course. But you may be surprised to find that even "Pass the potatoes, please" can make you feel valued or deprecated, depending on the tone of voice, the facial expression, the timing (did it interrupt you or serve as a way of ignoring something you said?).

When dinner is about half finished, change the game. Listen to what you are saying to others. Is your remark likely to make the other person feel better about himself? Does his reply or his facial expression fit that prediction? If not, your face or tone or gestures may be communicating some message of which you are not aware. Try to be spontaneous and say what you would have said if you weren't trying this experiment. That won't be easy. Just being aware of what you say will make you tend to say pot-building things. But then that is another value of the experiment.

Tomorrow night explain this little game to the other members of the family. If they are old enough, let them read this chapter before dinner. Then all of you try the experiment at the same time. After dinner, talk together about what you discovered and how you felt.

Feelings of worth can only flourish in an atmosphere where individual differences are appreciated, mistakes are tolerated, communication is open, and rules are flexible—the kind of atmosphere that is found in a nurturing family. It is no accident that the children of these families usually feel good about themselves, or that the children of troubled families so often feel worthless, growing up as they must amid "crooked" communication, inflexible rules, criticism of their differentness, and punishment for their mistakes.

These same differences in self-worth can be seen in the adults in nurturing and troubled families. But here I think it is not so much that the family affects the adult's pot (although that certainly happens) as that high-pot parents are more likely to create nurturing families, and low-pot parents troubled families.

After years of working with families, I find that I no longer feel like blaming parents, no matter how foolish or destructive their actions. Instead, I try to find ways to raise their pot. This is a good first step to improving the whole family situation.

Happily, it is possible to raise anyone's pot, no matter what his age. Since the feeling of worth has been learned, it can be unlearned, and something new can be learned in its place. The possibility for this learning lasts from birth to death, so it is never too late. At any point in a person's life he can begin to feel better about himself.

I mean this to be the most important message in this book: *there is always hope that your life can change because you can always learn new things.* Human beings can grow and change all their lives. It is a little harder as we grow older, and it takes a little longer. But knowing that change is possible, and wanting to do it, are two first big steps. We may be slow learners, but we are all educable.

I want to close this chapter with a bit of prose which contains my feelings and ideas about self-worth.

MY DECLARATION OF SELF-ESTEEM

I am me.

In all the world, there is no one else exactly like me. There are persons who have some parts like me, but no one adds up exactly like me. Therefore, everything that comes out of me is authentically mine because I alone chose it.

I own everything about me—my body, including everything it does; my mind, including all its thoughts and ideas; my eyes, including the images of all they behold; my feelings, whatever they may be—anger, joy, frustration, love, disappointment, excitement; my mouth, and all the words that come out of it, polite, sweet or rough, correct or incorrect; my voice, loud or soft; and all my actions, whether they be to others or to myself.

I own my fantasies, my dreams, my hopes, my fears.

I own all my triumphs and successes, all my failures and mistakes.

Because I own all of me, I can become intimately acquainted with me. By so doing I can love me and be friendly with me in all my parts. I can then make it possible for all of me to work in my best interests.

I know there are aspects about myself that puzzle me, and other aspects that I do not know. But as long as I am friendly and loving to myself, I can courageously and hopefully look for the solutions to the puzzles and for ways to find out more about me.

However I look and sound, whatever I say and do, and whatever I think and feel at a given moment in time is me. This is authentic and represents where I am at that moment in time.

When I review later how I looked and sounded, what I said and did, and how I thought and felt, some parts may turn out to be unfitting. I can discard that which is unfitting, and keep that which proved fitting, and invent something new for that which I discarded.

I can see, hear, feel, think, say, and do. I have the tools to survive, to be close to others, to be productive, and to make sense and order out of the world of people and things outside of me.

I own me, and therefore I can engineer me.

I am me and I am okay.*

*Reprinted by permission of the publisher from V. Satir, "A Goal of Living," ETCETERA, December 1970.

Communication: Talking and Listening

I see communication as a huge umbrella that covers and affects all that goes on between human beings. Once a human being has arrived on this earth, *communication is the largest single factor determining what kinds of relationships he makes with others and what happens to him in the world about him.* How he manages his survival, how he develops intimacy, how productive he is, how he makes sense, how he connects with his own divinity—all are largely dependent on his communication skills.

Communication is the gauge by which two people measure one another's "pot level," and it is also the tool by which that level can be changed for them both. Communication covers the whole range of ways people pass information back and forth; it includes the information they give and receive, and the ways that that information is used. Communication covers how people make meaning of this information.

All communication is learned. By the time we reach the age of five, we probably have had a billion experiences in sharing communication. By that age we have developed ideas about how we see ourselves, what we can expect from others, and what seems to be possible or impossible for us in the world. Unless we have some exceedingly unusual experiences, those ideas will become fixed guides for the rest of our lives.

Once a person realizes that all of his communication is learned, he can set about changing it if he wants to. It will be helpful to remember that every baby who comes into this world comes only with raw materials. He has no self-concept, no experience of interacting with others, and no experience in dealing with the world around him. He learns all these things through communication with the people who are in charge of him from his birth on.

Patterns of Communication

After thirty years of listening to literally thousands of interactions among people, I gradually became aware of certain seemingly universal patterns in the way people communicated.

Whenever there was any stress, over and over again I observed four ways people had of handling it. These four patterns occurred only when one was reacting to stress *and at the same time* felt his self-esteem was involved—"his pot got hooked." In addition, the "hooked" one felt he could not say so. Presence of stress alone need not hook your pot, incidentally. Stress might be painful or annoying, but that isn't the same as doubting your own worth.

The four patterns of communication (which will be dealt with in detail later in this chapter) are: *placating, blaming, computing,* and *distracting.*

As I went into this more deeply I began to see that the self-esteem (pot) became hooked more easily when a person had not really developed a solid, appreciative sense of his own worth. Not having his own, he would use another's actions and reactions to define himself. If someone called him green, he would agree with no checking and take the other's comment as one fitting him. He was green because the other person said so. It's easy for anyone with doubts about his own worth to fall into this trap.

Do you know your internal feeling when your pot gets hooked? When mine does, my stomach gets knots, my muscles get tight, I find myself holding my breath, and I sometimes feel dizzy. While all this is going on I find that my thoughts concern the pot dialogue I am having with myself. The words are variations of "Who cares about me? I am unlovable. I can never do anything right. I am a nothing." Descriptive words for this condition are embarrassed, anxious, incompetent.

What I say at this point might be quite different from anything I am feeling or thinking. If I feel the only way out of my dilemma is to make things right with you so you will think I am lovable, etc., I will say whatever I think would fit. It would not matter if it were true or not. What matters is my survival, and I have put that in your hands.

Suppose, instead, I keep my survival in my hands. Then when my pot is hooked, I can say straight out what I think and feel. I might feel some initial pain at exposing my "weaknesses" and taking the risk that I believe goes with that, but I avoid the greater pain of hurting myself physically, emotionally, intellectually, socially, and spiritually, as well as avoiding giving you double-level messages.

It's important at this point to understand that every time you talk, all of you talks. Whenever you say words, your face, voice, body, breathing, and muscles are talking, too. A simple diagram is as follows:

Verbal communication   =   words

Body/sound communication   = facial expression
body position
muscle tonus
breathing tempo
voice tone

What we are essentially talking about in these four patterns of communication are *double-level* messages. In all four instances your voice is saying one thing, and the rest of you is saying something else. Should you be interacting with someone who responds in double-level messages, too, the results of your interactions are often hurtful and unsatisfactory.

The troubled families I have known all have handled their communication through double-level messages. Double-level messages come through when a person holds the following views:

1. He has low self-esteem (low pot) and feels he is bad because he feels that way.
2. He feels fearful about hurting the other's feelings.
3. He worries about retaliation from the other.
4. He fears rupture of the relationship.
5. He does not want to impose.
6. He does not attach any significance to the person or the interaction itself.

In nearly all of these instances the person is unaware that he is giving double-level messages.

So the listener will be confronted by two messages, and the outcome of the communication will be greatly influenced by his response. In general, these are the possibilities: pick up the words and ignore the rest; pick up the non-word part and ignore the words; ignore the whole message by changing the subject, leaving, going to sleep, or commenting on the double-level nature of the message.

For example, if I have a smile on my face and the words, "I feel terrible," come out of my mouth, how will you respond? Picking up on the possibilities outlined in the last paragraph, you might respond to the words and say, "That's too bad," to which I can respond, "I was just kidding." Your second choice is to respond to the smile and say, "You look great," in which case I can say, "How can you say that!" Your third choice is to ignore the whole thing and go back to your paper, in which case I would respond, "What's the matter? Don't you give a damn?" Your fourth choice is to comment on my double message: "I don't know what you're telling me. You're smiling, yet you tell me you're feeling bad. What gives?" In this case I have a chance to respond, "I didn't want to impose on you," and so on.

Let yourself imagine what kinds of results there could be if each of the above were the basis of communication between two people.

I feel terrible

It is my belief that any family communication not leading to realness or straight, single levels of meaning cannot possibly lead to the trust and love that, of course, nourish members of the family.

Remember that what goes on in a moment in time between two people has many more levels than are visible on the surface. The surface represents only a small portion of what is going on, much in the same way that only a very small part of an iceberg is visible.

Thus in the following:

"Where were you last night?"

"You are always nagging me!"

Something is happening to each person in relation to himself.

Something is happening to the perception by each of the other.

The ensuing direction of the relationship can go toward distrust, personal low pot, frustration, or, on the other hand, it can be the beginning of new depth and trust.

Let's take a closer look at these universal patterns

of response people use to get around the threat of rejection. In all cases the individual is feeling and reacting to the threat, but because he doesn't want to reveal "weakness" he attempts to conceal it in the following ways:

1. *Placate* so the other person doesn't get mad;
2. *Blame* so the other person will regard you as strong (if he goes away it will be his fault, not yours);
3. *Compute* with the resultant message that you are attempting to deal with the threat as though it were harmless, and you are trying to establish your self-worth by using big words;
4. *Distract* so you ignore the threat, behaving as though it were not there (maybe if you do this long enough, it really will go away).

Our bodies have come to accommodate our feeling of self-worth whether we realize it or not. If our self-worth is in question, our bodies show it.

With this in mind I have devised certain physical stances to help people get in touch with parts of themselves that are obvious to other people but not to themselves. All I did was exaggerate and expand the facial and voice messages into the whole body and make it so exaggerated that nobody could miss it.

To help clarify the responses (we are actually going to play out these roles in communication games in the next chapter), I have included a simple word-diagram with each descriptive section.

PLACATER

(1) Words   agree   ("Whatever you want is okay. I am just here to make you happy.")

Body   placates   ("I am helpless.")

Insides   ("I feel like a nothing; without
                           him I am dead. I am worthless.")

The *placater* always talks in an ingratiating way, trying to please, apologizing, never disagreeing, no matter what. He's a "yes man." He talks as though he could do nothing for himself; he must always get someone to approve of him. You will find later that if you play this role for even five minutes, you will begin to feel nauseous and want to vomit.

A big help in doing a good placating job is to think of yourself as really worth nothing. You are lucky just to be allowed to eat. You owe everybody gratitude, and you really are responsible for everything that goes wrong. You know you could have stopped the rain if you used your brains, but you don't have any. Naturally you will agree with any criticism made about you. You are, of course, grateful for the fact that anyone even talks to you, no matter what they say or how they say it. You would not think of asking anything for yourself. After all, who are you to ask? Besides, if you can just be good enough it will come by itself.

Be the most syrupy, martyrish, bootlicking person you can be. Think of yourself as being physically down on one knee, wobbling a bit, putting out one hand in a begging fashion, and be sure to have your head up so your neck will hurt and your eyes will become strained so in no time at all you will begin to get a headache.

When you talk in this position your voice will be whiny and squeaky because you keep your body in such a lowered position that you don't have enough air to keep a rich, full voice. You will be saying "yes" to everything, no matter what you feel or think. The placating stance is the body position that matches the placating response.

BLAMER

(2)	Words	disagree	("You never do anything right. What is the matter with you?")
	Body	blames	("I am the boss around here.")
	Insides		("I am lonely and unsuccessful.")

The *blamer* is a fault-finder, a dictator, a boss. He acts superior, and he seems to be saying, "If it weren't for you, everything would be all right." The internal feeling is one of tightness in the muscles and in the organs. Meanwhile the blood pressure is increasing. The voice is hard, tight, and often shrill and loud.

Good blaming requires you to be as loud and tyrannical as you can. Cut everything and everyone down.

As a blamer it would be helpful to think of yourself pointing your finger accusingly and to start your sentences with "You never do this or you always do that or why do you always or why do you never . . ." and so on. Don't bother about an answer. That is unimportant. The blamer is much more interested in throwing his weight around than really finding out about anything.

Whether you know it or not, when you are blaming you are breathing in little tight spurts, or holding your breath altogether, because your throat muscles are so tight. Have you ever seen a really first-rate blamer whose eyes were bulging, neck muscles and nostrils standing out, who was getting red and whose voice sounded like someone shoveling coal? Think of yourself standing with one hand on your hip and the other arm extended with your index finger pointed straight out. Your face is screwed up, your lips curled, your nostrils flared as you tell, call names, and criticize everything under the sun. Your blaming stance looks like this:

You don't really feel you are worth anything, either. So if you can get someone to obey you, then you feel you count for something.

COMPUTER

(3) Words	ultra- reasonable	("If one were to observe carefully, one might notice the workworn hands of someone present here.")
Body	computes	("I'm calm, cool, and collected.")
Insides		("I feel vulnerable.")

The *computer* is very correct, very reasonable with no semblance of any feeling showing. He is calm, cool, and collected. He could be compared to an actual computer or a dictionary. The body feels dry, often cool, and disassociated. The voice is a dry monotone, and the words are likely to be abstract.

When you are a computer, use the longest words possible, even if you aren't sure of their meanings. You will at least sound intelligent. After one paragraph no one will be listening anyway. To get yourself really in the mood for this role, imagine that your spine is a long, heavy steel rod reaching from your buttocks to the nape of your neck, and you have a ten-inch-wide iron collar around your neck. Keep everything about yourself as motionless as possible, including your mouth. You will have to try hard to keep your hands from moving, but do it.

When you are computing, your voice will naturally go dead because you have no feeling from the cranium down. Your mind is bent on being careful not to move, and you are kept busy choosing the right words. After all, you should never make a mistake. The sad part of this role is that it seems to represent an ideal goal for many people. "Say the right words; show no feeling; don't react."

Your computer position stance will look like this:

DISTRACTER

(4) Words   irrelevant (the words make no sense)

    Body   angular and off somewhere else

    Insides   ("Nobody cares. There is no place for me.")

Whatever the *distracter* does or says is irrelevant to what anyone else is saying or doing. He never makes a response to the point. His internal feeling is one of dizziness. The voice can be singsong, often out of tune with the words, and can go up and down without reason because it is focused nowhere.

When you play the distracting role, it will help you to think of yourself as a kind of lopsided top, constantly spinning, but never knowing where you are going, and not realizing it when you get there. You are too busy moving your mouth, your body, your arms, your legs. Make sure you are never on the point with your words. Ignore everyone's questions; maybe come back with one of your own on a different subject. Take a piece of imaginary lint off someone's garment, untie shoelaces, and so on.

Think of your body as going off in different directions at once. Put your knees together in an exaggerated knock-kneed fashion. This will bring your buttocks out, and make it easy for you to hunch your shoulders and have your arms and hands going in opposite directions.

At first this role seems like a relief, but after a few minutes of play, the terrible loneliness and purposelessness arise. If you can keep yourself moving fast enough, you won't notice it so much.

You will look like this:

As practice for yourself, take the four physical stances I have described, hold them for just sixty seconds and see what happens to you. Since many people are unaccustomed to feeling their body reactions, you may find at first that you are so busy thinking you aren't feeling. Keep at it, and you will begin to have the internal feelings you've experienced so many times before. Then the moment you are on your own two feet and are freely relaxed and able to move, you find your internal feeling changes.

It is my hunch that these ways of communicating are learned early in childhood. As the child tries to make his way through the complicated and often threatening world in which he finds himself, he uses one or another of these means of communicating. After enough use he can no longer distinguish his response from his feeling of worth or his personality.

Use of any of these four responses forges another ring in an individual's feeling of low self-worth or low pot. Attitudes prevalent in our society also reinforce these ways of communicating—many of which are learned at our mother's knee.

"Don't impose; it's selfish to ask for things for yourself," helps to reinforce placating.

"Don't let anyone put you down; don't be a coward," helps to reinforce blaming.

"Don't be so serious. Live it up! Who cares?" helps to reinforce distracting.

At this point you may well be wondering if there is any hope for us at all if these four crippling modes of communication are all we have. Of course they are not.

There is a fifth response that I have called *leveling* or flowing. In this response all parts of the message are going in the same direction—the voice says words that match the facial expression, the body position, and the voice tone.

Relationships are easy, free and honest, and there are few threats to self-esteem. With this response there is no need to blame, retreat into a computer, or to be in perpetual motion.

Of the five responses only the leveling one has any chance to heal ruptures, break impasses, or build bridges between people.   And lest leveling seem too unrealistic to you, let me assure you that you can still placate if you choose, blame if you like, be on a head trip, or be distracting. The difference is you know what you are doing and are prepared to take the consequences for it.

So when you are leveling you apologize in reality when you realize you've done something you didn't intend. You are apologizing for an act not for your existence. There are times when you need to criticize and evaluate. When you do this in a leveling way, you are evaluating an act, not blaming the person, and there is usually a new direction you have to offer. There are times when you're talking about intellectual kinds of things such as giving lectures, making explanations, giving directions, and so on, where precise word meanings are essential. When you are leveling in this area, you are still showing your feelings, moving freely while you're explaining. You aren't coming off like a machine. So many people who make their livings with their brains—scientists, mathematicians, accountants, teachers, and therapists—come off like machines and epitomize the computing response. In addition, there are times when you want to or need to change the subject. In the leveling response you can say what you want to instead of hopping all over the place.

The leveling response is real for whatever is. If a leveler says, "I like you," his voice is warm and he looks at you. If his words are, "I am mad as hell at you," his voice is harsh, and his face is tight. The message is single and straight.

Another aspect of the leveling response is that it represents a truth of the person at a moment in time. This is in contrast, for example, to a blaming response where the person is feeling helpless, but is acting angry—or is hurting, but is acting brave.

A third aspect of the leveling response is that it is whole, not partial. The body, sense, thoughts, and feelings all are shown, in contrast to computing, for example, where nothing moves but the mouth and that only slightly.

There is an integration, a flowing, an aliveness, an openness and what I call a *juiciness* about a person who is leveling. You trust him, you know where you stand with him, and you feel good in his presence. The position is one of wholeness and free movement. This response is the only one that makes it possible to live in an alive way, rather than a dead way.

Now, to help you distinguish more clearly between a given subject and the different ways of expressing oneself about that subject, let me present five ways of apologizing in the five ways of communicating. This can also serve as a kind of demonstration before actually playing the games in the next chapter. Let's imagine that I have just bumped your arm.

Placating (looking down, wringing hands): "Please forgive me. I am just a clumsy oaf."

Blaming: "Ye gods, I just hit your arm! Keep it in next time so I won't hit it!"

Computing: "I wish to render an apology. I inadvertently struck your arm in passing. If there are any damages, please contact my attorney."

Distracting (looking at someone else): "Gee, some guy's mad. Must've got bumped."

Leveling (looking directly at the person): "I bumped you. I'm sorry. Are you hurt?"

Let's take another imaginary situation. I am your father, and there is something wrong in what you, my son, are doing.

Placating (coming up with a hushed voice, downcast face): "I'm — uh — uh — gosh, gee, Jim, I — am sorry — you feeling okay? You know — promise me you won't get mad — no, you're doing okay, it's just — maybe you could do a little better? Just a little, maybe? Hm?"

Blaming: "For Christ's sake, don't you know anything, you dumb cluck?"

Computing: "We are making a survey of our family efficiency. We find that in this department, namely with you, that efficiency is beginning to go down. Would you have any comments to make?"

Distracting (talking to his other son, standing next to Jim): "Say, Arnold, is your room about the same as Jim's? No, nothing wrong—I was just taking a walk through the house. Tell Jim to see his mother before he goes to bed."

Leveling: "Jim, your room is in bad shape. You haven't made your bed since yesterday. We need to stop, take a look, and see what's wrong."

It's anything but easy to break old habit patterns and become a leveler. One way in which you might be helped to achieve this goal is through learning what some of the fears are that keep you from leveling. To thwart the rejection we so fear, we tend to threaten ourselves in the following ways:

1. I might make a mistake.
2. Someone might not like it.
3. Someone will criticize me.
4. I might impose.
5. He will think I am no good.
6. I might be thought of as imperfect.
7. He might leave.

When you can tell yourself the following answers to the foregoing statements, you will have achieved real growth:

1. You are sure to make mistakes if you take any action, especially new action.
2. You can be quite sure that there will be someone who won't like what you do. Not everyone likes the same things.
3. Yes, someone will criticize you. You really aren't perfect. Some criticism is useful.
4. Sure! Every time you are in the presence of another person, speak to him, and interrupt him, you impose!
5. So maybe he will think you're no good. Can you live through it? Maybe sometimes you aren't so hot. Sometimes the other person is "putting his trip on you." Can you tell the difference?
6. If you think of yourself as needing to be perfect, the chances are you will always be able to find imperfection.
7. So he leaves. Maybe he should leave, and anyway, you'll live through it.

These attitudes will give you a good opportunity to stand on your own two good feet. It won't be easy and it won't be painless, but it might make the difference as to whether or not you grow.

With no intention of being flippant, I do think that most of the things we use to threaten ourselves and that affect our self-worth turn out to be tempests in teapots. One way I helped myself through these threats was to ask myself if I would still be alive if all these imagined threats came true. If I could answer yes, then I was okay. I can answer yes to all of them now.

I will never forget the day I found out that lots of other people worried about these same silly threats as I did. I had thought for years I was the only one, and I kept myself busy trying to outwit them, and at the same time doing my best to conceal the threats. My feeling was—what if somebody found out? Well, what if somebody did? We all use these same kinds of things to threaten ourselves.

By now you must realize that this isn't some kind of a magical recipe, but the leveling response is actually a way of responding to real people in real life situations that permit you to agree because you really do, not because you think you should; disagree because you really do, not because you think you won't make points unless you do; use your brain freely, but not at the expense of the rest of you; to change courses, not to get you off the hook, but because you want to and there is a need to do so.

What the leveling response does is make it possible for you to live as a whole person—real, in touch with your head, your heart, your feelings, and your body. Being a leveler enables you to have integrity, commitment, honesty, intimacy, competence, creativity, and the ability to work with real problems in a real way. The other forms of communication result in doubtful integrity, commitment by bargain, dishonesty, loneliness, shoddy competence, strangulation by tradition, and dealing in a destructive way with fantasy problems.

It takes guts, courage, some new beliefs, and some new skills to become a leveling responder. *You can't fake it.*

Unfortunately there is little in society that reinforces this leveling response. Yet people are actually hungry for this kind of straightness and honesty. When they become aware of it and are courageous enough to try it, distances between people are shortened.

I did not come to this formulation via religion or through the study of philosophy. I came to it through a tough, trial-and-error way, trying to help people who had serious life problems. I found that what healed people was getting them to find their hearts, their feeling, their bodies, their brains, which once more brought them to their souls and thus to their humanity. They could then express themselves as whole people, which, in turn, helped them to greater feelings of self-worth (high pot), to nurturing relationships and satisfying outcomes.

None of these results is possible through the use of the four crippling ways of communication. I have found these, incidentally, as inevitable outcomes of the way authority is taught in famliies and reinforced by much of our society. What is so sad is that these four ways have become the most frequently used among people and are viewed by many as the most possible ways of achieving communication.

From what I have seen I've made some tentative conclusions about what to expect when I meet new groups of people. Fifty percent will say yes no matter what they feel or think (placate); 30 percent will say no, no matter what they feel or think (blame); 15 percent will say neither yes nor no and will give no hint of their feelings (compute); and 1/2 percent will behave as if yes, no, or feeling did not exist (distracting). That leaves only 4 1/2 percent whom I can expect to be real and to level. My colleagues tell me I am optimistic, saying the leveling response is probably found in only 1 percent of our population. Remember this is not validated research. It is only a clinical hunch. In the vernacular it would seem we are all a bunch of crooks—hiding ourselves and playing dangerous games with one another.

At this point I want to make an even more drastic statement. If you want to make your body sick, become disconnected from other people, throw away your beautiful brain power, make yourself deaf, dumb, and blind, using the four crippling ways of communication will in great measure help you to do it.

I feel very strongly as I write this. For me, the feelings of isolation, helplessness, feeling unloved, low pot, or incompetence comprise the real human evils of this world. Certain kinds of communication will continue this and certain kinds of communication can change it. What I am trying to do in this chapter is make it possible for each person to understand the leveling response so he can recognize and use it.

I would like to see each human being value and appreciate himself, feel whole, creative, competent, healthy, rugged, beautiful, and loving.

Despite the fact that I have exaggerated these different ways of communication for emphasis, and they may even seem amusing, I am deadly serious about the killing nature of the first four styles of communication.

In the next chapter, when you play the games I have invented, you will be able to experience exactly what these ways of communication are like, and you will be able to understand very quickly the toll they take of your body, the distrust that is formulated in your relationships with others and the blah, disappointing, and many times disastrous outcomes that ensue.

The second article included in this section is derived from a transcription of an impromptu talk by Virginia Satir after she conducted a very moving family interview and professional workshop. I was present at the workshop and again was struck by the amazing way she made rapid contact with all members of the workshop and the family. I think this article conveys more of Virginia's essence than anything she has written to date.

When I Meet a Person

People have often asked me how I look at people and what I see when I look. Many times what I think people are really asking is what kind of beliefs I have about people. And so today — seated in a lovely home looking out over the redwoods in Santa Cruz, California, in the presence of Dr. Robert Spitzer, who is publisher of Science and Behavior Books, and Peggy Granger, who is on the editorial staff, and Richard Bandler, who is in charge of production — I will try to answer by recording this tape.

I will try to do this in a way that I think might help people understand more about some of the things that I do when I'm working with people. And I will treat this in an extemporaneous fashion, trying to put together what I do as thoughts occur to me. I am quite aware that many of the ways I feel and things I do may not be all that's there, but I will share with you the best that I know at this point.

I would like to start with what goes on in me when I think about using myself as a helper to another person. In the first place, the person and his family — because I almost always think in the family context — would not be coming to me unless they had some kind of pain or some kind of problem that they wanted to solve. In some way I feel them as having said to themselves, "We've reached the end of our ability to cope, and we are searching for some way to cope better." People don't always put it in that language. Sometimes they only say, "I hurt" or "Somebody is doing something wrong." But the way I hear it is as a search for a new ability to cope better with their lives, and to have more joy and pleasure and less pain and perhaps more productivity. So I first think about these people; and, by the way, I think I apply these thoughts to myself as well as to others, only my thoughts become a little more sharply defined when I'm using them in a treatment context.

I see all people as representations of life, in whatever form that happens to be. When people are in need or are having some kind of problem, their manifestation of themselves— the way they look and sound and talk—can be pretty ugly, pretty beautiful, or pretty painful. But underneath all this I see the living human who, I feel, if he were in touch with the life that he is and has, would use himself differently. So that means that with every human being that I encounter, I mentally take off his outside and try to see his inside, which is that piece of the self that I call self-worth or self-esteem, and to which I have given the affectionate name "pot." This "pot" is searching for some way of manifesting itself. And that means that when I meet a person, I meet him with that awareness. There is in the person that which probably even he has not touched. He not only hasn't touched it; he doesn't even know it's there. But I know it's there. And this conviction in me is so strong that it is a given for me. So I never ask *if* that person has life; I ask only how it can be touched.

Yesterday I did an interview with a family and it is fresh in my mind at the moment. What I am going to try to do is describe in the best way I can what happened between the family and me. And I'll try to supply my understanding of what was going on in me, and how I used that to reach the self-worth of each member of the family. This was a family that had an adult male and an adult female who were husband and wife. These two adults were also father and mother of five children, the oldest eighteen and the youngest five. Of course, they had some kind of problem or they wouldn't have come in for treatment, so that was also obvious.

To start off, I was not so much concerned with a particular problem as with trying to understand and learn about how each person in this family lived his life, both with the others and with himself. For me, there are always two lives going on all the time—mine with myself, and mine with the other people who are significant to me. So I came to meet this family. I didn't know what I was going to find. I did not know how these particular family members were going to manifest themselves; I only knew that they were hurting and that they had something in them that could be touched and developed and that could grow.

The first thing I did was to take the first step toward meeting each one. Something that I am quite aware of is that people aren't usually related to themselves as people of worth. I feel that no changes can be made in people unless they begin to feel themselves as having worth, and that I as the therapist become the first means by which a person comes in touch with his own feeling of worth. So my meeting with this family is the beginning of this. I extended my hand to the husband-father, and subsequently did the same with all the rest of the family. I would like to say a little bit about what it was like for me when I did that. In the first place—and you might think along with me—suppose you are someone I am just meeting. You are with a group of people, perhaps members of your family, and I stand in front of you and reach out my hand to you at arm level. And as I reach for your hand and you give it to me, I feel the connection. At that moment in time, I am looking at you; I am in touch with your skin feelings and my skin feelings and for that moment there is no one else in the world except you and me. You are the receiver of my full attention at that moment. You can feel that what I am connecting with is your personhood, and I feel that I am giving mine to you. A smile accompanies this, and my smile is saying "hello" to you and to your life as a representation of all life. This kind of experience makes it possible for me to feel that I am connected with another form of life, another manifestation of life—yours. I regard life manifestation as the basis of what personhood is all about. As I do this with each member of your family, I am also aware within myself that I am enjoying having the contact—full contact—which in some way also affirms me. I am a living being connected with another living being. It is like the platform or the base from which we are going to go. This is why I do not start out my treatment session with a discussion of the problem, but rather make this basic connection on a human level with everyone. Of course, people are coming in for some help; and if they knew what sort of help they needed, they would probably be doing it themselves and not seeking me. They have come to the end of their coping and they want some help, but probably all that they are aware of is that they have pain.

As I am making this first contact with them and listening to their responses to me and feeling me, in a few moments I hear responses from the people to one another. I begin to get a feeling for what they have done, how they have used their experiences from the time they popped out of the womb until now. Some of you may be familiar with the stances I use for shorthand purposes—the ways in which people communicate with one another, the responses I have labeled as *placating, blaming, super-reasonable, irrelevant,* and *real.* At the beginning of treatment I do not expect the family to display many "real" responses, because the fact that they haven't arrived at that point is probably one of the reasons they are coping in the way that they are. But I also want to underscore the fact that I see the people in front of me as doing the very best they can with what they have learned; and I believe that what they have learned represents the best way they know how to survive. Some of you may be aware that I have translated the various kinds of responses into body positions. So, within a few moments, I am making mental pictures of the people in front of me in physical postures that represent their ways of communicating.

For example, in the family I saw yesterday, I saw the man as making super-reasonable responses. That meant that in my imagination he was standing there very erect, with very little movement, speaking in a rather monotonous way. I saw the woman kneeling before him in a placating position, but at the same time—behind her back—pointing an accusing finger at him. I saw the oldest daughter standing and super-reasonable like her father, looking at neither parent but with one finger barely poking out, pointing at her father. And I saw the next girl very deliberately and in a very obvious way pointing her finger at her mother. The next child was a boy, and I saw him standing very close to his mother and placating her. Then I saw the next child as giving out irrelevant responses by moving all over the place and not being able to fix on anyone. I also saw the youngest child, a five-year-old girl, as being irrelevant.

As I saw these pictures in my mind, it was important to respect them as representing the best ways that these people had developed to cope. Their ways of placating, blaming, and being super-reasonable or irrelevant had formed a kind of system which meant that no one in the family could really approach the personhood of another. They were likely to mishear one another; they were seeing roles rather than real people. So my search and my efforts would be directed to helping these people to become real with one another. I looked at this family, and my insides felt them respond to my contact. Full contact, by the way, carries the message of caring—caring in a deep, personal sense—and I regard that contact as a vital basis for developing any changes. There has to be high trust. If people in the family group do not find me trustworthy, I don't think we are going to be able to effect any changes.

I remember that as I entered the room yesterday, the family was spread around on chairs, looking very much like targets on a rifle range. There was a table in front of them and as I looked at this scene, I felt that it would be very awkward to work in. I feel very strongly that where people are sitting (far apart or close together) and the way they are sitting is very important. I need to make the place where I work comfortable—that is, to arrange it so that I can see everybody and am not much farther than arm's length from anyone. And there must be enough space for me and the other people to move about. This space is necessary because sometimes I will have family members work in pairs, or I will do "sculpturing" or some other kind of activity which requires space. A table or other obstacle makes movement difficult. So, yesterday, I moved the table and fixed it so that I was no more than a small step away from making touch contact with everyone in the group.

The little five-year-old was on my right. At one point I noticed that she was moving back a little bit. By this time I had the feeling that she was regarded as the troublemaker in the family and was rather on the outside. So I just slipped my hand around her back—she had a nice, round back—and I found myself feeling the enjoyment of touching her. I think she felt this as a message of encouragement to be a part of the group. Throughout the interview there was much more of this.

I would like to take a brief moment here to say that you can touch in all kinds of ways. In training therapists, I have told them that to develop "eyes and ears" in their fingers is an important thing to do. People in families are touching all the time—slapping, pushing, shoving, holding. I'm sure all of you know that touches have different meanings. So it isn't a matter of giving a touch; it's a matter of the message in the touch. I referred earlier to developing trust. What that literally means is that the atmosphere, through trust, has to be such that people can begin to talk about what I call "unspeakable things"—the things that are close to their hearts—what they worry about, what they fear, and what they hope for. I don't know if I can state this strongly enough to really get the message across to you. To me, that people *do* say what was once unspeakable is much more important than *what* they say. Sometimes it takes a little while for people to get the feeling that whatever they say can be heard and understood, and that it does not have to be run through any censorship system about what is right. I don't know of any way in which I can help a person get to himself unless he can let out whatever is there. That is not a usual thing in this society, as many of you doubtless know. But in order to create the context and the working way for change to take place, it seems to me that no one can be penalized in any way for what he says—at least not by me. Instead I must take whatever someone says and make this a living account of where the person is at that moment; and have what he says understood by him as well as everyone else. This means that a great deal of clarifying and interpreting must go on in order that a family can understand what each member is really trying to say.

As yesterday's interview proceeded, I put a question to each person in the family: "What do you hope will happen to you as a result of your coming here?" I suppose the usual question a therapist might ask is, "What is the problem?" I *am* interested in finding out where people are locked in, but I also feel that my way of asking about this and what I ask helps the person to center more on himself. And it also goes a little way toward diminishing the "vibes" that are usually there—usually some form of "Well, if he or she were better, I would be better," or something of that sort. In this instance I started out with the oldest daughter. At this moment I don't know why I did, except that at the time it seemed to be the right place to start. She said that she would like to see the family not fight so much. I went on to her sister, who said the same thing. I asked other family members if they had noticed that there was a lot of fighting going on and if they felt they too would like that to change. Everyone acknowledged this. So, the next picture that emerged in my mind was of the two older girls fighting with one another. It seemed at that point that they were the focus around which the family's problems centered. If these two girls didn't fight, then something else would be better. What this introduced was how people in this family could feel comfortable about expressing their anger. When I put my questions to the father, his answer was on the level of perhaps educating the family to some things they had previously not known. Because I like to make an "alive" picture as quickly as possible, it seemed natural at that point to ask the two older girls to get up and point their fingers at each other in order to see what other family members did when this happened. I find that words are more useful when there is a picture; I call this "sculpturing" or "posturing." I found that when I asked the two girls to point at each other, they were very reluctant to do so. They talked about how they fought, but actually putting themselves in the position of doing it made it more real. They seemed embarrassed.

One of the important things that I try to do is help people to be free (that word *free* can be misunderstood, but I'm going to use it anyway). I try to help people start playing with new ideas about behavior, and I try to give them the kind of encouragement that breaks through their taboos. So, since there was embarrassment, I stood behind the girl who seemed most embarrassed and supported her, standing close to her back and taking her arm and helping it to go out in a pointing direction. Then I did the same thing for the other girl. I was essentially taking the first step toward breaking this family's rule that you shouldn't be angry. This then led to the matter of what the others in the family do when there is fighting. Here were the two girls standing and pointing at each other, and everyone in the family had seen this before. So, my next question to the husband-father was, "What do you do when this happens?" He tried to tell the girls to stop, but it didn't do any good. I had him come up with his finger pointing and when he saw that this did no good either, he dropped his arm and sat down. One of the girls said the wife-mother "came on a little stronger," so I had her come in with her finger pointing. I asked some of the other children what usually happened, and they said they tried to stay out of it. The oldest boy now went to his mother's side, so he came in like an auxiliary father, trying to help her with the problem between the two girls.

This kind of sculpturing has value because it makes explicit what is going on. And it also does something else. In my way of seeing it, this is like bringing a familiar picture to life. But this time when it comes alive, it is not to show how bad people are, but instead to help them see what is going on. There is oftentimes a good bit of humor in this. I remember at one point asking the oldest girl to put out her finger. Her hand was a little wobbly, so I supported it and asked her to make believe there really was a pistol at the end of her hand. Lighthearted things like this tend to help neutralize the negative self-worth effect and to increase the ability of the person to look and see. For me, it is very important to make the separation between the person with his values and how he is using himself. What I am doing is bringing people in touch with the various ways they can use themselves; and I try to do this in ways that raise their feelings of self-worth. People often ask me if I feel drained after an interview. My answer is "No." I *would* get drained if I kept asking myself all kinds of questions like "Am I doing it right? Will people love me? Am I going to come out with a cure?" If I started to do that (which I call "potting myself"), I would lose track of the system and process that are going on and I would be on *my* story rather than the story of the family.

This leads me now to something else. I consider myself the leader of the *process* in the interview but *not* the leader of the *people*. I check out everything I do with them before I do it, so what I am is a strong leader for the process. This is based on the fact that I am the one who knows what the process I am trying to produce is all about. So I have to be a strong leader in relation to that. Also, I want to help people to become their own designers of their own choice-making; and before they can do that , they need to be free to take risks. So, my checking out with them their willingness to undertake anything is a very important piece of this interaction.

With yesterday's family, the wife-mother said that she started her marriage by always trying to please her husband. That had been what she was taught to do, but she was tired of it. So I asked her if she would be willing to make a little picture with me and she agreed to do it. I asked her to get down on her knees and to look up at her husband, whom I asked to stand on a stool. Then I asked the wife if what she was doing felt like anything she had ever felt before. She said that it did but she didn't want it to be like that anymore. Then I asked her husband how he felt up there, and he said he didn't like her being down there and he didn't like being on top. So then I asked them to fix it so they would both be comfortable. Of course, they ended up being eye-to-eye, both on the same level. It was following this that some expressions of hope began to appear on their faces.

But I was talking before about being the leader, and I would like to enlarge on that. If I have something to offer you, I need to tell you about it; I need to show you; I need to ask you if what I offer has any value to you. But what is important is that if I am introducing something new to you and I ask you too soon if you are willing to do it—that is, before I have gotten your understanding, trust, and willingness to take risks—then you will not be in a place where you feel that you can take a chance.

This brings up something else. People often say to me, "Well, what if something you do backfires?" And I answer, "That's not unusual." It is what happens in life when you try something that doesn't work. And you have some choices after that. You can call yourself bad names for trying it out, or you can use it as a life experience and learn from it. Nothing backfired in yesterday's interview because it seemed that I was in the flow and had nice things going. That is the whole point. As a therapist, I try to be aware of what is happening and keep it flowing rather than try continually to keep score of what is right or wrong.

This might be a good place to say that when I am speaking to a family, I am not trying to solve a specific problem such as should they get a divorce or should they have a baby. I am not working for that. What I am working for is to help people seek a different kind of coping process. I do not see myself as wise enough to know what is the best thing for a person to do. Should the wife ask her mother-in-law to leave? Should she *demand* that she leave? Should the wife leave her husband if the mother-in-law doesn't leave? These kinds of questions are not mine to answer. My task is to help each person with his own coping so that he can decide to do the things that work for him.

In yesterday's family, it came out that the second girl had occasionally talked of committing suicide, and there were a lot of hate responses going on between her and her mother. Instead of responding to that hate, what I read in my insides was that these two people were very much wanting to get a connection with each other but there were all kinds of barriers between them. I had learned earlier that the wife-mother had viewed this particular child as having the same problems she had had, and was feeling very bad about seeing them in her child. Apparently the mother was trying to solve the problems in herself by trying to solve them in her daughter. This, of course, was why these two could not get together.

What I did was to ask the two of them to move toward one another, because by this time the trust level was sufficiently established so that they would be willing to take this risk. First I had them move to where they could see each other clearly, approximately at arm's length, and then I had them look at each other. I then had them close their eyes and I asked each of them to tell me what she saw. This was very interesting because when the wife-mother closed her eyes, she said she saw a little baby whom she hadn't cared for very well, and that she was feeling very guilty. She began to sob a little. When I asked the daughter what she had seen, she said first that she just saw her mother. But then, after her mother had spoken, the girl said, "Well, she always sees me as a baby." What I was aware of at this point was that these two were not seeing each other as they really were at this point in time; they were seeing each other in terms of past experience. And if they didn't change, they would continue to see this way. One of the criticisms that the daughter had made earlier was that her mother was always treating her like a little baby. So, after this disclosure, I pointed out to the mother that she was indeed seeing this thirteen-year-old as a baby. Then, after having asked the mother her age, I pointed out to the daughter that she was seeing a thirty-six-year-old person. I stated that there were these two *ladies* (I used that word), Cynthia and June, who were looking at each other; and I wondered out loud if they not could see each other as Cynthia and June. Then I asked them to look again and tell me, after shutting their eyes, what they saw. They were what I call "being brought up to date." As June—the mother—spoke, she said she saw this thirteen-year-old who was attractive and that it was a whole new awareness for her. The daughter said she saw her mother and the look in her eyes, which seemed to be a look of caring for her and which she liked. And both of them at that point said they felt a whole lot different about one another.

The family then moved on to another situation involving the older daughter and her father. She was almost eighteen, and her father was still insisting that she come home early. It turned out that this man, because of his psychological and physical problems, had not yet come to a place where he could see himself as supporting his family by working. So his wife was working from 2:30 in the afternoon until midnight or so, which meant that the bulk of the management of the family was in the hands of the husband. He had worked out with the older daughter that she always cooked the dinner. Apparently she did the shopping, too. He always asked her to come in early, and she felt that this was an affront—a kind of invasion. I was then able to ask these two to sit in front of one another and just try to hear one another. I guided their listening and (I am sure this is something that you have seen often) helped them to see that they were not talking to each other in terms of what the other was saying but only in terms of what each wanted to get across. After this, it seemed as though both the daughter and her father had come to a new understanding.

It was quite clear at this point that both the husband and wife were very fearful about what would happen to their children. Another piece of information that came out was that both of them had parents who had left them early, and they were both brought up by grandparents who apparently were very anxious about them. This anxiety was transferred. Without this being clear before, most of the children in the family heard the parents' efforts to care for them as something against them. They had not been in touch with this other part. At the same time, the parents had been hearing their children as being quarrelsome and unappreciative. So we were able to make some new connections.

Throughout the interview, my mental picture was one of content flowing out and connections being made. Using myself in a very active way, I could pick out times (as with the mother and daughter) to make a new connection. During the flow of touching in the family, the mother said that she hoped that her youngest son would hug her. He always came in and just gave her a "little old hug" and she always felt cheated. So the whole question of affection in the family and how people could be affectionate was brought up. This had had a taboo on it. At the end of the interview—because I was enjoying the family and feeling affectionate feelings toward them—it was natural for me to hug the members of the family and to feel the response from them. Just after I had hugged the mother and gone to the two sisters, I heard a little snickering by the two boys, aged eighteen and twelve. What crossed my mind was that these two boys were at a period where it might be awkward for them to engage in this kind of thing even though I felt they wanted some kind of expression of affection from me. So, when I turned to the first of them, I commented that I had heard the snickering and that maybe this was a bit much for them, but I wanted them to know that I had these feelings. Then I gave them each an extra-warm handshake and a pat on the shoulder, trying to respect where they were at that point and at the same time to convey my message. What was interesting also was that the father was the last one I went to; and I had the feeling that he was almost standing in line waiting and would be willing to hug but couldn't quite ask. So when I made the overture to him, he came readily to be hugged. I know that men very often have had experiences in the past where it wasn't manly to have such feelings, and so I found myself telling the father that Bob Hope had spoken so many years ago about an individual who "had not been cuddled and so he curdled." This helped the father to put an acceptable face on this display of affection.

The observers watching the family yesterday could see life

begin to be much more evident in these people. And I am aware right now that when I think about my treatment sessions, I think of them as experiences in human contact which for me—without being in any sense mystical—create a feeling that I have had a journey and an adventure with other live beings. And I always hope that as a result of our journey, the people are feeling more alive, more lovable, more hopeful, more creative, and are seeing new ways to use themselves. There are lots and lots of times when I see people only one time, and my hope is that every interview will result in a new window for each person to look through with the result of feeling better about himself and gaining the ability to do things more creatively with other members of his family. So this is really what I mean by saying that I am dealing with a coping process rather than a problem-solving process.

I would like to return to my use of the communication stances as aids to developing changes in the coping process. I mentioned the four stances which I expect to see in some combination with all of the people who are experiencing problems in coping. Placating, blaming, being super-reasonable, and being irrelevant all appeared in yesterday's family. Incidentally, one of the things I have become increasingly conscious of is that the American dream about what a person should be really fits my category of the super-reasonable response. This response is: "For goodness sake, don't show any feeling!" This to me is sad, but it is also true.

At this point I will digress a moment and state that the stances are not rigid and unchangeable. Each of these ways of communicating can be "renovated." If you are handling your responses by placating, one of the ravages going on within you is that you keep giving yourself messages that you don't count for very much. However, if you know how, you can renovate this ability to be tender and bring it into your awareness instead of just feeling an automatic given that you always have to please everyone.

Renovated blaming becomes your ability to stand up for yourself. Everyone needs to be able to do that, but you must do it realistically rather than automatically.

Renovated super-reasonableness becomes the creative use of your intelligence. Using your intelligence is delightful; but if it is used only to protect yourself, it becomes rather boring.

Renovated irrelevancy becomes your ability to be spontaneous and to give yourself direction in awareness and in reality.

In any case, dealing with a super-reasonable person—like the father in yesterday's family—the therapist faces a most difficult problem. Super-reasonable people sit very still and upright; they move their faces very little, their voices are usually in a monotone, and they always talk very reasonably. What you get is this feeling of a kind of drying-up about the person; he is all locked in. As it happened, the father had been a Fundamentalist minister, and he had strong feelings about what was right and wrong. I noticed that he responded to all my overtures—the handshake, the questions, and the statements I made—in the same way. I felt that he listened, but I wasn't always sure he understood. I did find—and continue to find—with people who organize their responses in this fashion that lots of words are used to say things. It is important for me to try to tune in wherever I can in a way that is going to touch the person. And so when someone is organized by using big words and being reasonable, it is natural for me to come in on that level. Oftentimes therapists get bored by people who talk a lot. However, I need to have them talk enough so that I can understand what they are doing. In the case of this man, he had told me about his repeated efforts to try to do what he wanted to do and how they had failed. Again, this was said in his dry, rather matter-of-fact voice. As I listened to him, I became aware that it sounded as though he had stopped trying. I asked him what had happened to his dreams. It sounded a little to me as if he had given up on his dreams. I began to see a light come into his eyes. The bottom half of his face didn't change particularly, but his eyes became a little wider and there was a little light in them. As I listened to his response, he said it was true that he didn't have any more dreams and that they were dead.

So, I use these stances and ways of communicating that I hear and see in my mind as my guidelines for the kinds of interventions I make with people. It is a little like tuning in to a place where they can hear me and they can begin to hear themselves. And, of course, if this is done in a trusting, understanding, hearing context, then it happens. By the end of yesterday's interview, the husband's whole face was beginning to respond, not just his eyes.

And I might say here—I think it is true of me and of others too—that when I am listening to somebody, I am also looking at him and am aware of all his moving parts. I am aware of all the changes that may be going on. So, with me—as I mentioned at the beginning—when you are talking to me, I am listening with my full self, with all of my senses.

By the way, there is an important thing that I would like to mention. I call it the "energy field." I think it is important because it goes along with touching. Around any well-integrated person there is a circular field that is about three feet in diameter. At the edge of this field, you can feel vibrations—at least *I* can! These vibrations are like unacknowledged territorial lines around the person. And when he is relatively well put-together, those lines feel like elastic. If you come up to them, first of all you can physically feel them; you can feel that you are bumping against something. If it feels elastic, you know that you are there and that maybe you can reach over. I respect these lines. That's why I stay at arm's length. If I go closer to a person, I have already experimented as to whether or not his boundary will let me in. There seems to be a relation between the development of trust and the elasticity of this boundary. It occurs to me just now that when I am dealing with people who are very, very much out of contact with themselves, their energy field is only about two or three inches in diameter. I have to go a long way before I can feel any kind of vibration at all. It is a kind of deadness. I am virtually face to face with them before I get any kind of feeling of presence at all. Now when people have very violent insides, their field extends to about six feet and I am very aware of that. We tend to overuse the word *vibrations;* but I know about what that feels like, and I am very respectful of that boundary. It is imaginary, but I can feel it in my body. And when I'm around people in whom there is a lot of violence, I never get myself beyond that until I can begin to feel the elasticity. I don't know if I am explaining this suitably, but it is a little like using your body to determine how far you can go. This is very relevant to the whole touching business because my touching doesn't take place unless I know that the other person's boundary is elastic.

Sight is also a part of this. The distance that you can see someone—*really* see him—is probably nine or ten feet. But at ten feet the outlines and the nuances aren't there. You can see fairly well at six feet; at about three feet you can see much better. So I want to get where I can be seen and heard as soon as I can. But the process of going is many times also the process of connecting—the slow way. You can't judge this by what you *should* do; you have to judge it by the way you feel. I know some people who watched me work with a family and saw me touch. And they said, "Aha! I see! All you have to do is touch." But I would tell them that touch has to be used just as carefully with people as with a hot stove. You are quite literally feeling your way. And this is one of the reasons that when I work with therapists and train them, I try to train their body awareness. Maybe you who are now hearing this know already what I mean about the business of boundaries. For example, when people get into murderous rages, it helps me to be in a position of helping but not crowding. I don't think the touch connection works in that kind of situation. Perhaps some of you have noticed that when someone is in a rage and you touch him, you're going to get hit. And the hit is not because the person wants to kill you (although he could) but because at that time those vibrations are for him and not for you.

I wondered then about the other members of the family and their dreams. So for a few moments we talked about dreams that had not come to life. The wife's dream was of being able to have a life with her husband different from the one she had. But what I really want to emphasize here is that if I hear a person handling his responses in a super-reasonable fashion, my tuning-in is at the level of the intellect but in such a way as to give the person an experience of really being heard and seen. If I shift to a person who—like the wife—is placating, I try to get in touch with what she hoped for herself and lead her to talk about some of her yearnings and loneliness. The wife did this, but it wouldn't have appeared unless I had asked.

In terms of blamers—like the second oldest child—I have to get in touch with the longing to be connected. This was my approach yesterday when, rather than dealing with all the hate feelings, we focused instead on her own feelings about herself. What I found myself doing in each case was trying to help the person stabilize. Sometimes I did this with a touch of my hand, or perhaps just by getting the person to by physically still for a moment in order to focus.

This is important to share with you because as I sit with a family, my body tells me a great deal about where those people are and where their boundaries are. For example, the boundary is very, very close around a super-reasonable person. This is probably one of the reasons people say that he is not "available." The boundary around an irrelevant person is all broken; you can't tell where it is. The boundary around a blamer is very far out, and you can step over it lightly. The placater is a very interesting person. His boundary is made out of liquid—out of whipped cream that is beginning to melt. It is there, but you can't tell much from it. So, even though this is a somewhat picturesque way of talking about a person and his presence, it is something of which I am very aware and it needs to be honored. Perhaps a poetic way of putting it is this: What you are feeling at any point in time is how much of a person's life is willing to make itself known, with what fear, with what protectiveness. And if you want to connect with that, you must be able to respect it.

My hands are my most valuable treatment asset. Also my body and my skin, in sensing what is going on; and my eyes in seeing; and the connections that all of these make. But hands are *so* important! This is one of the reasons I try to help people to educate their hands. Something else I do in affectional relationships with people is to help them to educate their bodies and also to be aware of spaces. I am quite convinced that that's what this business of making connections really means. What I have just said helps me make a definition of *intimacy*. It is simply the freedom to respect the spaces between people—to go in when there is an invitation, and not to invade when there isn't one. That is real intimacy.

Now I would like to answer a question that people often ask me, and it is: "How long is an interview?" It is as long as is necessary to make it possible to find and open a new window for people to look thorugh. Which means they go out of my office with a new awareness that they can use. It can be small or big, but that awareness carries with it some kind of hope; and the hope is that they can do something different about themselves —that life can be different for them in some way. Now, for me, an interview can last anywhere from two to three hours. I am not doing office practice anymore, but when I was, I had three hours as my minimum time for an initial interview. I wanted people to have something new that they could experiment with and live with. And I would time the ensuing sessions to occur whenever it looked as if there needed to be another step. This pattern is not rigid, but my thought is that every entity has a life of its own; and there is nothing that says I am going to be around tomorrow to see you again, or even that you are going to be around. So we have a closing on something as the family and I leave one another. That doesn't mean that all the work is finished. Of course, it never means that, because can't we go on growing forever? But it does mean that at the end of this time we have together, something new has been added that can be useful.

For example, with the family I saw yesterday, the ending for me was my telling them that I enjoyed being with them and being a part of their life for two hours; and that I would have really liked to have been able to continue to be a part, but my life needs didn't make that possible. If by chance we were to meet again, I would like it very much. The idea is that an interview has a life of its own and the next interview will have still another life. Because if you are really growing, each interview will have still another life. Because if you are really growing, each interview is totally different. People are in different places and the therapist is in a different place. At any rate, that is how I like to look at it.

Also, more and more now I am combining several families into groups of families so that I can go even more deeply into things that it takes a larger group for—family reconstructions and something I call "parts parties," all of which I will discuss on subsequent tapes.

Right now as I am talking, I am aware again that I peeked (and you peeked with me) at a slice of life shared by you and me. Just as I did with the family yesterday, I tried to use myself creatively to open some doors. The promise I make to people is that I will try to tell everything I know and show everything I can; and that is the promise I can make. I cannot even promise that I'll tell *all* that is in me. I can tell you only what I know is there. Many of you who are listening to this tape may hear things that I never intended, but which may be there anyway. So I always leave room for that kind of thing.

Now as I come to the end of my tape, my hope for you is that maybe there are some new windows for you. This has been a creative act for me because I've never done this before, and I've learned something about what I've said. I hope it will be useful to you. And suddenly I am aware that nowhere on this tape have I told you my name. I'd like you to know what my name is. It is Virginia Satir.

Part III

- Excerpts from

The Gestalt Approach
&
Eye Witness to Therapy

by *Fritz Perls* M.D., Ph.D.

Fritz Perls

Fritz Perls had an extraordinary life. He was forced to flee Nazi Germany and leave behind his traditional psychoanalytic practice. In South Africa he had time to paint, learn to fly an airplane, and find personal bravery as an Army physician. He founded the first South African psychoanalytic institute, but realized that the country would not change politically and so left it for America.

By this time, Fritz had put together the basis of what became Gestalt therapy. In *Ego, Hunger, and Agression* (1942) we can see some of the origins of the thoughts contained in the selections below. Today it seems as if almost every therapist "does some Gestalt."

My first experience with Fritz was in a professional workshop at Esalen in Big Sur, California. There were fifteen of us—a few fellow psychiatrists, some social workers, and scattered psychologists. Each of the fifteen of us underwent great changes, breaking through self-defeating torture games we had imposed on ourselves. I was fascinated by what I have come to call "Fritz's Game of Lourdes." Fritz worked in a group. He had technical reasons for using the group, but he often said two things: "The group keeps me honest" and "I love to show off." He knew he was a virtuoso and enjoyed demonstrating his skill. He was fond of saying that the only tools he needed to work were a box of Kleenex, cigarettes, and an empty chair—the famous "hot seat." One by one we took our turns working with Fritz in front of the group. Usually he began by having us increase our awareness in the here and now. He used the hot seat in a variety of ways, but chiefly to increase awareness of parts of the personality and facilitate integration of conflicting parts. It was a scary business working with Fritz. (He would have me rephrase that statement as "I scared myself," and he would focus on *how*.) We always found it impossible to anticipate what he would do next.

I remember clearly my first time in the hot seat. I didn't want to make a fool of myself (that's an expression he would like). I told him I wanted to work on a dream I had had as a young boy. I was familiar with his dream work from reading his *Gestalt Therapy Verbatim*, and was prepared to act out all the different people and objects in my dream. We are the sole playwright of each of our dreams; and though it may appear that we are simply the protagonist, we are also every character and object— each of them representing disowned aspects of ourselves. Well, as always, Fritz came at me that day from an unpredictable direction. He had me move to the hot seat and be the *entire* dream! This seemed like a totally bewildering assignment—to be the concept of the dream and talk to myself as a little boy. But I got into it immediately and enjoyed telling the boy that he had dreamed me only once, but that I would frighten him for the rest of his life. Fritz had me move back and forth, getting in touch with an unsuspected part of myself that enjoyed frightening another part. He then directed my attention to my voice, which had a hypnotic quality. I was told to hypnotize the group and, in so doing, I became aware of my fear of the unknown and my desire to control.

Fritz had an uncanny ability to communicate with a person's unconscious and help the person break through impasses. After some preliminary work, he had one woman at the workshop jump from her left foot to her right. He urged her to exaggerate this activity. Gradually losing an initial inhibitedness, she grew able to jump with abandon (at least during the week I knew her). Apparently she had achieved awareness and integration of aggressive and passive parts of her personality. (Which were probably related to male and female components and to her mother and father as well; but Fritz seldom reduced the impact of his work by offering theoretical explanations.)

With another woman, at a crucial point in her work, Fritz had her sit on the floor and try to push her way out through his legs, which he draped over her. With considerable struggle she emerged and seemed to be a much more vibrant and assertive person. Perhaps her struggle was a symbolic rebirth.

The following excerpts from *The Gestalt Approach and Eye Witness to Therapy* show some of the methods in Fritz's "madness." Fritz felt that a careful study of his writings and films would make his work understandable to all and allow general application of it. He was fond of a Zen saying that grew to have great meaning for me: "Maya, maya, all is play. Only a few wise men know it." He never explained exactly what this meant to him, but I see it as tying in very nicely with his work. Fritz saw many of us as caught up in our roles and giving survival significance to our career, marriage, appearance, or possessions. He could well be called the master of the mini-satori—a sudden insight that changes one's life perspective. Scrooge experienced this kind of change in Dickens's *Christmas Carol,* when he broke out of the role of miser and encountered people directly. This kind of shift from one state of consciousness to another, from one value system to another, has great interest for me. I think we are seeing such shifts in attitudes toward race, sex, nationalism, and ecology. I am hopeful that the liberating and enlightening satoris which Fritz helped people achieve will be generalized to all of us.

INTRODUCTION

Modern man lives in a state of low-grade vitality. Though generally he does not suffer deeply, he also knows little of true creative living. Instead of it, he has become an anxious automaton. His world offers him vast opportunities for enrichment and enjoyment, and yet he wanders around aimlessly, not really knowing what he wants and completely unable, therefore, to figure out how to get it. He does not approach the adventure of living with either excitement or zest. He seems to feel that the time for fun, for pleasure, for growing and learning, is childhood and youth, and he abdicates life itself when he reaches "maturity." He goes through a lot of motions, but the expression on his face indicates his lack of any real interest in what he is doing. He is usually either poker-faced, bored, aloof, or irritated. He seems to have lost all spontaneity, all capacity to feel and express directly and creatively. He is very good at talking about his troubles and very bad at coping with them. He has reduced life itself to a series of verbal and intellectual exercises; he is drowning himself in a sea of words. He has substituted psychiatric and pseudo-psychiatric explanations of life for the process of living. He spends endless time trying either to recapture the past or to mold the future. His present activities are merely bothersome chores he has to get out of the way. At times, he is not even aware of his actions at the moment.

All this may seem a sweeping statement, but the time has come when such a statement needs to be made. The last fifty years have seen an enormous growth in man's understanding of himself. They have seen an enormous growth in our understanding of the mechanisms—both physiological and psychological—by which we maintain ourselves under the constantly changing pressures and conditions of life. But they have seen no corresponding increase in our capacity to enjoy ourselves; to use our knowledge for our own interests; to expand and widen our sense of aliveness and growth. Understanding human behavior for the sake of understanding it is a pleasant intellectual game, an amusing or tortured way of whiling away time, but it has no necessary relationship to or usefulness in the daily business of living. As a matter of fact, much of our neurotic dissatisfaction with ourselves and our world stems from the fact that, while we have swallowed whole many of the terms and concepts of modern psychiatry and psychology, we have not digested them, tested them, or used our verbal and intellectual knowledge as the tool of power it is supposed to be. On the contrary, many of us use psychiatric concepts as rationalizations, as ways of perpetuating unsatisfactory present behavior. We justify our current unhappiness by our past experiences, and wallow in our misery. We use our knowledge of man as an excuse for socially destructive and self-destructive behavior. We have graduated from the infant's "I can't help myself," to the adult's "I can't help myself because . . . my mother rejected me when I was a child; because I never learned to appreciate my Oedipus complex; because I'm too introverted." But psychiatry and psychology were never meant to be after-the-fact justifications for continuing neurotic behavior, behavior which does not permit the individual to live up to the maximum of his capacities. The aim of these sciences is not merely to offer explanations of behavior, it is to help us arrive at *self-knowledge, satisfaction and self-support.*

Perhaps one of the reasons psychiatry in particular has lent itself to this perversion is that too many of the classical theories of psychiatry have been petrified, by their proponents, into dogma. In the effort to fit all the different shapes and sizes of human behavior into the Procrustes' bed of theory, many psychiatric schools either ignore or condemn those aspects of man's ways of living which stubbornly resist explanation in terms of their own pet arguments. Instead of abandoning or changing a theory when it no longer adequately conforms with the facts, and when it no longer adequately serves to solve difficulties, they twist the facts of behavior to suit the theory. This serves neither to increase understanding nor to help man solve his problems.

This book is an exploration of a somewhat new approach to the entire subject of human behavior—both in its actuality and its potentiality. It is written from the belief that man can live a fuller, richer life than most of us now do. It is written from the conviction that man has not yet even begun to discover the potential of energy and enthusiasm that lies in him. The book endeavors to bring together a theory and a practical application of that theory to the problems of daily life and to the techniques of psychotherapy. The theory itself is grounded in experience and observation; it has grown and changed with years of practice and application, *and it is still growing.*

FOUNDATIONS

Gestalt Psychology

Any reasonable approach to psychology not hiding itself behind a professional jargon must be comprehensible to the intelligent layman, and must be grounded in the facts of human behavior. If it is not, there is something basically wrong with it. Psychology deals, after all, with the one subject of most interest to human beings—ourselves and others. The understanding of psychology, and of ourselves, must be consistent. If we cannot understand ourselves, we can never hope to understand what we are doing, we can never hope to solve our problems, we can never hope to live rewarding lives. However, such understanding of the 'self' involves more than the usual intellectual understanding. It requires feeling and sensitivity too.

The approach here presented rests on a set of premises that are neither abstruse nor unreasonable. On the contrary, they are, by and large, common sense assumptions which experience can easily verify. As a matter of fact, although they are frequently expressed in complicated terminology which serves the triple function of confusing the reader, inflating the self-importance of the writer and obscuring the issues they are meant to enlighten, these assumptions underlie a large part of contemporary psychology. Unfortunately, too many psychologists take them for granted and push them into the background, while their theory gallops further and further away from reality and the observable. But if we bring these premises, simply expressed, out into the open, we will be able to use them continually as a yardstick against which to measure the reliability and the utility of our concepts, and we will be able to undertake our exploration with both pleasure and profit.

Gestalt Psychology

Let us introduce the first premise through an illustration. We said earlier that the approach outlined in this book is in many ways new. This does not mean that this approach has no relationship to any other theory of human behavior or to any other applications of theory to the problems of daily life or psychotherapeutic practice. Nor does it mean that this approach is composed exclusively of new and revolutionary elements. Most of the elements in it are to be found in many other approaches to the subject. What is new here is not necessarily the individual bits and pieces that go to make up the theory, *rather it is the way they are used and organized which gives this approach its uniqueness and its claim on your attention.* The first basic premise of this book is implicit in that last sentence. The premise is that it is the organization of facts, perceptions, behavior or phenomena, and not the individual items of which they are composed, that defines them and gives them their specific and particular meaning.

Originally, this concept was developed by a group of German psychologists working in the field of perception, who showed that man does not perceive things as unrelated isolates, but organizes them in the perceptual process into meaningful wholes. A man coming into a room full of people, for example, does not perceive merely blobs of color and movement, faces and bodies. He perceives the room and the people in it as a unit, in which one element, selected from the many present, stands out, while the others recede into the background. The choice of which element will stand out is made as a result of many factors, all of which can be lumped together under the general term *interest.* As long as there is interest, the whole scene will appear to be organized in a meaningful way. It is only when interest is completely lacking that perception is atomized, and the room is seen as a jumble of unrelated objects.

Let us see how this principle operates in a simple situation. Suppose that the room is a living room, and the occasion is a cocktail party. Most of the guests are already present; the latecomers are gradually dribbling in. A new arrival enters. He

Gestalt Psychology

is a chronic alcoholic, and he wants a drink desperately. To him, the other guests, the chairs and couches, the pictures on the walls—all will be unimportant and will recede into the background. He will make straight for the bar; of all the objects in the room, that one will be foreground to him. Now another guest comes in. She is a painter, and the hostess has just purchased one of her works. Her primary concern is to find out how and where her picture is hanging. She will select the painting from all the other objects in the room. Like the alcoholic, she will be completely unconcerned with the people, and will head for her work like a homing pigeon. Or take the case of the young man who has come to the party to meet his current girl friend. He will scan the crowd, will search among the faces of the guests until he finds her. She will be foreground, everything else background. For that peripatetic guest who flits from group to group, from conversation to conversation, from bar to couch, from hostess to cigarette box, the room will appear to be patterned differently at different times. While he is talking with one group, that group and that conversation will be foreground. When, towards the end of his chat, he feels tired and decides to sit down, the one vacant seat on the sofa will be foreground. As his interest shifts, his perception of the room, the people and objects in it, and even himself, changes. Foreground and background are interchanged, they do not remain static as they do, for example, to the young swain, whose interest is fixed and invariable. Now comes our last guest. He, like so many of us at cocktail parties, didn't want to come in the first place and has no real interest in the entire proceedings. For him the entire scene will remain disorganized and meaningless unless and until something happens to make him focus his interest and attention.

The school of psychology which developed out of these observations is called the Gestalt School. Gestalt is a German word for which there is no exact English equivalent. A gestalt is a pattern, a configuration, the particular form of organization of the individual parts that go into its make up. The basic premise of Gestalt psychology is that human nature is organized into

Gestalt Psychology

patterns or wholes, that it is experienced by the individual in these terms, and that it can only be understood as a function of the patterns or wholes of which it is made.

Homeostasis

Our next premise is that all life and all behavior are governed by the process which scientists call homeostasis, and which the layman calls adaptation. The homeostatic process is the process by which the organism maintains its equilibrium and therefore its health under varying conditions. Homeostasis is thus the process by which the organism satisfies its needs. Since its needs are many, and each need upsets the equilibrium, the homeostatic process goes on all the time. All life is characterized by this continuing play of balance and imbalance in the organism. When the homeostatic process fails to some degree, when the organism remains in a state of disequilibrium for too long a time and is unable to satisfy its needs, it is sick. When the homeostatic process fails, the organism dies.

A few simple examples will serve to make this clear. The human body functions efficiently only when the level of sugar in the blood is kept within certain limits. If the blood sugar content falls below these limits, the adrenal glands secrete adrenalin; the adrenalin makes the liver turn its stores of glycogen into sugar; this sugar passes into the blood and brings the blood sugar up. All of this occurs on a purely physiological basis; the organism is not aware of what is happening. But a drop in the blood sugar level has still another effect. It is accompanied by the sensation of hunger, and the organism satisfies its dissatisfaction and disequilibrium by eating. The food is digested, a certain amount of it becomes sugar, and the sugar is restored to the blood. Thus, in the case of eating, the homeostatic process demands awareness and some deliberate action on the part of the organism.

Homeostasis

When the blood sugar rises excessively, the pancreas secretes more insulin, and this causes the liver to remove sugar from the blood. The kidneys also help to remove this excess; sugar is excreted into the urine. These processes, like the first ones we described, are purely physiological. But the blood sugar content can be lowered deliberately, as the result of an act of awareness. The medical term for that chronic failure of homeostasis which results in a constant excess of blood sugar is diabetes. The diabetic's system apparently cannot control itself. However, the patient can supply a control by artificially adding insulin through injection. This reduces the blood sugar content to the proper level.

Let us take another example. For the organism to be in good health, the water content of the blood must also be kept at a certain level. When it drops below that level, sweating, salivation and the excretion of urine are all diminished, and the body tissues pass some of their water into the blood stream. So the body sees to it that it conserves water during such an emergency period. This is the physiological side of the process. But when the water content of the blood drops too low, the individual feels thirst. He then does what he can to maintain the necessary balance. He takes a drink of water. When the water content of the blood is excessive, all these activities are reversed, just as they are in the case of the blood sugar. Even more simply we could say this: The physiological term for loss of water in the blood is dehydration; chemically it can be expressed as the loss of a certain number of units of H_2O; sensorially it is felt as thirst, with its symptoms of mouth dryness and restlessness; and psychologically it is felt as the wish to drink.

Thus we might call the homeostatic process the process of *self-regulation*, the process by which the organism interacts with its environment. Although the examples I have given here involve complex activity on the part of the organism, they both deal with the simplest and most elemental functions, all of which operate in the service of survival for the individual and, through him, of the species. The need to maintain the level of blood sugar

Homeostasis

and water within certain limits is basic to all animal life. But there are other needs, not so closely related to questions of life and death, in which the process of homeostasis also functions. The human being can see better with two eyes than with one; but if one eye is destroyed, the victim is able to continue living. He is no longer a two-eyed organism. He is a one-eyed organism and he soon learns to function efficiently within this situation, to gauge what his new needs are and to find the adaptive means for satisfying them.

The organism has psychological *contact* needs as well as physiological ones; these are felt every time the psychological equilibrium is disturbed, just as the physiological needs are felt every time the physiological equilibrium is disturbed. These psychological needs are met through what we might call the psychological counterpart of the homeostatic process. Let me make it very clear, however, that this psychological process cannot be divorced from the physiological one; that each contains elements of the other. Those needs that are primarily psychological in nature and the homeostatic or adaptive mechanisms by which they are met constitute part of the subject matter of psychology.

Human beings have thousands of such needs on the purely physiological level. And on the social levels, there are other thousands of needs. The more intensely they are felt to be essential to continued life, the more closely we identify ourselves with them, the more intensely we will direct our activities towards satisfying them.

Here again, the static concepts of the older psychologies have stood in the way of understanding. Noting certain common drives among all living creatures, the theoreticians postulated the "instincts" as the guiding forces in life, and described neurosis as the result of the repression of those instincts. Mac-Dougall's list of instincts included fourteen. Freud considered the two basic and most important to be Eros (sex or life) and Thanatos (death). But if we could classify all the disturbances of the organismic balance, we would find thousands of instincts, and these would differ among themselves in intensity.

Homeostasis

There is still another weakness in this theory. We can agree, I think, that the need to survive acts as a compelling force in all living creatures and that all show, at all times, two important tendencies: to survive, as individuals and as species, and to grow. These are fixed goals. But the ways in which they are met vary, from situation to situation, from species to species, from individual to individual. If a nation's survival is threatened by war, its citizens will take up arms. If an individual's survival is threatened because his blood sugar level is too low, he will look for food. Scheherezade's survival was threatened by the Sultan, and to meet the threat she told him stories for a thousand and one nights. Shall we then say that she had a story telling instinct?

The whole instinct theory tends to confuse needs with their symptoms, or with the means we use to achieve them. And it is from this confusion that the conception of the repression of instincts arose.

For the instincts (if they exist) cannot be repressed. They are out of reach of our awareness, and thus out of reach of our deliberate action. We cannot repress the need to survive, for example, but we can and do interfere with its symptoms and signs. This is done by interrupting the ongoing process, by preventing ourselves from carrying out whatever action is appropriate.

But what happens if several needs (or instincts, if you prefer) come into existence simultaneously? The healthy organism seems to operate within what we might call a hierarchy of values. Since it is unable to do more than one thing properly at a time, it attends to the dominant survival need before it attends to any of the others; it operates on the principle of first things first. Once in Africa I observed a group of deer grazing within a hundred yards of a pack of sleeping lions. When one of the lions awoke and began to roar in hunger, the deer took speedy flight. Now try for a moment to imagine yourself in the deer's place. Suppose you were running for your life. Soon you would run out of breath, then you would have to slow down or stop

Homeostasis

altogether until you got a second wind. At that point, breathing would have become a greater emergency—a greater need—than running, just as running had previously become a greater need than eating.

Formulating this principle in terms of Gestalt psychology, we can say that the dominant need of the organism, at any time, becomes the foreground figure, and the other needs recede, at least temporarily, into the background. The foreground is that need which presses most sharply for satisfaction, whether the need is, as in our example, the need to preserve life itself, or whether it is related to less physically vital areas—whether it is physiological or psychological. It seems to be a need of mothers, for example, to keep their infants happy and contented; discomfort in the child produces discomfort in them. The mother of a young baby may be able to sleep soundly through the noises of rumbling trucks or even through crashing, deafening peals of thunder, but she will waken in an instant if her baby—in another room at the end of a long hall—so much as whimpers.

For the individual to satisfy his needs, to close the gestalt, to move on to other business, he must be able to sense what he needs and he must know how to manipulate himself and his environment, for even the purely physiological needs can only be satisfied through the interaction of the organism and the environment.

The Holistic Doctrine

One of the most observable facts about man is that he is a unified organism. And yet this fact is completely ignored by the traditional schools of psychiatry and psychotherapy which, no matter how they describe their approach, are still operating in terms of the old mind-body split. Since the emergence of psychosomatic medicine, the close relationship between mental and physical activity has become increasingly apparent. And yet,

The Holistic Doctrine

because of the persistence of psycho-physical parallelism, even this advance in understanding has not achieved as much as it should. It is still tied to the concepts of causality, treating functional disease as a physical disturbance caused by a psychic event.

What seems to have happened in the development of psychological thinking is as follows. We observe that man is able to function on two qualitatively different levels; the level of thinking and the level of acting. We are struck by the differences between the two and by their apparent independence from one another. And so we postulate that they are different orders of matter. Then we are compelled to postulate the existence of some as yet undiscovered structural entity, the mind, which is described as the seat of mental activity. Since the development of depth psychology, springing out of the observation that man is not purely a rational creature, the mind, which previously had been considered exclusively as the font of reason, now becomes also the seat of the murky unconscious and a structure which is capable of exercising its will, not only over the body, but also over itself. Thus, the mind can repress thoughts and memories it finds offensive. It can convert symptoms from one area of the body to another. It is the little deus ex machina which controls us in every respect.

Because the quantitative analysis of physiological processes progressed so much more rapidly than the quantitative analysis of mental processes, we also tended to accept considerably more as given about the body than about the mind. We do not quarrel with the scientific facts of physiology and anatomy. We can describe the heart, the liver, the muscular and circulatory systems, and we know how they operate. We recognize that the ability to perform certain physical and physiological activities is built into man, and we have lost our sense of wonder at our marvelous efficiency. We know, too, a great deal about the brain and the way it functions, and we are learning more every day. But until we have gone further in this study, we will still have limited understanding of another one of man's basic

The Holistic Doctrine

built-in capacities: the ability to learn and manipulate symbols and abstractions. That ability seems to be associated with the greater development and complexity of his brain. And it is as natural to man as is his ability to clench his fists or walk or have sexual intercourse.

This symbol using capacity shows itself in what we call mental activity, whether it is directed towards the production of scientific theories or towards the production of a trite statement about the weather. Even what we consider a low order of mental activity requires a great deal of ability to deal with symbols and to combine abstractions. Comparably, even what we consider a low order of physical activity—the state of sleep, for example—requires a considerable use of our built-in physiological capacities. The muscles are not as active during sleep as they are in the waking state, but some degree of activity there inevitably is.

Given, then, that the human being has a built-in ability to use symbols and to abstract (and even the most rigid behaviorist has to admit this; if the ability did not exist he could not conduct an argument about its existence) what is the human being doing when he uses it? He is, I maintain, acting in effigy. He is doing *symbolically* what he could do *physically*. If he thinks about a scientific theory, he could write it down or explain it verbally. Writing and speaking are physical actions. That he can think up scientific theories is truly remarkable—but it is really no more remarkable than the fact that he can write or speak.

Thinking, of course, is not the only mental activity we engage in. The mind has other functions, too.

There is the function of attention. When we say, "I put my mind on a problem," we do not mean that we take some physical body from inside ourselves and deposit it heavily and with a thud on that problem. We mean "I concentrate much of my activity and my sensory perceptions on this problem."

We also talk of awareness, which could be described as the fuzzy twin of attention. Awareness is more diffuse than attention—it implies a relaxed rather than a tense perception by

The Holistic Doctrine

the whole person.

And we talk of will. Here the area of attention or awareness is highly limited in scope, and the person focuses on initiating and carrying through a certain set of actions directed towards certain specific goals.

In all of these mental activities, the relationship between what we do and what we think is very clear. When we are aware of something, or focus attention on it, or attempt to exert our will on it, there are at least some overt signs by which the spectator can see that these processes are at work. The man who is concentrating hard on understanding what someone else is saying is likely to be sitting forward in his chair; his whole being seems to be aimed and directed towards that in which he is interested. The man who makes up his mind not to take that fifth piece of candy is likely to make a motion towards it, and to stop his hand suddenly and withdraw it before it reaches the candy dish.

But let me return to the area of thinking. It is here that most of the confusion arises. We understand thinking to include a number of activities—dreaming, imagining, theorizing, anticipating—making maximum use of our capacity to manipulate symbols. For the sake of brevity, let us call all of this *fantasy* activity rather than thinking. We tend to attach the notion of reason to thinking and of unreason to dreaming, and yet the two activities are very much alike. Let me make it very clear, however, that I do not mean, by using the word fantasy, to imply that there is anything unreal, eerie, strange, or false about these activities. Fantasy activity, in the broad sense in which I am using the term, is that activity of the human being which through the use of symbols tends to reproduce reality on a diminished scale. As activity involving the use of symbols, it derives from reality, since symbols themselves are initially derived from reality. Symbols begin as labels for objects and processes; they proliferate and grow into labels for labels and labels for labels for labels. The symbols may not even be approximated in reality, but they start in reality.

The Holistic Doctrine

The same thing is true of fantasy activity, which is internal symbol-using activity. Here the reality reproduction may stray far from its origins, from the reality with which it was originally connected. But it is in some way always related to a reality which has a meaningful existence for the person into whose fantasy activity it enters. I do not see a real tree in my mind's eye, but the correspondence between the real tree in my garden and my fantasy tree is sufficient to make it possible for me to connect one with the other. When I mull over a problem, trying to determine which course of action I will take in a given situation, it is as if I were doing two very real things. Firstly, I have a conversation about my problem—in reality I might have this conversation with a friend. Secondly, I reproduce in my mind's eye the situation into which my decision will precipitate me. I anticipate in fantasy what will happen in reality, and although the correspondence between my fantasy anticipation and the actual situation may not be absolute, just as the correspondence between the tree in my mind's eye and the tree in my garden is not absolute, just as the correspondence between the word "tree" and the object tree is only approximate, it is close enough for me to base my actions upon it.

Thus mental activity seems to act as a time, energy, and work saver for the individual. The lever, for example, works on the principle that a small force applied at one end of the instrument produces a large force at the other. If I put one end of a lever under a five-hundred pound rock and bear down heavily on the other end of the tool, I can move an object so heavy that it would otherwise resist all my attempts to change its position.

When I fantasize, or put my attention on a problem, I use a small amount of my available energy internally in order to produce a larger amount of efficiently distributed body or external energy. We think about problems in fantasy in order to be able to solve them in reality. Instead of simply going to the supermarket with absolutely no idea of what she will purchase, the housewife decides beforehand what she needs and she is thus able to act more efficiently once she gets to the store. She does

The Holistic Doctrine

not have to rush from display case to display case, deciding at each step of the way whether or not she needs the particular item available for purchase. She saves time, energy, and activity.

Now we are ready to formulate a definition of the functions of the mind and a definition of mental activity as a part of the whole organism we call the human being. Mental activity seems to be activity of the whole person carried on at a lower energy level than those activities we call physical. Here I must stop to point out that by using the word "lower" I am implying no value judgment at all. I simply mean that the activities we call mental require less expenditure of the body substance than do those we call physical. All of us take it for granted that the sedentary professor can get along on fewer calories than the ditch-digger. As water changes to steam by the application of heat, so covert body activity changes to the latent, private activity we call mental by a diminution of intensity. And conversely, as steam turns into water by the application of cold, so the latent, private activity we call mental changes into overt body activity by an increase of intensity. The organism acts with and reacts to its environment with greater or lesser intensity; as the intensity diminishes, physical behavior turns to mental behavior. As the intensity increases, mental behavior turns into physical behavior.

One further example should serve to make this concept entirely clear. When a man is actually attacking an enemy, he shows enormous overt body activity. He contracts his muscles, his heart beats faster, adrenalin is poured into his blood stream in large quantities, his breathing becomes rapid and shallow, his jaws are clenched and rigid, his whole body becomes tense. When he talks about how much he dislikes this enemy he will still show a large number of overt physical signs, although there will be fewer of these than when he is actually fighting. When he feels anger, and thinks about attacking an enemy, he still shows some overt physical signs. But these signs are less visible and less intense than they were when he was actually fighting, or when he was talking about it. His behavior is now of still lower

The Holistic Doctrine

intensity. His overt physical activity has changed to covert mental activity.

Our capacity to act on a level of diminished intensity—to engage in mental behavior—is of tremendous advantage not only for the individual human being in solving his own particular problems, but for the entire species. The energy man saves by thinking things out instead of acting them out in every situation can now be invested in enriching his life. He can make and use tools which further save him energy and therefore offer him even greater opportunities for enrichment. But these are not the only advantages. Man's ability to abstract and to combine abstractions, his capacity to invent symbols, to create art and science—all these are intimately connected with his ability to fantasize. The basic ability to create and use symbols is enhanced by the real products of symbol using. Each generation inherits the fantasies of all preceding generations, and thus accumulates greater knowledge and understanding.

This conception of human life and behavior as made up of levels of activity does away once and for all with the disturbing and unsatisfying psycho-physical parallelism with which psychology has been coping ever since its birth. It enables us to see the mental and physical sides of human behavior not as independent entities which could have their existence apart from human beings or from one another, which was the inevitable and logical conclusion to the older psychologies, but to look at the human being as he is, as a whole, and to examine his behavior as it manifests itself on the overt level of physical activity and the covert level of mental activity. Once we recognize that thoughts and actions are made of the same stuff, we can translate and transpose from one level to another.

Thus we can introduce finally into psychology a holistic concept—the concept of the unified field—which scientists have always longed to find and towards which the contemporary psychosomaticists have been groping.

In psychotherapy, this concept gives us a tool for dealing with the whole man. Now we can see how his mental and

The Holistic Doctrine

physical actions are meshed together. We can observe man more keenly and use our observations more meaningfully. For how much broader now is the surface which we can observe! If mental and physical activity are of the same order, we can observe both as manifestations of the same thing: man's being. Neither patient nor therapist is limited by what the patient says and thinks, both can now take into consideration what he *does.* What he does provides clues as to what he thinks, as what he thinks provides clues as to what he does, and what he would like to do. Between the levels of thinking and doing there is an intermediate stage, the stage of playing at, and in therapy, if we observe keenly, we will notice that the patient plays at a lot of things. He himself will know what his actions, his fantasies and his play-actings mean, if we but call them to his attention. He himself will provide his own interpretations.

Through his experience of himself on the three levels of fantisizing, play-acting, and doing, he will come to an understanding of himself. Psychotherapy then becomes not an excavation of the past, in terms of repressions, Oedipal conflicts, and primal scenes, but an experience in living in the present. In this living situation, the patient learns for himself how to integrate his thoughts, feelings, and actions not only while he is in the consulting room, but during the course of his everyday life. The neurotic obviously does not feel like a whole person. He feels as if his conflicts and unfinished business were tearing him to shreds. But with his recognition that he is, being human, a whole, comes the ability to regain that sense of wholeness which is his birthright.

Contact Boundary

No individual is self-sufficient; the individual can exist only in an environmental field. The individual is inevitably, at every moment, a part of some field. His behavior is a function

Contact Boundary

of the total field, which includes both him and his environment. The nature of the relationship between him and his environment determines the human being's behavior. If the relationship is mutually satisfactory, the individual's behavior is what we call normal. If the relationship is one of conflict, the individual's behavior is described as abnormal. The environment does not create the individual, nor does the individual create the environment. Each is what it is, each has its own particular character, because of its relationship to the other and the whole. The study of the human organism alone, of what goes on entirely inside him, is the province of anatomy and physiology. The study of the environment alone, of what goes on entirely outside him is the province of the physical, geographical and social sciences. In these sciences, elements of the total field—which includes both the individual and the environment—can be abstracted and studied alone because the concern of these fields is precisely with those elements which exist independently of one another. The structure of the human eye has no influence on the structure of the objects it sees. Nor does the structure of these objects affect the structure of the eye. But psychology cannot make such abstractions, nor can it deal with structure per se. The study of the way the human being functions in his environment is the study of what goes on at the contact boundary between the individual and his environment. It is at this contact boundary that the psychological events take place. Our thoughts, our actions, our behavior, and our emotions are our way of experiencing and meeting these boundary events.

With this concept we come to a parting of the ways with the older psychologies. They established another split. Like the mind-body split, they proceeded to treat their postulated abstraction as a factual reality, and then compounded the confusion in their effort to extricate themselves from the mess they had gotten themselves into. They split experience into inside and outside and then were faced with the insoluble question of whether man is ruled by forces from without or from within. This either-or approach, this need for a simple causality, this

Contact Boundary

neglect of the total field, makes problems out of situations which are in reality indivisible.

True enough, I can divide the sentence "I see a tree" into subject, verb and object. But in experience, the process cannot be split up in this way. There is no sight without something to be seen. Nor is anything seen if there is no eye to see it. Yet by splitting experience into inside and outside in this way, and then dealing with their abstractions—inside and outside—as if they were experiential realities, scientists had to find some explanation of each. And of course, in actuality, neither can be explained without the other.

To explain the inner experience, the theory of the reflex arc was devised: first the stimulus (the outside) reaches the receptor (the sensory organs), then impulses are carried through the intermediate system (the nerves) to the effector (the muscles). True enough, we act through two systems, the sensoric and the motoric. But the organism reaches out towards the world with both. His sensory system provides him with an *orientation*, his motor system with a means of *manipulation*. Neither is a function of the other, neither is temporally or logically prior to the other, they are both functions of the total human being.

With this new outlook, the environment and the organism stand in a relationship of mutuality to one another. Neither is the victim of the other. Their relationship is actually that of dialectical opposites. To satisfy its needs, the organism has to find its required supplements in the environment. The system of orientation discovers what is wanted; all living creatures are observably able to sense what the outside objects are that will satisfy their needs. The hungry puppy is not confused by the myriad of shapes, smells, noises and colors in the world; he goes directly for his mother's teat. This is the foreground figure.

Once the system of orientation has done its job, the organism has to manipulate the object it needs in such a way that the organismic balance will be restored, the gestalt will be closed. The mother wakened by her crying baby will not be

Contact Boundary

content to lie comfortably back in her bed listening to her off-spring wail. She will do something to eliminate the disturbance. She will try to satisfy the baby's needs, and when they are satisfied, she too can return to sleep. The puppy, having found the teat, will suck.

These concepts, too, have meaning in psychotherapy. First of all, the conception that effective action is action directed towards the satisfaction of a dominant need gives us a clue as to the meaning of specific forms of behavior. Secondly, it gives us a further tool for an understanding of neurosis. If, through some disturbance in the homeostatic process, the individual is unable to sense his dominant needs or to manipulate his environment in order to attain them, he will behave in a disorganized and ineffective way. He will be trying to do too many things at once.

You will, I am sure, have noticed in your own experience that if your attention is divided between two objects of interest, you cannot concentrate properly on either. This inability to concentrate is a frequent complaint of the neurotic. When there are more than two objects demanding our attention, or if the object of interest is hazy, we feel confused. If there are two inconsistent situations requiring our attention we speak of conflict. If these are permanent and apparently insoluble, we regard them as neurotic conflicts.

The neurotic has lost the ability (or perhaps he never developed it) to organize his behavior in accordance with a necessary heirarchy of needs. He literally cannot concentrate. In therapy, he has to learn how to distinguish the myriad of needs from one another, and how to attend to them, one at a time. He must learn to discover and identify himself with his needs, he must learn how, at every moment, to become totally involved in what he is doing; how to stick with a situation long enough to close the gestalt and move on to other business. *Organization plus environment equals field.*

Let me return for a moment to the discussion of the organism's relationship to the field, or, in more specific terms, the individual's relationship to his environment. Not only does

Contact Boundary

he have needs and a system of orientation and manipulation with which to achieve their satisfaction, he has attitudes towards those things in the environment that can help or hinder his search for satisfaction. Freud described this by saying that objects in the world receive a cathexis. In Gestalt terms, we would say that these objects become figure. Those that are desirable because they help to satisfy the individual's needs and to restore the disturbed equilibrium are said to have a positive cathexis. Water has a positive cathexis for a thirsty man, a soft bed for a tired man. Those that are undesirable because they threaten the individual or tend to upset his equilibrium, or do not satisfy his needs, have a negative cathexis. For the hunter threatened by a rampaging elephant, the elephant has a negative cathexis.

Man is suspended between *impatience* and *dread.* Each need requires immediate gratification without any lapse of time. Impatience, then, is the emotional form which excitement— produced by the presence of a need and the disturbance of balance—assumes first. Impatience is the basis of positive cathexis. Dread, on the other hand, is the basis of all negative cathexis; it is the anti-survival experience. The dreadful is experienced as vague, undifferentiated danger; as soon as there is an object to cope with, dread diminishes into fear. As the positive cathexis indicates the life supporting supplements, so negative cathexis indicates danger, diminished support, or even death. In any case, it threatens that some or all of our existence is at stake, whether it is the physical being (illness), sexual integrity (castration), self-concept (humiliation), weltanschauung (existential confusion), security (economic depression), or any one of a number of other things.

The individual wants to appropriate or take over those objects or people in the environment which have a positive cathexis; the young man in love wants to marry the girl of his choice, the hungry man wants to eat. In trying to acquire the positively cathexed objects, the individual *contacts* his environment, he reaches out towards it. On the other hand, the individual has an entirely different orientation towards those objects or

Contact Boundary

people that have a negative cathexis. These he wants to annihilate or remove from the field. This applies to our fantasy as well as to the actual world. The farmer will try to shoot the fox that is raiding his chicken coop. We try to remove "bad" thoughts and unwanted emotions from our "minds" as if they were actual enemies.

The safest way to annihilate the enemy is, of course, to destroy him or render him harmless. This means destroying those of his qualities that support his threat against us. When Delilah cut off Sampson's hair, she did just that. The next best thing would be to frighten or threaten him, to chase him out. In addition to these methods of destruction, we can cope with the negatively cathexed situation or object by magic annihilation or by flight from the danger field. Both are means of *withdrawal.*

Magic annihilation is well known in psychotherapy under the name of *scotoma*, that is, blind spot. There are people who literally do not see what they don't want to see, don't hear what they don't want to hear, don't feel what they don't want to feel—all this in order to shut out what they consider to be dangerous—the objects or situations that have a negative cathexis for them. Magic annihilation is a partial withdrawal, a substitute for actual withdrawal.

In this age of psychoanalysis, we tend to think of withdrawal as one of the symptoms of neurosis. But this is a misunderstanding of the phenomenon. Withdrawal per se is neither good nor bad, it is simply a means of coping with danger. The question of whether or not it is pathological can only be answered by our answers to these questions: withdrawal from what, withdrawal to what, and withdrawal for how long?

The same thing applies to contact. Contact itself is neither good nor bad, although in our age of concern for "social adjustment" we tend to value the capacity to make contact almost above all others. Yet some forms of contact are anything but healthy. You yourself must have known people who simply have to stay in continual contact with you: the hangers-on. Every psychotherapist knows that they are as

Contact Boundary

difficult to treat as the deeply withdrawn personalities. There are some people who feel compelled to stay in contact with their fixed ideas; they are as disturbed as the schizophrenics who withdraw almost completely.

Hence, not every contact is healthy and not every withdrawal unhealthy. One of the characteristics of the neurotic is that he can neither make good contact nor can he organize his withdrawal. When he should be in contact with his environment, his mind is somewhere else, and so he cannot concentrate. When he should withdraw, he cannot. Insomnia, a frequent complaint of the neurotic, is an example of the inability to withdraw, the phenomenon of boredom is another. Boredom occurs when we try to stay in contact with a subject that does not hold our interest. We quickly exhaust any excitement at our disposal; we get tired and lean back. We want to withdraw from the situations. If we cannot find a suitable excuse to do so, the over-contact becomes painful, and we express it in exactly these terms. We're "bored to death," or "bored to tears." If we let our tiredness take over, we will withdraw to our fantasy, to a more interesting contact. That our tiredness is really only a temporary matter is apparent from the renewed interest we feel when we suddenly find ourselves leaning forward to listen attentively to a more fascinating speaker. Once again we are in contact—we are "all there."

Contact and withdrawal are dialectical opposites. They are descriptions of the ways we meet psychological events, they are our means of dealing at the contact boundary with objects in the field. In the organism/environment field the positive and negative (contact and withdrawal) cathexis behave very similarly to the attracting and repelling forces of magnetism. As a matter of fact, the whole organism/environment field is one unit which is dialectically differentiated. It is differentiated biologically into the organism and the environment, psychologically into the self and the other, morally into selfishness and altruism, scientifically into subjective and objective, etc.

Contact Boundary

When the cathected object, whether its cathexis is positive or negative, has been appropriated or annihilated, contacted or withdrawn from, or dealt with in some way satisfactory to the individual, both it and the need with which it is associated disappear from the environment; *the gestalt is closed.* The cathected object and the need have an almost mathematical relationship to one another; if the need is a minus, the cathected object is a plus. If a man is thirsty, he feels a lack of fluid, his need is experienced as a minus in him. At that time a glass of water has a positive cathexis for him, and it is experienced as a plus. The exact number of units of fluid he needs can be measured, and when he gets that number from the environment his needs are satisfied. The sum, as it were, of the need and the cathected object is zero.

This contact with and withdrawal from the environment, this acceptance and rejection of the environment, are the most important functions of the total personality. They are the positive and negative aspects of the psychological processes by which we live. They are dialectical opposites, part of the same thing, the total personality. Those psychologists who maintain a dualistic conception of man see them operating as opposing forces which tear the individual into pieces. We, on the other hand, see them as aspects of the same thing: *the capacity to discriminate.* This capacity can become confused and can function badly. When it does, the individual is unable to behave appropriately and consequently we describe him as a neurotic. But when the capacity to discriminate functions well, the components of acceptance and rejection, of contact and withdrawal, are always present and active.

Indeed, this function seems to be part of the very rhythm of life itself. During the day, when we are awake, we are in touch with the world, we are in contact with it. During the night when we are asleep, we withdraw, we give up contact. In summer we are usually more outgoing than in winter. Wintertime withdrawal is perfectly exemplified by those animals which hibernate, sleeping through the entire season.

Contact Boundary

Contacting the environment is, in a sense, forming a gestalt. Withdrawing is either closing it completely or rallying one's forces to make closure possible. The prize-fighter makes contact with his opponent's jaw but he does not leave his fist there. He withdraws it for the next blow. If contact is over-prolonged, it becomes ineffective or painful; if withdrawal is overprolonged, it interferes with the processes of life. Contact and withdrawal, in a rhythmic pattern, are our means of satisfying our needs, of continuing the ongoing processes of life itself.

Now we have the hierarchy of needs, the equipment—sensory and motor—with which to satisfy them, the positive and negative cathexes of the field, contact and withdrawal, impatience and dread. This brings us to the question of the force which basically energizes all our action. That force seems to be emotion. For although modern psychiatry treats emotions as if they were a bothersome surplus that had to be discharged, emotions are the very life of us. We can theorize and interpret the emotions any way we will. But this is a waste of time. For emotions are the very language of the organism; they modify the basic excitement according to the situation which has to be met. Excitement is transformed into specific emotions, and the emotions are transformed into sensoric and motor actions. The emotions energize the cathexes and mobilize the ways and means of satisfying needs.

Here again are some cues for psychotherapy. Earlier, we described neurosis as the illness which arises when the individual somehow interrupts the ongoing processes of life and saddles himself with so many unfinished situations that he cannot satisfactorily get on with the process of living. The interruptions we described as psychological, or neurotic, were, as contrasted with those that we call physiological, of the kind that take place either on the level of awareness or on a level which can be made aware. We now see something else about the neurotic. His contact—withdrawal rhythm is out of kilter. He cannot decide for himself when to participate and when to withdraw because

Contact Boundary

all the unfinished business of his life, all the interruptions to the ongoing process, have disturbed his sense of orientation, and he is no longer able to distinguish between those objects or persons in the environment which have a positive cathexis and those which have a negative cathexis; he no longer knows when or from what to withdraw. He has lost his freedom of choice, he cannot select appropriate means to his end goals, because he does not have the capacity to see the choices that are open to him.

NEUROTIC MECHANISMS

Birth of Neurosis

The individual's chance of physical survival is almost nil if he is left entirely to himself. Man needs others to survive physically. His psychological and emotional survival chances are even lower if he is left alone. On the psychological level, man needs *contact* with other human beings as much as, on the physiological level, he needs food and drink. Man's sense of relatedness to the group is as natural to him as his sense of relatedness to any one of his physiological survival impulses. Indeed, this sense of identification is probably his primary psychological survival impulse.

The gestalt approach, which considers the individual as a function of the organism/environment field, and which considers his behavior as reflecting his relatedness within that field, gives coherence to this conception of man as both an individual and as a social creature. The older psychologies described human life as a constant conflict between the individual and his environment. We see it, on the other hand, as an interaction between the two, within the framework of a constantly changing field. And since the field is constantly changing, out of its own nature and out of what we do to it, the forms and techniques of interaction must necessarily be fluid and changeable themselves.

What concerns us as psychologists and psychotherapists, in this ever changing field, are the ever-changing constellations of the ever-changing individual. For he must change constantly if he is to survive. It is when the individual becomes incapable of altering his techniques of manipulation and interaction that neurosis arises. When the individual is frozen to an outmoded way of acting, he is less capable of meeting any of his survival

Birth of Neurosis

needs, including his social needs. And the very large number of alienated, unidentified and isolated individuals we find around us is ample evidence that this inability can easily arise. If we look at man in his environment, as both an individual and a social creature, as part of the organism/environment field, we cannot lay the blame for this alienation either at the door of the individual or of the environment. In our first chapter, in talking about the old mind-body problem, we pointed out that a causal relationship cannot exist among the elements that go to make up the whole. And since individual and environment are merely elements of a single whole, the field, neither of them can be held responsible for the ills of the other.

But both of them are ill. A society containing a large number of neurotic individuals must be a neurotic society; of the individuals living in a neurotic society, a large number must be neurotic. The man who can live in concernful contact with his society, neither being swallowed up by it nor withdrawing from it completely, is the well-integrated man. He is self-supportive because he understands the relationship between himself and his society, as the parts of the body instinctively seem to understand their relationship to the body-as-a-whole. He is the man who recognizes the contact boundary between himself and his society, who renders unto Caesar the things that are Caesar's and retains for himself those things that are his own. The goal of psychotherapy is to create just such men.

The ideal of a democratic community, on the other hand, is to create a society with the same characteristics, a community in which, as its needs are determined, each member participates for the benefit of all. Such a society is in concernful contact with its members. In such a society, the boundary between the individual and the group is clearly drawn and clearly felt. The individual is not subservient to the group nor is the group at the mercy of any individual. The principle of homeostasis, of self-regulation, also governs such a society. As the body responds to its dominant needs first, so would the society respond to its dominant needs first. If a fire threatened the

Birth of Neurosis

whole community, everyone would help to extinguish the flames and salvage life and property. But, as the human-body-as-a-whole fights to preserve the integrity of any of its members when that one is under attack, so, in a well-regulated or self-regulated community, if the fire threatened only one home, the home owner's neighbors and, if necessary, the entire community would join with him in fighting it. The members of the community and its rulers would mutually identify with one another, and the members would identify with each other.

Man seems to be born with a sense of social and psychological balance as acute as his sense of physical balance. Every movement he makes on the social or psychological level is a movement in the direction of finding that balance, of establishing equilibrium between his personal needs and the demands of his society. His difficulties spring not from the desire to reject such equilibrium, but from misguided movements aimed towards finding and maintaining it.

When these movements bring him into severe conflict with society because, in his search for the contact boundary, (the point of balance) he has overshot the mark and impinged too heavily on society, we call him a criminal. The criminal is the man who has arrogated to himself functions traditionally defined as the prerogatives of the state. The man who arrogates these functions to himself is, in our society, a criminal.

When, on the other hand, man's search for balance leads him to draw back further and further, leads him to permit society to impinge too heavily on him, to overwhelm him with its demands and at the same time alienate him from social living, to push and passively mold him, we call him a neurotic. The neurotic cannot see his own needs clearly and therefore cannot fulfill them. He cannot distinguish properly between himself and the rest of the world, and he tends to see society as larger than life and himself as smaller. The criminal cannot see the needs of others—and therefore stamps on them—because he too cannot properly distinguish between himself and the rest of the world. As contrasted with the neurotic, he tends to see himself as larger

Birth of Neurosis

than life and society as smaller.

What is it, then, in the organism/environment field, that permits such disturbances in balance to arise? Sociologists will examine this question in terms of the environment. Psychologists, psychiatrists and psychotherapists examine it by examining what happens in the individual.

It seems to me that the imbalance arises when, simultaneously, the individual and the group experience differing needs, and when the individual is incapable of distinguishing which one is dominant. The group can mean the family, the state, the social circle, co-workers—any or all combinations of persons who have a particular functional relationship with one another at any given time. The individual, who is part of this group, experiences the need for contact with it as one of his primary psychological survival impulses, although of course he does not experience the need as acutely at all times. But when, at the same time, he experiences a personal need, the satisfaction of which requires withdrawal from the group, trouble can begin. In the situation of conflict of needs the individual has to be able to make a clear-cut decision. If he does this, he either stays in contact or he withdraws; he temporarily sacrifices the less dominant need to the more dominant, and that is that. Neither he nor the environment suffers any severe consequences. But when he cannot discriminate, when he cannot make a decision, or feel satisfied with the decision he has made, he can neither make a good contact nor a good withdrawal, and both he and the environment are affected.

There seems to be, in all human beings, an inborn tendency towards ritual, which can be defined as an expression of man's sense of social identification, his need for contact with a group. We find this tendency not only among primitives, but among highly civilized groups as well. The play of children is made up largely of ritual acting and repetition. Parades, festivals, religious services, all are expressions of this need. In a perverted way, the need for ritual seems to underlie the obsessional and compulsive neuroses—those that display

Birth of Neurosis

themselves in such seemingly ridiçulous needs as the compulsion to wash one's hands every twenty minutes. Obsessional rituals of this sort always have social as well as personal roots. But they maintain social form without social content, and at the same time, they are incapable of satisfying the individual's changing needs. They are the most sterile kind of expression—rendering nothing either to Caesar or to the self.

But normal people, too, seem to feel the need for ritual. If at an important occasion there were no ritual at all—no toast, no handshake, no speech, no processional, no ceremony of any kind—the whole thing would seem meaningless and flat. The ritual seems to give such experience order, form and purpose. In gestalt terms, we could say that it makes the gestalt clearer, makes the figure stand out more sharply. All of us, for example, seem to feel the need for some ritual in dealing with death. Even the most sophisticated citizen of the world would find it shocking if we simply bundled our corpses up in bags and disposed of them.

At the same time that it satisfies a deep-seated need in the individual, the ritual has social value as well. For ritual reinforces the survival value of group living. It joins people together. Drill, for example, increases the coordination of its participants, and at the same time increases their capacity to act as a group in defense of their group needs. Magic—which is simply fantasized manipulation of the environment—serves to enhance the value of the group as a tool for the achievement of goals. It is used to evoke the support of beneficial powers (those that have a positive cathexis) and to annihilate dreaded powers (those that have a negative cathexis). Whatever the value for the group may be, ritual will—and it is meant to—interrupt at least some of the spontaneous and personal processes of the individuals in the group. Once engaged in ritual, all other activity is disesteemed as profane. The highest concentration, such as that befitting a dominant survival need, is demanded and achieved with solemnity and awe. Only a full participation of the entire personality will result in that religious feeling of intensified

Birth of Neurosis

existence, of exaltation, of integration, without diminishing the full awareness of both the individual and the group, both the self and the other, and the full awareness of the individual that he is part of the group.

But such intensification of feeling is possible only if his full participation is uninterrupted. If there is any interruption at all—either from the environment, or if the individual interrupts in fantasy—the meaningfulness and integration of the entire activity is gone.

Now suppose that in the process of group activity, or ritual, the individual suddenly becomes aware of a personal survival need which appears more dominant than attention to the ritual. Suppose, for example, a chorus is in the middle of its performance, and one of its members suddenly finds that he has to urinate. His survival need profanely intrudes upon the solemn act. We then have three possibilities: the individual may withdraw (but quietly, so as not to call attention to himself), he may push his need completely into the background and force it, at least temporarily, out of existence, or he may vacillate in his attention from his own needs to the needs of the group. In this last case he tries to stay in contact with the ritual, to accord it the position of dominance, but he cannot, and a traumatic conflict between dread and impatience may occur. The sufferer might verbalize his experience thusly: "I want to urinate; I wish I could interrupt the session, but we want to go on. We don't like to be disturbed. And it isn't nice to disturb the others. So I wish I did not need to urinate, and I have to control myself. I wish my bladder would not bother me. It really is a nuisance."

In this apparently harmless statement lie hidden a whole series of confusions that can lead to neurosis. The speaker is apparently unable to distinguish properly between himself and his environment, and his statement contains all four of the mechanisms of meeting boundary disturbances that Gestalt therapy believes lay behind neurosis. This does not mean, of course, that he who utters it is a confirmed neurotic. It does mean that the attitudes which lie behind the statement, if they

Birth of Neurosis

are unchecked, if they represent a continual pattern of thought and behavior, can develop into full-fledged neurotic attitudes. So let us leave our sufferer for a moment to discuss what these neurotic mechanisms are and how they develope. Then we can return to him and see how this simple situation can be the model for the development of neurotic patterns.

All neurotic disturbances arise from the individual's inability to find and maintain the proper balance between himself and the rest of the world, and all of them have in common the fact that in neurosis the social and environmental boundary is felt as extending too far over into the individual. The neurotic is the man on whom society impinges too heavily. His *neurosis* is a defensive maneuver to protect himself against the threat of being crowded out by an overwhelming world. It is his most effective technique for maintaining his balance and his sense of self-regulation in a situation where he feels that the odds are all against him.

Although we assume that the neuroses, the boundary disturbances, operate primarily through four mechanisms which can be distinguished, one from the other, it would be unrealistic to say that any particular kind of neurotic behavior was an example only of the operation of any single one of them. Nor would it be reasonable to say that any single confusion about the boundary—any single disturbance of the balance in the organism/environment field—produces neurosis or is evidence of a neurotic pattern. There are, to be sure, certain situations where this does occur, and they lead to what psychiatry calls the *traumatic neuroses*. The traumatic neuroses are essentially patterns of defense that originate in an attempt by the individual to protect himself from a thoroughly terrifying intrusion of society or clash with the environment. For example, the two year old child whose parents lock him in a dark closet overnight has been subjected to an almost insupportable strain. He has been reduced by their behavior to nothing—indeed, to less than nothing; to an object of manipulation with neither rights nor powers of his own. There is no "he" any more, there is only "they" and what

Birth of Neurosis

"they" can do. In defending himself against this situation, the child is likely to develop rigid patterns of behavior. And these may persist long after the danger is past. They were called into action by a trauma, but they continue to operate even when the trauma itself has disappeared from existence.

But the boundary disturbances that lie behind most neuroses are usually less dramatic than this. They are nagging, chronic, daily interferences with the processes of growth and self-recognition through which we reach self-support and maturity. And whatever form these interferences and interruptions of growth may take, they result in the development of continuing confusion between the self and the other.

Introjection

All of us grow through exercising the capacity to discriminate, itself a function of the self-other boundary. We take from the environment, we give back to it. We accept or reject what the environment has to offer. We can only grow if, in the process of taking, we digest completely and we assimilate thoroughly. What we have really assimilated from our environment becomes ours, to do with as we please. We can retain it, or we can give it back in its new form, its distillation through us. But what we swallow whole, what we accept indiscriminately, what we ingest and do not digest, is a foreign body, a parasite that is making its home in us. It is not part of us, even though it may look as if it is. It is still part of the environment.

Physically, this process of growth by assimilation—by destructuring and digesting—is easy to see. We grow and maintain ourselves not through the food we swallow whole, but through the food we chew (which begins the process of destructuring) and digest (which continues the process by further changing the food into chemical particles which the body can use). Physical food, then, properly digested and assimilated,

Introjection

becomes part of us—it is converted into bone, muscle, and blood. But food which is swallowed whole, which we shove down our gullets, not because we want it, but because we have to eat it, lies heavily on the stomach. It makes us uncomfortable, we want to throw it up and get it out of our systems. If we do not, if we suppress our discomfort, nausea, and desire to get rid of it, then we finally succeed either in painfully digesting it or else it poisons us.

The psychological process of assimilating is very much the same as its physiological counterpart. Concepts, facts, standards of behavior, morality, and ethical, esthetic or political values—all these come to us originally from the outside world. There is nothing in our minds that does not come from the environment, but there is nothing in the environment for which there is not an organismic need, physical or psychological. These must be digested and mastered if they are to become truly our own, truly a part of the personality. But if we simply accept them whole-hog and uncritically, on someone else's say-so, or because they are fashionable or safe or traditional or unfashionable or dangerous or revolutionary—they lie heavily on us. They are really undigestible. They are still foreign bodies even though they may have taken up residence in our minds. Such undigested attitudes, ways of acting, feeling and evaluating, psychology calls *introjects*, and the mechanism by which these alien accretions are added to the personality we call introjection.

I am not saying that this process of swallowing whole does not occasionally serve a useful purpose. The student who crams the night before an examination in order to get a passing grade in a very dull subject has a legitimate reason for his actions. But if he deludes himself into thinking that he has really learned anything from his cramming, he will be in for a bad shock when, six months later, he is again quizzed on the same subject. For by that time he will have lost the greatest part of what he "learned."

Nor am I saying that the individual should reject any psychological food that comes from the outside world. It is as

Introjection

impossible to feed off oneself psychologically as it is to feed off oneself physically. What I am saying is that the psychological food with which the outside world presents us—the food of facts and attitudes on which our personalities are built—has to be assimilated in exactly the same way as is our actual food. It has to be destructured, analyzed, taken apart, and then put together again in the form in which it will be of most value to us. If it is merely swallowed whole, it contributes not at all to the development of our personalities. On the contrary, it makes us something like a house so jampacked with other people's possessions that there is no room for the owner's property. It turns us into waste baskets of extraneous and irrelevant information. And what makes it most tragic is the fact that if this material were to be tempered, altered and transformed through us, it could be of enormous value to us.

The dangers of introjection, then, are twofold. First of all, the man who introjects never gets a chance to develop his own personality, because he is so busy holding down the foreign bodies lodged in his system. The more introjects he has saddled himself with, the less room there is for him to express or even discover what he himself is. And in the second place, introjection contributes to personality disintegration. If you swallow whole two incompatible concepts, you may find yourself torn to bits in the process of trying to reconcile them. And this is a fairly common experience today.

Our society, for example, teaches all of us from infancy two entirely different and apparently opposing sets of attitudes. One is the Golden Rule, "do unto others as you would have them do unto you." The other is the law of the survival of the fittest, which has been reduced to the slogan, "dog eat dog." If we were to introject both of these bits of dogma, we would wind up trying to be, at the same time, kind, gentle, undemanding, and wantonly aggressive. We would love our neighbors, but we wouldn't trust them any further than we could throw them. We would emulate the meek, and at the same time would be ruthless and sadistic. Those who do introject both of these concepts, or

Introjection

any other set of warring ideas, make a battleground of their own personalities. And the neurotic's internal conflict is usually fought to a stalemate, where neither side wins, where the personality is immobilized for any further growth and development.

Introjection, then, is the neurotic mechanism whereby we incorporate into ourselves standards, attitudes, ways of acting and thinking, which are not truly ours. In introjection, we have moved the boundary between ourselves and the rest of the world so far inside ourselves that there is almost nothing of us left. To go back to the example in our last chapter of our suffering singer's statement, "It isn't nice to disturb the others," is an example of introjection. Who, after all, said that—he or they? Does he really believe that his own needs are so unimportant that the needs of the group must always be given preference? When the introjector says, "I think," he usually means, "they think."

Projection

The reverse of introjection is *projection.* As introjection is the tendency to make the self responsible for what actually is part of the environment, so projection is the tendency to make the environment responsible for what originates in the self. Clinically, we recognize that the disease of paranoia, which is characterized by the development of a highly organized system of delusions, is the extreme case of projection. The paranoiac has been found to be, in case after case, a highly aggressive personality who, unable to bear the responsibility for his own wishes, feelings, and desires, attaches them to objects or people in the environment. His conviction that he is being persecuted is in fact the statement that he would like to persecute others.

But projection exists in much less extreme forms than this, and we have to be careful to distinguish between projection, which is a pathological process, and assumption based on

Projection

observation, which is normal and healthy. Planning and anticipating, skirmishing and maneuvering in a game of chess and
many other activities all involve behavior based on observation
and assumptions about the outside world. But these assumptions
are recognized as assumptions. The chess player who thinks
ahead several moves is making a whole group of assumptions
about his opponent's mental processes based on his observations. Essentially, he is saying, "If I were he, this is what I would
do." But he recognizes that he is making assumptions which will
not necessarily govern his opponent's behavior, and he recognizes
that these assumptions are his own.

On the other hand, the sexually inhibited woman who
complains because everyone is making passes at her, or the cold,
withdrawn, haughty man who accuses others of being unfriendly
to him—these are examples of neurotic projection. In these
cases the individuals have made assumptions based on their own
fantasies and have failed to recognize that they are only assumptions. In addition, they have further refused to recognize the
origin of their assumptions. Artistic creation, too, demands a
kind of assumptive –projective behavior. The novelist often
literally projects himself into his characters and becomes them
while he is writing about them. But again, he does not suffer
from the confusion of identity which characterizes the projecting neurotic. He knows where he leaves off and his characters
begin, although in the heat of creative activity he may temporarily lose his sense of boundary and become someone else.

The neurotic does not use the mechanism of projection
only in relation to his dealings with the world outside himself.
He also uses it on himself. He has a tendency not only to disown
his own impulses, but also to disown those parts of himself in
which the impulses arise. He gives them, as it were, an objective
existence outside himself so that he can make them responsible
for his troubles without facing the fact that they are part of him.
Instead of being an active participant in his own life the projector becomes a passive object, the victim of circumstances.

Our singer's plaintive statement about his bladder, "It

Projection

really is a nuisance," is a neat little example of projection. The *it* has reared its ugly head; our fellow is on the verge of being victimized by his own bladder. "It just has to happen to me; I have to suffer," he is saying. We are witnessing the birth of a tiny bit of paranoia. For just as the answer to the introjector's question "who said that?" is "they," so the answer to the projector's statement is, "it's your bladder, it's you that wants to urinate." When the projector says "it" or "they" he usually means "I."

In projection, then, we shift the boundary between ourselves and the rest of the world a little too much in our own favor—in a manner that makes it possible for us to disavow and disown those aspects of our personalities which we find difficult or offensive or unattractive. And usually, by the way, it is our introjects that lead us to the feelings of self-contempt and self-alienation that produce projection. Because our hero has introjected the notion that good manners are more important than the satisfaction of pressing personal needs, because he has introjected the belief that one should learn to "grin and bear it," he must project or even expel those impulses in him which are at odds with what he now considers external activities. So no longer does he want to urinate; he is a good boy, he wants to stay with the group and continue singing. But that nasty, inconsiderate bladder, which just happens to have its residence in him, and which he now conceives of as being an introject—a foreign element introduced forcibly into him against his will—wants him to urinate. Like the introjector, he is incapable of distinguishing between those facets of his total personality which are really his and those which are imposed on him from the outside. He sees his introjects as himself and he sees those parts of himself which he would rather be rid of as undigested and indigestible introjects. By projecting, he hopes to rid himself of his fancied introjects, which are, in fact, not introjects at all, but aspects of himself.

The introjecting personality, who becomes a battleground for warring unassimilated ideas, is paralleled by the projecting

Projection

personality, who makes the world the battleground on which his private conflicts must be fought out. The over-wary, over-cautious person, who tells you he wants friends and wants to be loved, but who tells you at the same time that "you can't trust anyone, they're all out for what they can get," is a projector par excellence.

Confluence

When the individual feels no boundary at all between himself and his environment, when he feels that he and it are one, he is in *confluence* with it. Parts and whole are indistinguishable from one another. Newborn infants live in confluence; they have no sense of any distinction between inside and outside, between the self and the other. In moments of ecstacy or extreme concentration, grown people, too, feel confluent with their environment. Ritual demands this sense of confluence, in which boundaries disappear and the individual feels most himself because he is so closely identified with the group. Part of the reason ritual produces a sense of exaltation and heightened experience is that normally we feel the self-other boundary quite sharply, and its temporary dissolution is consequently felt as a tremendously impactful thing. But when this sense of utter identification is chronic and the individual is unable to see the difference between himself and the rest of the world, he is psychologically sick. He cannot experience himself because he has lost all sense of himself.

The person in whom confluence is a pathological state cannot tell what he is and he cannot tell what other people are. He does not know where he leaves off and others begin. As he is unaware of the boundary between himself and others, he cannot make good contact with them. Nor can he withdraw from them. Indeed, he cannot even make contact with himself.

Confluence

We are built from millions of cells. If we were a confluence, we would be a jelly-like mass and no organization would be possible. If, on the other hand, every cell were separated from one another by a porous membrane, and this membrane is the place of contact, of discrimination, as to what is "accepted" and what is "rejected."

If our component parts, however, which operate not only as parts of the total human being but also perform their own particular functions, are brought together and kept together in pathological confluence, neither will be able to perform its own job properly. Let us take as an example some chronic inhibition. Suppose that on several occasions you wanted to cry, but you prevented yourself from doing it by deliberately contracting the muscles of your diaphragm. Suppose further that this pattern of behavior, which originally arose as a conscious effort to suppress the need to cry, became habitual and unaware. The breathing and the need to cry would have become confused and confluent with one another. You would then have lost both activities—the capacity to breathe freely and the capacity to cry. Unable to sob, you would never release and work through your sorrow; probably after a while you would even forget what you were sad about. The need to sob and the contraction of the diaphragm as a defense against the expression of this need together form a single stabilized battle line of activity and counteractivity, and this perpetual warfare goes on constantly, and in isolation from the rest of the personality. The man who is in pathological confluence ties up his needs, his emotions, and his activities in one bundle of utter confusion until he is no longer aware of what he wants to do and how he is preventing himself from doing it. Such pathological confluence lies behind many of the diseases now recognized as psychosomatic. The breathing-sobbing confusion we mentioned above may lead to asthma, if it persists long enough.

Pathological confluence has serious social consequences, too. In confluence, one demands likeness and refuses to tolerate any differences. We often find this in parents who consider

Confluence

their children to be merely extensions of themselves. Such parents lack the appreciation that their children are bound to be unlike them in at least some respects. And if the children are not confluent, and do not identify with their parents' demands, they will meet with rejection and alienation: "You are not my son." "I don't love such a naughty child."

If the members of the United Nations were to appreciate or even esteem the differences between the nations that go to make up the organization, they would have good contact, and there would be a good chance of working out the problems that now beset the world. But as long as differences are not tolerated, and as long as each nation demands that all the others should share its outlook, point for point, conflict and confusion will continue. As long as differences are not appreciated, they are likely to be persecuted. The demand for total agreement, for confluence, is like the statement, "If you won't be my friend, I'll crack your skull open!"

Our singer's statement, "We want to go on," when in fact it is they who want to go on and not he—he wants to leave and urinate—is a statement of confluence; a statement that he no longer knows how to distinguish between himself and the rest of the group. When the man who is in pathological confluence says "we" you can't tell who he is talking about; himself or the rest of the world. He has completely lost all sense of boundary.

Retroflection

The fourth neurotic mechanism can be called *retroflection*, which literally means "turning back sharply against." The retroflector knows how to draw a boundary line between himself and the environment, and he draws a neat and clean one right down the middle—but he draws it down the middle of himself. *The introjector does as others would like him to do, the projector does unto others what he accuses them of doing to*

Retroflection

him, the man in pathological confluence doesn't know who is doing what to whom, and the retroflector does to himself what he would like to do to others. When a person retroflects behavior, he treats himself as he originally wanted to treat other persons or objects. He stops directing his energies outward in attempts to manipulate and bring about changes in the environment that will satisfy his needs; instead, he redirects his activity inwards and substitutes himself in place of the environment as the target for behavior. To the extent that he does this, he splits his personality into doer and done to. He literally becomes his own worst enemy.

Obviously, no human being can go through life giving free reign to every one of his impulses. At least some of them have to be held in check. But deliberately resisting destructive impulses with the recognition that they are destructive is quite different from turning them against oneself. The harrassed mother at the tail end of a long and hectic day in which the washing machine went berserk and tore the clothes, her five year old son went berserk and scribbled with red crayon all over the living room wall, the man who was supposed to fix the vacuum cleaner didn't show up and her husband came home an hour late for dinner is likely to feel absolutely murderous. It would not be advisable for her to kill the child or her husband, but it would be equally foolish for her to cut her own throat.

How does the mechanism of retroflection display itself? As introjection displays itself in the use of the pronoun "I" when the real meaning is "they;" as projection displays itself in the use of the pronouns "it" or "they," when the real meaning is "I;" as confluence displays itself in the use of the pronoun "we" when the real meaning is in question; so retroflection displays itself in the use of the reflective, "myself."

The retroflector says, "I am ashamed of myself," or "I have to force myself to do this job." He makes an almost endless series of statements of this sort, all of them based on the surprising conception that he and himself are two different people. What does our singer say? "I must control myself."

Retroflection

The confusion between the self and the other that lies behind neurosis shows itself also in utter confusion about the self. To the neurotic, the self is a beast or an angel—but the self is never myself.

Freud in describing the development of personality contributed to this confusion. He talked about the ego, (the "I") the id, (the organic drives) and the super-ego, (the conscience) and described the individual's psychic life as a constant conflict between them—clenched in an endless and unbreakable embrace with himself— man struggles until death. The retroflector seems to be acting in accordance with the Freudian picture of man. But stop to consider for a moment what the super-ego actually is. If it is not part of the self, the "I," the ego, it must of necessity be a bundle of introjects, of unassimilated attitudes and approaches imposed on the individual by the environment. Freud talks of introjection as part of the moral process of growth; he says for example that the child introjects the "good" parent images and establishes them as his ego-ideals. The ego, then, becomes a bundle of introjects too. But study after study of neurotic personalities shows us that problems arise not in relation to a childhood identification with "good" parents, but in relation to identification with the "bad" parents. The child does not, in fact, introject the attitudes and ethics of the "good" parents. He assimilates them. He may not be aware in complicated terms and psychiatric jargon of what he is doing, but he is translating the attitudes that lie behind his parents' satisfying behavior into terms which he can understand; reducing them, as it were, to the least common denominator, and then assimilating them in their new form, a form which he can use. He cannot comparably reduce his parents' "bad" attitudes; he has no means for coping with them, and certainly no built-in desire to cope with them. So he must take them over as undigested introjects. And that is where the trouble begins. For now we have a personality made up, not of ego and super-ego, but of I and not I, of self and self-image, a personality so confused that it has become incapable of distinguishing one from the other.

Retroflection

Indeed, this confusion of identification is in fact neurosis. And whether it displays itself primarily through the use of the mechanism of introjection or of projection or of retroflection or of confluence, its hallmark is disintegration of the personality and lack of coordination in thought and action.

Therapy consists in rectifying false identifications. If neurosis is the product of "bad" identifications, health is the product of "good" identifications. That leaves open, of course, the question of which are the good identifications and which are the bad. The simplest and, I think, the most satisfactory answer—and one based on observable reality—is that "good" identifications are those which promote the satisfactions and goal-fulfillments of the individual and his environment. And "bad" identifications are those which result in stunting or thwarting the individual, or destructive behavior toward his environment. For the neurotic not only makes himself miserable, he punishes all those who care for him by his self-destructive behavior.

In therapy, then, we have to re-establish the neurotic's capacity to discriminate. We have to help him to rediscover what is himself and what is not himself; what fulfills him and what thwarts him. We have to guide him towards integration. We have to assist him in finding the proper balance and boundary between himself and the rest of the world. It is simple to say, "just be yourself," but for the neurotic, a thousand obstacles bar the way. Understanding now, as we do, the mechanisms through which the neurotic is preventing himself from being himself, we can settle down to try to remove the road blocks, one by one. For this is what should happen in therapy, and therapy is what we shall now discuss.

HERE AND NOW THERAPY

Implicit in the emphasis of orthodox psychotherapy is the point of view that the neurotic is a person who once had a problem, and that the resolution of this past problem is the goal of psychotherapy. The whole approach to treatment through memory and the past indicates this assumption, which runs directly counter to everything we observe about neurosis and the neurotic. From the Gestalt viewpoint the neurotic is not merely a person who once *had* a problem, he is a person who has a *continuing* problem, here and now, in the present. Although it may well be that he is acting the way he is today "because" of things that happened to him in the past, his difficulties today are connected with the ways he is acting today. We cannot get along in the present, and unless he learns how to deal with problems as they arise, he will not be able to get along in the future.

The goal of therapy, then, must be to give him the means with which he can solve his present problems and any that may arise tomorrow or next year. That tool is self-support, and this he achieves by dealing with himself and his problems with all the means presently at his command, right now. If he can become *truly aware* at every instant of himself and his actions on whatever level—fantasy, verbal or physical—he can see how he is producing his difficulties, he can see what his present difficulties are, and he can help himself to solve them in the present, in the here and now. Each one he solves makes easier the solution of the next, for every solution increases his self-support.

If therapy is successful the patient will inevitably have taken care of the tag ends of his past unsolved problems, because these tag ends are bound to cause trouble in the present, and so

Here and Now Therapy

they are bound to come up in the course of the therapeutic session, disguised in any number of different ways—disassociations, nervous habits, fantasies, etc. But these tag ends of the past are also current problems which inhibit the patient's participation in the present.

The neurotic is, by accepted definition, a person whose difficulties make his present life unsuccessful. In addition, by our definition, he is a person who chronically engages in self-interruption, who has an inadequate sense of identity (and thus cannot distinguish properly between himself and the rest of the world), who has inadequate means of self-support, whose psychological homeostasis is out of order, and whose behavior arises from misguided efforts in the direction of achieving balance.

Within this general framework, we can see what must be done. The neurotic finds it difficult to participate fully in the present—his past unfinished business gets in his way. His problems exist in the here and now—and yet too often only part of him is here to cope with them. Through therapy, he must learn to live in the present, and his therapeutic sessions must be his first practice at this hitherto unaccomplished task. Gestalt therapy is therefore a "here and now" therapy, in which we ask the patient during the session to turn all his attention to what he is doing at the present, during the course of the session—right here and now.

Gestalt therapy is an experiential therapy, rather than a verbal or an interpretive therapy. We ask our patients not to talk about their traumas and their problems in the removed area of the past tense and memory, but to *re-experience* their problems and their traumas—which are their unfinished situations in the present—in the here and now. If the patient is finally to close the book on his past problems, he must close it in the present. For he must realize that if his past problems were really past, they would no longer be problems—and they certainly would not be present.

In addition, as an experiential therapy, the Gestalt technique demands of the patient that he experience as much of himself as he can, that he experience himself as fully as he can in the here and now. We ask the patient to become aware of his

Here and Now Therapy

gestures, of his breathing, of his emotions, of his voice, and of his facial expressions as much as of his pressing thoughts. We know that the more he becomes aware of himself, the more he will learn about what his self is. As he experiences the ways in which he prevents himself from "being" now—the ways in which he interrupts himself—he will also begin to experience the self he has interrupted.

In this process, the therapist is guided by what he observes about the patient. We shall discuss the therapist's role in more detail in a later chapter. Here let it suffice to say that the therapist should be sensitive to the surface the patient presents so that the therapist's broader awareness can become the means by which the patient is enabled to increase his own.

The basic sentence with which we ask our patients to begin therapy, and which we retain throughout its course—not only in words, but in spirit—is the simple phrase: "Now I am aware." The now keeps us in the present and brings home the fact that no experience is ever possible except in the present. And the present, itself, is of course an ever changing experience. Once the now is used, the patient will easily use the present tense throughout, work on a phenomenological basis and, as I will show later, provide the material of past experience which is required to close the gestalt, to assimilate a memory, to right the organismic balance.

The "I" is used as an antidote to the "it" and developes the patient's sense of responsibility for his feelings, thoughts and symptoms. The "am" is his existential symbol. It brings home whatever he experiences as part of his being, and, together with his now, of his becoming. He quickly learns that each new "now" is different from the previous one.

The "aware" provides the patient with the sense of his own capacities, and abilities, his own sensoric and motor and intellectual equipment. It is not the conscious—for that is purely mental—it is the experience sifted, as it were, only through the mind and through words. The "aware" provides something in addition to the conscious. Working, as we do, with what the

Here and Now Therapy

patient has, his present means of manipulation, rather than with what he has not developed or what he has lost, the "aware" gives both therapist and patient the best picture of the patient's present resources. For awareness always takes place in the present. It opens up possibilities for action. Routine and habits are established functions, and any need to change them requires that they should be brought into the focus of awareness afresh. The mere idea of changing them presupposes the possibility of alternative ways of thinking and acting. Without awareness, there is no cognition of choice. Awareness, contact, and present are merely different aspects of one and the same process—self-realization. It is here and now that we become aware of all our choices, from small pathological decisions (is this pencil lying straight enough?) to the existential choice of devotion to a cause or avocation.

How does this "now I am aware," this here and now therapy work in action? Let us take the example of a neurotic whose unfinished business is the unfinished labor of mourning a dead parent. Aware or unaware, such a patient fantasizes that his guiding parent is still around; he acts as if the parent were still alive and conducts his life by outdated directions. To become self-supportive and to participate fully in the present as it is, he has to give up this guidance; he has to part, to say a final good-bye to his progenitor. And to do this successfully, he has to go to the deathbed and face the departure. He has to transform his thoughts about the past into actions in the present which he experiences as if the now were the then. He cannot do it merely by re-recounting the scene, he must re-live it. He must go through and assimilate the interrupted feelings which are mostly of intense grief, but which may have in them elements of triumph or guilt or any number of other things. It is insufficient merely to recall a past incident, one has to *psychodramatically* return to it. Just as talking about oneself is a resistance against experiencing oneself, so the memory of an experience—simply talking about it—leaves it isolated as a deposit of the past—as lacking in life as the ruins of Pompei. You are left with the opportunity to make

Here and Now Therapy

some clever reconstructions, but you don't bring them back alive. The neurotic's memory is more than simply a hunting ground for the archeologists of man's behavior we call psychoanalysts. It is the uncompleted event, which is still alive and interrupted, waiting to be assimilated and integrated. It is here and now, in the present, that this assimilation must take place.

The psychoanalyst, out of the vast stores of his theoretical knowledge, might explain to the patient: "You are still tied to your mother because you feel guilty about her death. It was something you wished for in childhood and repressed, and when your wish came true, you felt like a murderer." And there may be elements of truth in what he says. But this kind of symbolic or intellectual explanation does not affect the patient's feelings, for these are the result not of his sense of guilt, but of his interruption of it when his mother died. If he had permitted himself fully to experience his guilt then, he would not feel distressed now. In Gestalt therapy we therefore require that the patient psychodramatically talk to his dead mother.

Because the neurotic finds it difficult to live and experience himself in the present, he will find it difficult to stick to the here and now technique. He will interrupt his present participation with memories of the past, and he will persist in talking about them as if they were indeed past. He finds it less difficult to associate than to concentrate and, in concentrating, to experience himself. Whether concentrating on his body sensations or his fantasies—although at first he will find this a miserable task—his unfinished business makes concentration a major project for him. He no longer has a clear sense of the order of his needs—he tends to give them all equal value. He is like the young man Stephen Leacock once spoke about who got on his horse and galloped off madly in all directions.

It is not a desire to make his life miserable that lies behind our request to make him capable of concentrations If he is to move towards full participation in the present, to take the first step towards productive living, he must learn to direct his energies—that is, to concentrate. He will be able to move from

Here and Now Therapy

"now I need this" to "now I need that," only if he truly experiences each now and each need.

In addition, the concentration technique (focal awareness) provides us with a tool for therapy in depth, rather than in breadth. By concentrating on each symptom, each area of awareness, the patient learns several things about himself and his neurosis. He learns what he is actually experiencing. He learns how he experiences it. And he learns how his feelings and behavior in one area are related to his feelings and behavior in other areas.

Let me return for a moment to that classical psychosomatic manifestation, the headache. Patients frequently list this as one of their most annoying symptoms. They complain that their headaches bother them and now, when they come for treatment, they want to bother us with their symptoms. They are, of course, welcome to do so. But we in turn bother them— we ask them to take more responsibility and less aspirin. We do this by asking them to discover through experiencing how they produce their headaches. (The "aha" experience of discovery is one of the most powerful agents for cure). We ask them first to localize the pain and to stay, or sit, or lie with the tension. We ask them to concentrate on the pain, not to dispose of it. In the beginning only a few will be able to stand the tension. Most patients will tend to interrupt immediately with explanations, associations, or by pooh-poohing what we are doing. Consequently, the therapist has to work through one way of interrupting after another, and he has to change these interruptions into "I" functions. This means that even before we work on the headache itself, we have already done a considerable amount of integration. Suppose, for example, the therapist asks the patient to stay with his pains and the patient says, as often happens, "this is all nonsense." If he learns to say, instead, "what you are trying to do is all nonsense," he is taking a tiny step forward. With such a small step we have transformed a minute particle of "it" into a *contact function*, into a self-expression. We might even follow up his statement and ask the patient to elaborate on

Here and Now Therapy

it. This would give him an opportunity to come out with a lot of his unspoken skepticism, distrust, and so on, and all of these are part of the unfinished businesses that are preventing his total participation in the present.

But finally the patient will be able to stay with his headache, and with his pains, which he can now localize. This staying with is opening up the possibility for development of contact with the self. If he stays with his pains he may find that he has been contracting some muscles or that he feels a numbness. Let us say that he discovers his pains are associated with muscle contractions. Then we will ask him to exaggerate the contracting. He will then see how he can voluntarily create and intensify his own pains. He might then say, as a result of his discoveries up to now, "It's as if I were screwing up my face to cry." The therapist might then ask, "Would you like to cry?" And then, if we ask him to direct that remark directly to us, to say it to our face, he might well burst out crying and weeping. "I won't cry, damn you! Leave me alone, leave me alone!" Apparently, then, his headache was an interruption of the need to cry. It has become apparent that he has lost his need to interrupt his crying by giving himself headaches. At best, the patient may lose his need to cry, too, for if the therapy can be concentrated on this one factor for a long enough period of time, he may be able to work through the past interruptions that also led to the need to cry in the present. But even before this stage, progress has been made. The patient has transformed a partial involvement (headache) into a total involvement (weeping). He has transformed a psychosomatic symptom into an expression of the total self, because in his short outburst of despair he was wholly and totally involved. So through the concentration technique the patient has learned how to participate fully in at least one present experience. He has learned at the same time something about his process of self-interruption and the ways in which these self-interruptions are related to the totality of his experience. He has discovered one of his means of manipulation.

Here and Now Therapy

The neurotic is, as we said, a self-interrupter. All schools of psychotherapy take this fact into account. Freud, as a matter of fact, built his therapy around a recognition of this phenomenon. Of all the possible forms of self-interruption he chose a very decisive one, which he called the Censor. He said, "Do not interrupt the free flow of your associations." But he also assumed that the Censor was the servant of embarrassment, and thus spoke Freud: "Do not be embarrassed." Precisely with these two taboos he interrupted the patient's experience of his embarrassment and his experience of its dissolution. This results in a desensitization, an inability to experience embarrassment, or even (and this applies still more to patients in Reichian therapy) in overcompensating brazenness. What has to be tackled in therapy is not the censored material but the censoring itself, the form that self-interruption takes. Again, we cannot work from the inside out, but only from the outside in.

The therapeutic procedure (which is the re-establishment of the self by integrating the dissociated parts of the personality) must bring the patient to the point where he no longer interrupts himself, that is, to the point where he is no longer neurotic. How can we do this without making the mistake of interrupting the interruption? We have previously mentioned Freud's command, "do not censor," which is in itself a censoring of the censor, an interruption of the process of censoring. What we have to do is notice and deal with the *hows* of every interruption, rather than with the censor—which is Freud's postulated *why* of interruption. If we deal with the interruptions per se, we deal with the direct clinical picture, with the experience the patient is living through. Again, we deal with the surface that presents itself. There is no need to guess and to interpret. We hear the interruption of a sentence or we notice that the patient holds his breath or we see that he is making a fist, as if to hit someone, or swinging his legs as if to kick, or we observe how he interrupts contact with the therapist by looking away.

Is he aware of these self-interruptions? This must be our first question to him in such a situation. Does he know that this

Here and Now Therapy

is what he is doing? As he becomes more aware of the ways in which he interrupts himself, he will inevitably become more aware of what he is interrupting. As our example of the headache showed, it was in staying with his interruption, his headache, that he discovered how he was using this mechanism to interrupt his own crying. This example shows how, by concentrating on the interruption per se—on the hows of it, not its whys—the patient comes to an awareness of the fact that he is interrupting himself, and becomes aware of what he is interrupting. He also becomes able to dissolve his interruptions and to live through and finish up one unfinished experience.

The neurotic mechanisms of introjection, projection, and retroflection are themselves mechanisms of introjection, and often developed in response to interruptions from the outside world. In the normal process of growth, we learn through trial and error, through testing our lives and our world as freely and uninterruptedly as possible.

Imagine a kitten climbing a tree. It is engaged in experimenting. It balances itself, it tests its strength and its agility. But the mother cat will not leave it alone; she insists that it come down. "You may break your neck, you naughty kitten," she hisses. How this would interrupt the kitten's pleasure in growing! It would even interrupt the growth process itself. But cats, of course, do not behave so stupidly. They leave the pursuit of safety to the human beings.

On the contrary, the cat, like any other animal and any sensible human being, will consider it the essence of up-bringing to facilitate the transformation of external into self-support. The newly born kitten can neither feed, transport nor defend itself. For all this it needs its mother. But it will develop the means to do these things itself, partly through developing its inborn instincts, and partly through environmental teaching. In the human being, the transition from external to self-support is, of course, more complicated. Consider only the need to change diapers, to dress, to cook, to choose a vocation, or to gain knowledge.

Here and Now Therapy

Since we are forced to learn so much more through education than by using our inherited instincts, much of the animal's intuition as to what is the right procedure is missing. Instead, the "right" procedure is established by composite fantasies which are handed over and modified from generation to generation. They are mostly support functions for social contact, such as manners and codes of behavior (ethics), means of orientation (reading, weltanschauungen), standards of beauty (aesthetics), and social position (attitudes). Often, however, these procedures are not biologically oriented, thus disrupting the very root of our existence and leading to degeneration. Psychiatric case histories show over and over how our depreciatory orientation towards sex can produce neurosis. But whether these procedures are anti-biological or anti-personal or anti-social, they are interruptions in the on-going processes which, if left alone, would lead to self-support.

Such interruptions are the nightmares of Junior's upbringing. There are the *interruptions of contact,* the "don't touch that!" and the "don't do that!" that fly around his ears day in and day out. Or "leave me alone! Can't I have a moment's peace," interrupt his wish to interrupt mamma. His *withdrawals* are also interrupted. "You stay here now, keep your mind on your homework and don't dream," or "you can't go out to play until you finish your dinner."

Shall we then follow a policy of utter non-interruption? Like any other animal, Junior has to test the world, to find his possibilities, to try to expand his boundaries, to experiment with how far he can go. But at the same time he has to be prevented from doing serious harm to himself or others. He has to learn to cope with interruptions.

The real trouble begins when the parents interfere with the child's maturation, either by spoiling him and interrupting his attempts to find his own bearings or by being overprotective, and destroying his confidence in his ability to be self-supportive within the limits of his development. They regard the child as a possession to be either preserved or exhibited. In the latter case,

Here and Now Therapy

they will tend to create precocity by making ambitious demands on the child, who at that time lacks sufficient inner support to fulfill them. In the former case, they will tend to block maturation by giving the child no chance to make use of the inner supports he has developed. The first child may grow up self-sufficient, the second dependent—neither self-supportive.

Our patients come to us having incorporated their parent's interruptions into their own lives—and this is introjection. Such patients are the ones who say to us, for example, "grown men don't cry!" They come to us having disowned the offending parts of themselves—the ones that were interrupted in their childhood—this is projection. "These darn headaches! Why do I have to suffer from them!" They may turn the qualities their parents called bad, and the display of which they interrupted, against themselves. This is retroflection. "I must control myself. I must not let myself cry!" They may have become so confused by their parents' interruptions that they give up their identity completely and forget the difference and the connection between their internal needs and the external means of satisfying them. This result is confluence. "I always get a headache when people yell at me."

Through making our patients aware, in the here and now, by concentration, of what these interruptions are, of how these interruptions affect them, we can bring them to real integrations. We can dissolve the endless clinch in which they find themselves. We can give them a chance to be themselves, because they will begin to experience themselves; this will give them a true appreciation both of themselves and others, and will enable them to make good contact with the world, because they will know where the world is. Understanding means, basically, seeing a part in its relation to the whole. For our patients, it means seeing themselves as part of the total field and thus becoming related both to themselves and to the world. This is good contact.

SHUTTLING, PSYCHODRAMA AND CONFUSION

There is one obvious limitation to the awareness technique used alone. It would probably take years to achieve its results, as do most of the orthodox therapies, and at that rate, psychiatry could never catch up with the constantly increasing number of people who are mentally disturbed and the still more rapidly increasing number of people who live far below their potentials. Although the analytical approach has failed to provide us with a tool that can cope with the social emergency, the awareness technique by itself would be equally limited.

But, having recognized the relationship between fantasy and actuality, we can make full use in therapy of fantasizing and all its increasing states of intensity towards actuality—a verbalized fantasy, or one which is written down, or one which is acted out as psychodrama. We can play at psychodrama with our patients, or we can ask them to play at this game alone, a game which we term "monotherapy."

In this latter case, the patient creates his own stage, his own actors, his own props, direction and expression. This gives him a chance to realize that everything he fantasizes is his, and gives him a chance to see the conflicts inside him. Monotherapy thus avoids the contamination, the precepts of others which are usually present in ordinary psychodrama.

We make use of several other techniques as well. The first I would like to discuss is the shuttle technique. As an approach, it is nothing new. The Freudians handle dreams in precisely this way, by asking the patient to shuttle between the manifest content of a dream and its associations. But the systematic application of the technique in Gestalt therapy and the

Shuttling, Psychodrama and Confusion

particular way in which it is applied are both new. I have already demonstrated its use in our experiment on acute anxiety, in which I asked the patient to shuttle his attention from his breathing to his muscles, from his muscles to his breathing, until the relationship between the two becomes clear and the patient can breathe freely. This shuttling helps us to break up patterns of confluence, such as we see in the headache that turns out to be a disguised crying.

One of my first "miracle" cures was due to an intuitive application fo this technique. A young man came for therapy whose major complaint was sexual impotence. He told me in great detail about his background, family situation, social activities, etc. But what was most interesting was his remark that although his health in general was good, he was under treatment by an ear-nose-and-throat specialist for chronic nasal congestion. This struck me as the most vital clue to his problem, and remembering the Fleiss-Freud observation that swelling of the nasal mucous membrane was often a displacement from the genital area, I asked him if he would be willing to stop medical treatment temporarily. He agreed. During his next session, I requested him to direct his concentration alternately to his nasal sensations and his non-existent genital sensations. And an extraordinary thing happened. The nasal swelling decreased and the tumescence of the penis increased. Now he could both breathe freely and have sexual relations. He had not only interrupted his penis erections and displaced both the sensation and the tumescence to his nose, he had even begun to compartmentalize his symptoms and to pander to his dissociations by having different specialists attend to them. While the ear-nose-and-throat doctor was used to working on dissociated symptoms and local "causes", the Gestalt approach enabled me to look for the total situation, to examine the structure of the field, to see the problem in its total context and to treat it in a unified way.

When we look at displacements in this way, it becomes evident that they cannot be dealt with where they occur because they have no functional meaning in that place. The displacement

Shuttling, Psychodrama and Confusion

must be brought back to where it belongs; it can only be resolved in the area where it has meaning. The patient who suffers from pains in the eyes which are due to the retention of tears, can dissolve his pains only in crying. The patient who has displaced from the testicles (in the vernacular, the balls) where there is retained semen—to the eyeballs (and I have had several such patients) will have to shift his pains back to where they belong before they can be dealt with. Not until then can he enjoy a good orgasm and lose his symptoms.

Now let me present another example, less dramatic but equally valid. Here we shuttle, not as the orthodox analyst does, between memory and associations, but between the re-living of a memory and the here and now. As I have previously mentioned, we treat all time during the therapeutic session as if it were here and now; for awareness and experience can only take place in the present. But even with the most vivid visualization and reliving of a memory, the knowledge that it is something from the past remains in the background. This is not true, however, with what we call the proprioceptions—the internal, muscular kinesthetic sense. The proprioceptions are timeless, and can only be experienced as here and now. Thus, if we shuttle between visualization and proprioception we will be able to fill in the blanks and complete the unfinished business of the past. The trained therapist will also take into account any involuntary movements the patient makes—shrugging his shoulders, kicking his feet, etc., and draw the patient's attention to them.

Suppose the patient has fantasized a return to a recent experience which bothered him. The first thing he says when he comes into the consulting room is that his job is getting on his nerves. Nobody, he says, treats him with enough respect. There isn't anything special that he can put his finger on, but the whole atmosphere is distasteful to him. Little things get him down. Something very unimportant happened in the company restaurant that very day. It disturbed him, and he cannot understand why he should have been so upset by it.

Shuttling, Psychodrama and Confusion

We ask him to return, in fantasy, to the experience that bothered him. This is what might happen:

Patient: I am sitting in our cafeteria. My boss is eating a few tables away.

Therapist: What do you feel?

Patient: Nothing. He is talking to someone. Now he is getting up.

Therapist: What do you feel now?

Patient: My heart is pounding. He is moving towards me. Now I am getting excited. He is passing me.

Therapist: What do you feel now?

Patient: Nothing. Absolutely nothing.

Therapist: Are you aware that you are making a fist?

Patient: No. Now that you mention it, though, I feel it. As a matter of fact, I was angry that the boss passed right by me but talked to someone else whom I dislike very much. I was angry at myself for being so touchy.

Therapist: Were you angry with anybody else, too?

Patient: Sure. With that guy the boss stopped to talk to. What right has he got to disturb the boss? See— my arm is shaking. I could hit him right now, the dirty apple-polisher.

We can now take the next step and shuttle between the patient's feelings and his projections. Still better, we could go over the scene again. The phrase "apple-polisher" makes us suspicious. Perhaps the patient was not angry with the boss when he felt the short pang of excitement or anxiety early in the scene.

Therapist: Let's go back to the moment when your boss gets up from the table. What do you feel when you visualize that?

Patient: Wait a minute . . . He is getting up. He is coming towards me. I am getting excited; I hope he will talk to me. I feel myself getting warm in the face. Now he is passing me. I feel very disappointed.

Shuttling, Psychodrama and Confusion

This was a minor traumatic situation for the patient. The excitement that was mobilized when the boss appeared could not find appropriate expression and the positive cathexis towards the boss (I hope he will talk to me) changed into a negative one—towards the patient's competitor. This negative cathexis, it later turned out, was actually directed towards the patient's projections, from experiencing and satisfying his own needs and desires.

The new patient usually finds considerable initial difficulty in working with the shuttle technique to recover missing abstractions. But with time it becomes easier, and it brings important rewards. Some patients, for example, never listen; others have no emotions to speak of; still others cannot verbalize; yet a fourth group has no power of self-expression at all. Let's work a bit on the theoretically simplest problem—the inability to express oneself.

Take the case of a fairly successful middle-aged man who seems to be in need of a wailing wall. He will start out by complaining to the therapist no end about his wife, his children, his employees, his competitors, etc. But we do not let him continue this indirect expression. We ask him either to visualize himself talking to them or, psychodramatically, to talk to the therapist as if he were the offending wife, children or whatever. As is our usual practice, we make it clear to him that he should not force himself to succeed—he should not interrupt himself. We make it clear to him that our experiments are carried out for the purpose of making him more aware of the ways in which he is blocking himself, and that what we want him to do is to convert the blocked areas, or repressions, into expressions.

In such a situation we actually have three positions among which to shuttle: the patient's complaining (his manipulation of the therapist for support), his inadequate self-expression (which is a lack of good contact and self-support), and his inhibitions (which are the patient's self-interruptions). The following is the kind of thing that might happen:

Shuttling, Psychodrama and Confusion

Patient: My wife has no consideration for me. (This is a complaint, one of his techniques of manipulating the outside world to give him the support he cannot give himself.)

Therapist: Can you imagine telling this to her face? (We are asking him here not to call on us for support, but to express himself directly.)

Patient: No, I can't. She'd interrupt me as soon as I began. (A complaint again.)

Therapist: Could you tell her that? (Again a request that he express himself directly.)

Patient: Yes. You never let me talk. (This is still a complaint, but at least it is direct. The therapist notes that the soft voice in which the patient uttered it belies his words.)

Therapist: Can you hear your voice? (Here we have shuttled from the complaint to the inadequate means of self-expression.)

Patient: Yes. Sounds rather weak, doesn't it? (A self-interruption.)

Therapist: Could you give an order—something starting with the words "you should?" (In other words, the therapist is asking the patient to express himself simply, directly and appropriately.)

Patient: No, I could not.

Therapist: What do you feel now? (Here we shuttle to the sensations that accompany the patient's actions.)

Patient: My heart is beating. I am getting anxious.

Therapist: Could you tell this to your wife?

Patient: No. But I'm getting angry. I feel like saying, "shut up for once." (And now we have something more than complaining, self-interrupting and inexpressiveness. We have an indirect self-expression.)

Therapist: You just said it to her.

Shuttling, Psychodrama and Confusion

Patient: (Shouting) Shut up, shut up! SHUT UP!! For heaven's sake, let me get a word in. (Explosive self-expression.)

The therapist says nothing; the patient is now on his way alone. And very soon he says: "No, I could not say 'shut up' to her, but now I can imagine interrupting her." And he begins to play-act that interruption: "Please, let me say something."

How far can we permit this acting to go? For acting out his neurotic tendencies is often harmful to the patient. Freud saw this and warned against the danger of acting out in daily life, outside the consulting room. He wanted the patient to keep in mind the neurotic tendency he was repeating. Our emphasis is a little different. We say that we want the patient to become aware, in the consulting room, of the meaning of what he is doing. And we believe that he can achieve this awareness by acting out—in therapy, on the fantasy level—whatever there is to be completed. This, as a matter of fact, is the basic concept of Gestalt therapy. The patient feels compelled to repeat in daily life everything that he cannot bring to a satisfactory conclusion. These repetitions are his unfinished business. But he cannot come to a creative solution in this way because he brings his interruptions along with his repetitions, his acting-out. Thus, if he is acting out a neurotic tendency in his extra-therapeutic life, we ask him, during his sessions, to repeat deliberately in fantasy, what he has been doing in actuality. In this way we can uncover the moment at which he interrupts the flow of experiences and thus prevents himself from coming to a creative solution.

Let's take an example almost directly opposite the one we described before. Our patient has difficulties with his wife which are unquestionably related to the fact that he is acting out his neurotic tendencies in every-day life. As therapy progresses he becomes more and more aware that there are many things he would like to say to her which he will not express; they would hurt her. But he still has not come to a creative solution, and he interrupts his direct expression by being indirectly sadistic. He is consistently late for dinner, he ignores

Shuttling, Psychodrama and Confusion

her, in general he behaves in a manner calculated to be irritating. If we ask him to act out in therapy what he cannot do in reality, to remove his interruptions and fantasize and express in her absence what he would say in her presence, were he not afraid, we will find initially the same reluctance to talk to her in fantasy as we find in actuality. But as the reluctance diminishes, and the patient is able to express—to the therapist, as if the therapist were his wife—more and more of his resentments, he will learn how to cope with them and he will have no need to return to his indirect sadism.

There are other patients who simply don't listen. They may drown the therapist with words. They may interrupt him. They may look attentive, but it is obvious that anything the therapist says goes in one ear and out the other. They may literally not hear him. They may misinterpret his requests and his statements. We let these patients shuttle between talking and listening to themselves. At first we ask them, after each of their sentences: "Are you aware of this sentence?" They usually remember having said the words, but they often say that they were not aware of them as they spoke. If there is a desensitization of the mouth, as there frequently is in these cases, we often ask the patient to become aware of his lips and tongue as he speaks. Once he has learned to listen and to feel himself speaking, he has made two important steps.

They can also now listen to others, and they have opened the road to the non-verbal in being and communicating. For their compulsive talk drowns out both their environment and their selves. It is their technique of self-interruption. What are they interrupting? Further investigations and experiments help us to find out.

Most often we discover that once we have prevented such patients from using up all their excitement—all their emotional investment—in constant chatter and verbalism, they show tremendous anxiety. Talking has become a compulsion with them, and like all compulsions there is great stress if it is interrupted.

Shuttling, Psychodrama and Confusion

There are, besides the shuttle techniques, still other short-cuts to awareness that we can use. The shuttle technique sharpens awareness by giving the patient a clearer sense of the relationships in his behavior. These other techniques, by encouraging self-expression, also produce both greater awareness and greater self-support. There are several schools besides ours which make use of the method of self-expression as a means to re-identification. All of them are essentially integrative approaches, but I would like to select Moreno's psychodramatic technique as one of the most lively and as a further demonstration of how we can apply the shuttle technique.

Moreno's way of handling the psychodramatic situation is essentially to ask the patient to switch over from one role to another—for instance, from the harrassed child to the nagging mother. That way the patient can realize that his nagging superego is his fantasized mother (his introjection), that actually he himself is doing the nagging, that he is not just listening to it but is nagging and being nagged at the same time. It's therapeutic significance is that it facilitates the release of the clinch, the constant quarrel between topdog and underdog, not by adjustment, but by integration.

The psychodramatic technique shows its value in the follow-up to the treatment of the headache we talked about in an earlier chapter. You will remember that ultimately this manifestation boiled down to the patient's statement of two mutually contradictory imperatives: "Don't cry," and "Leave me alone." Now the stage is set for a psychodrama in fantasy. The patient, realizing that the statement demonstrates a split in his own personality, can actually play out both the "don't cry" and the "leave me alone" roles. While he is playing the "don't cry" part, he may discover "I cry when I want to," or "I don't care if I am a sissy," and actually feel his defiance. While he is playing the "don't cry," part, he may feel his contempt for people who behave like sissies. And yet, a minute or two later, he may whisper, sympathetically, "don't cry." At that moment the negative cathexis—people who cry are fools and sissies—changes to a

Shuttling, Psychodrama and Confusion

positive one—I feel for people who cry—and the road opens for integration. Perhaps now he will experience his "leave me alone" as "don't interrupt my crying for the wrong reason, for the reason that I'm a sissy. Interrupt it by feeling sorry for me." And the session might finally end up with a need for confluence— "I cry because I have to leave you, but I don't want you to see it; I don't want to show you how much I need you."

We are now back where we started in the first place. We are back to the patient's lack of self-support. But there is a great difference. The patient is now miserable not, as Freud would say, for neurotic but for human reasons. In our language we would say that now he is no longer concerned with his dissociation, his headache, but with himself. He is, at this moment, fully unified, unhappy in his loneliness. But he expresses it, becomes fully aware of it, and now he may be ready to take the next step, to take responsibility for it and do something about it.

When the patient first came into the consulting room, bearing his headache with him, he was certainly not in *contact* with the therapist. He was in contact with his headache, and his headache was in contact with the therapist. He offered for contact his headache as others offer a mask or a facade. The patient will not part with the mask as long as his feeling of safety behind it outweighs the discomfort of wearing it, and he will certainly object to having his mask torn off his face. The fact that he brought his headache into therapy means that he was ready to acknowledge an unfinished situation; in this respect he was at one with the therapist. It is as if he said: "Make me feel so comfortable that I don't need this symptom or mask or personna or armor." But the therapist could not make him feel comfortable, for the patient was not in contact with him, but with his symptom, the headache.

This is a good example of how we work with psychosomatic symptoms in general. Although the interruption is taking place on the somatic level, where it displays itself in this case as a headache, we have to complete the picture by finding the fantasy that promotes the interruption. We invariably find,

Shuttling, Psychodrama and Confusion

when we do this, that the patient will fantasize some command which is opposed to his demand. In this case, the demand was "leave me alone." The commands were "don't cry!" and "a man doesn't cry," and "don't be a sissy!" There might even be a command reinforced by a threat: "If you don't stop crying I'll give you something to cry about!" In other words, the patient behaves as if somebody was ordering him to interrupt his tears. Whatever phrases were impressed on him in the past are now his, and he fantasizes and obeys them.

We can deal with these commands without delving into the unconscious, for there are two possibilities once we have reached this point. Either the patient is aware that he is making inhibiting demands on himself, which is usually the case, or he is not. In the latter case, he will be aware of the demands, but as a projection, as an assumption that the therapist is the one who is opposed to his crying. Once he has gathered enough strength to burst out into "leave me alone," he can take a stand against the counter demand, whether he localizes it as part of his own anti-self (an introjection) or in the therapist as the frustrator of his spontaneous feelings. If he localizes it in the therapist, the next step, (which again has nothing to do with the unconscious) is taken when the patient sees the paradox of accusing the therapist of wanting to interfere with his crying at the same time that he sees the possibility that the therapist might have been in favor of it. If the therapist has taken no sides in this controversy, which is, after all, not his but the patient's, the patient will discover for himself the absurdity of making the therapist responsible for his interruptions, and he will see the symptom as his own responsibility. And so, by the time the session is over, the patient is in *contact with himself,* and this is the first step to making contact with others.

You may have noticed that, in the dissolution of the headache, we made use of some of Reich's findings. I do not want to enter into the violent controversy over Reich or the equally sharp controversy over Hubbard, but I do at this point want to say that I have found their work in certain areas valuable

Shuttling, Psychodrama and Confusion

as an adjunct to the awareness technique. Wherever else they may have gone astray, Reich's work on motoric interruptions (the headache, for example) and Hubbard's work with the sensorially experienced return (the cafeteria episode, for example) and with verbal interruptions can provide the therapist with extremely useful tools in the restitution of the functions of the self.

The sensorially experienced return is not new. This method was described more than a decade ago, using the procedure of asking the patient to fill in more and more details of the actually visualized situation. This is re-experiencing on the fantasy level. As far as verbal interruptions are concerned, the idea of repetition has also been used extensively. Repeating over and over the significant maxims of the past, which are actually among the patient's introjections, can also have a therapeutic effect. These maxims apparently have had a profound effect on the patient, as we saw in the headache case. However, I differ from Hubbard in believing that these maxims have their effect not through a traumatic experience but through their every-day intrusion into the patient's life.

There is one disadvantage to any of these techniques: the patient must already be able to express himself to a certain degree. And for the psychodrama he must be able to identify with a role he dislikes. But even if the techniques provide us with no more than an experiment in ferreting out the patient's resistances against self-expression, they are very useful.

Another important therapeutic technique is the approach to the areas of confusion via the manifest interruptions. Confusion is a bad support for contact, and the patient's problem is often displayed in his areas of confusion. Before I discuss how this technique works, however, let me say that the experience of confusion is very, very unpleasant and, like anxiety, shame and disgust, we have a strong desire to annihilate it—by avoidance, by verbalism, or by any other kind of interruption. And yet a good part of the fight against neurosis is won merely by helping the patient to become aware of, to tolerate, and to stay with

Shuttling, Psychodrama and Confusion

his confusion and its correlative, blanking out. Although confusion is unpleasant, the only real danger is in interrupting it
and consequently becoming confused in action. For confusion,
like any other emotion, if left alone to develop uninterrupted,
will not remain confusion. It will be transformed into a feeling
which is experienced more positively and which can produce
appropriate action.

Confusion is generally associated with a lack of understanding accompanied by a need to understand. The only real
guarantee of total freedom from confusion is complete uncon-
cern with understanding. If I am among a group of people who
are talking about higher mathematics and I feel a lack of interest
it is possible to withdraw: "This is none of my business." But if,
for one reason or another, I become interested, my limited
knowledge of the subject is bound to make me confused. Confusion, in other words, usually results from an effort to make
contact in an area in which, for one reason or another, contact
is not possible—perhaps there is not enough understanding to
support good contact, perhaps there is not enough interest but
there is a need to show interest. Most people try to handle their
confusions, because they are so unpleasant, by interrupting
them with speculations, interpretations, explanations and rationalizations. This is the pattern of many neurotics, and especially
intellectuals. And it is almost encouraged by certain forms of
therapy. Much of Freudian analysis, for example, is based on
the error that symbolic, intellectual knowledge is equal to understanding. But such knowledge is usually itself an interruption, a
premature arresting of development, leaving behind itself a trail
of existential confusion. This in turn contributes to a lack of
self-support, to the need for external support, and to the development of a narrow orientation, which has to come from the
environment and not from the individual.

Although considerable attention has been paid to the
factor of confusion in dealing with psychosis, little attention
has been paid to its role in neurosis. Yet every patient in therapy
is himself a picture of confusion. And this the therapist cannot

Shuttling, Psychodrama and Confusion

fail to see if he will just observe what is going on right under his nose. Every "er" and "ah", every breaking up of a sentence , covers a small or large area of confusion. Each one is an attempt to hang on and maintain *contact,* while the patient's real need is to *withdraw.*

Once the patient has learned to accept the fact that he has areas of confusion, he will be willing to cooperate with the therapist. If he returns to the gaps in his speech he can recover much material which he blanked out or brushed aside during his interruption. Although this material will often be irrelevant, it provides all sorts of helpful clues as to what the patient is doing on the fantasy level. For during these times of confusion he is engaging in faded motoric behavior (all hiding under the collective name of thinking) and much of the activity which is missing in his day-to-day behavior and which constitutes some of the unfinished business of his neurosis, can be found tucked away in those crevices, right here and now.

Let me present a few examples of how this works in practice. The blank, as I said before, is the correlative of confusion. It is an interruption of confusion, the effort to wipe it out completely. This we see most often in dealing with the problem of visualization and visual imagination, areas of blind or nearly blind spots for many patients.

If we ask a patient to visualize something, he may tell us that his fantasy images are hazy. When we ask him to go on, he might continue and report that it is as if they are in a cloud or a fog. This fog or cloud the therapist considers to be a self-concept, a character structure, a system of verbalizations. Apparently the patient has to put a smoke screen around his images and shroud them in a cloud. And the therapist should not be deceived by the patient's complaint that he would like to be able to visualize clearly. Although this is doubtless true, it is not the whole story. We can assume that he must have at least some areas where he has to prevent himself from looking, otherwise he would not go to the trouble of making himself half fantasy blind. If the patient can stay with his fog long enough, it will clear up.

Shuttling, Psychodrama and Confusion

fall to pieces completely in the process, will acquire the courage to go into their junkyards and return more sane than when they went in. The most difficult part of the whole experiment is to abstain from an intellectualizing and verbalizing of the on-going process. For this would be an interruption and would put the experimenter in the position of being split between the explaining onlooker and the experiencing performer. The experience of the fertile void is neither objective nor subjective. Nor is it introspection. It simply is. It is awareness without speculation about the things of which one is aware.

The extremes of the reaction to the idea of the fertile void can be typified in the intellectualizer on the one hand and the artist on the other. The former might say: "Have you suddenly gone mad? This is utter nonsense." But the latter would probably greet the idea thusly: "What's all the excitement about? I spend most of my time in this state. If I'm working and I get stuck, I just relax or doze off and the block goes."

The aim of consulting the fertile void is basically to deconfuse. In the fertile void, confusion is transformed into clarity, emergency into continuity, interpreting into experiencing. The fertile void increases self-support by making it apparent to the experimenter that he has much more available than he believed he had.

Let us return for a moment to the approach to the areas of confusion through the interruptions in which they manifest themselves. Even in this work we can operate successfully only within an extremely limited space of time.[1] Three minutes is often all the area we can cover and recover in toto if we use a mental microscope. It is all very well for the Freudians to demand a recovery of the total life span as a goal for psychoanalysis, but try to experiment for yourself and see if you can recover exactly what you or someone else said or did only a few minutes ago. There are, of course, some people who can do this. They are the type whom Jaensch called eidetic persons. Goethe was such

1. This insight is the contribution of my colleage, Dr. Paul Weiss.

Shuttling, Psychodrama and Confusion

Take the case where the fog cleared into a whitish grey, which the patient reported was like a stone wall. The therapist asked the patient if he could fantasize climbing over that wall. And when the patient did, it developed that there were green pastures there. The wall had enclosed the patient's jail; he was a prisoner.

Our patient may have, on the other hand, a complete blank. He sees black. Suppose he describes the blackness as a black velvet curtain. Now we have our patient and a prop. We can ask him in fantasy to open the curtain. And often enough he will discover behind it that which he was hiding from himself. Perhaps his blackness is literally nothing, a blindness. We can still get some orientation by asking him to play the blind man.

The final step in dealing with the areas of confusion is an eerie experience, often approaching a miracle when it first occurs. Eventually, of course, it becomes routine and is taken for granted. We call it *withdrawal into the fertile void.*

To be able to withdraw into the fertile void two conditions must be obtained. One must be able to stay with one's techniques of interrupting it. Then one can enter the fertile void, which is a state something like a trance, but unlike the trance is accompanied by full awareness. Many people have the experience before falling asleep, and the phenomenon has been described as hypnogogic hallucination.

The person who is capable of staying with the experience of the fertile void—experiencing his confusion to the utmost—and who can become aware of everything calling for his attention (hallucinations, broken up sentences, vague feelings, strange feelings, peculiar sensations) is in for a big surprise. He will probably have a sudden "aha" experience; suddenly a solution will come forward, an insight that has not been there before, a blinding flash of realization or understanding.

What happens in the fertile void is a schizophrenic experience in miniature. This, of course, few people can tolerate. But those who find confidence, having successfully cleared away a few areas of confusion, and having found that they did not

Shuttling, Psychodrama and Confusion

a one. These people register with photographic fidelity on a pre-somantic level. They register everything they sense, meaningful or not, and they can consequently make use of all their recordings when they want to.

As for the rest of us, and we are the majority, we can restore quite a bit of the lost eidetical faculty through the fertile void and other means of eliminating the interruptions and blanks. One only has to consider that every one of us has developed his own style, his own character. Our patients' interruptions and dissociations will show up in their Rohrschach tests, their handwriting and their behavior. They will manifest themselves in the smallest details of thinking and feeling. If we change the patient's attitude about the interrupting behavior he presents in the consulting room, his changed attitude will eventually spread and finally engulf his style, his character, his mode of life. His behavior here and now is a microscopic cross section of his total behavior. If he sees how he structures his behavior in therapy, he will see how he structures it in every-day life.

"Fritz, Friend, and Freud" is a transcript of a film in which Fritz himself ends up in the hot seat and resolves some of his own "unfinished business." It is obviously very atypical of his work, but I include it here simply because it is my favorite.

FRITZ, FRIEND, AND FREUD

(Barbara is seated in the hot seat. She is a young woman who appears to be about 38 years old, with a rather diffident manner. She is a social worker, and has worked with Fritz before)

Barbara: I wanted to be a good girl and have a magnificent dream for you with lots of goodies in it. I didn't manage that, but something else happened which is maybe just as well. Last night I was in bed, and it's happened to me for a long time—though not very frequently—and what happens is I become totally paralyzed and I can't move at all. I can't move my toes and I can't open my eyes— I can't do anything. I'm just totally paralyzed. And I get very frightened and then it goes away. It seems like a very long time, but I think it's just a few minutes—maybe not even that long. But it's like I can't do anything, and what it made me think of was, uh, my inability to handle myself when I get frightened or angry. (Takes a long drag on her cigarette) I just get immobilized—so that I'm the same when I'm awake as when asleep, I'm still paralyzed.

Fritz: All right. Could you tell the whole story again and imagine that you are responsible for all that happens. For instance, "I paralyze myself."

Barbara: Um, all right. Um, I paralyze, I paralyze myself . . . I immobilize myself. I won't allow myself to feel any-thing or behave any way if it isn't civilized and good. I won't let myself run away when I'm afraid; I won't tell people I'm afraid. I won't, uh, fight back when I'm angry or hurt. I won't ever let people know that I have bad feelings. (Starts to cry) I won't let them know that I hate them sometimes, or that I'm scared to death and um . . . I put myself sometimes, to punish myself, in a state of panic where I'm scared to do anything. I'm scared to breathe, and then I torture myself with all the bad things I'll let happen to me. That's all I can think of right now. (Sniffs) Fritz, I don't want to cry because I think that crying is very bad for me. I think I hide behind my tears. But I don't know what I . . . hide.

Fritz, Friend, and Freud

(Barbara is slapping her thigh with her hand as she talks)

Fritz: Can you do this again? With your right hand. Talk to Barbara.

Barbara: (Slapping her thigh and laughing) Barbara, you need a spanking!

Fritz: Spank her.

Barbara: (Still slapping) You're a bad girl because you're phony and dishonest! You lie to yourself and to everybody else, and I'm tired of it because it doesn't work!

Fritz: What does Barbara answer?

Barbara: (Voice rising) She answers that she never learned how to do anything else.

Fritz: Say this in quotes.

Barbara: I never learned how to do anything else. I know about doing other things. I know that there are other things to do but I don't know how to do them.

Fritz: Say this again.

Barbara: I don't know how to do them! I can only do them when I'm in a protected, supporting kind of situation; then I can do it a little bit. But if I'm out in a cold situation by myself I'm too scared. And then I get into trouble. I get myself into trouble.

Fritz: Ya.

Barbara: And then I get mad at myself after I've gotten myself into trouble, and then I punish and punish and punish. (Spanks thigh again) And it's like there is no end to it, and I'll never be satisfied. (Starts to cry)

Fritz: Say this to Barbara. I'll never be satisfied with you, whatever you do I'm never satisfied.

Barbara: Barbara, I'm never satisfied with you. No matter what you do it's never good enough!

Fritz: Can you say this to your mother or father as well?

Barbara: Mother, no matter what I do or have done, it's never been good enough.

Fritz: Can you also say this to her? Mother, whatever you do it's never good enough.

Fritz, Friend, and Freud

Barbara: Uh huh. Mother, whatever you do, it isn't good enough.

Fritz: Tell her what she should do.

Barbara: Mother, you should try to know me. You don't know me. I'm a stranger, and you let me pretend . . . you know, and I have a whole personality just for you. And that's not me. I'm not at all the kind of person that think I am.

Fritz: What would she answer?

Barbara: Of course I understand you, you're my daughter. I understand everything about you. And I know what's good for you!

Fritz: Talk back.

Barbara: Mother, you don't know what's good for me! Your ways don't work for me. I don't like them and I don't respect your attitudes. I just don't think they're productive. I think that they leave you alone, and you never get close to people. You always disapprove of them too much. You don't like anybody, and I don't want to be that kind of person . . .

Fritz: Tell her more what she should do. What kind of person she should be.

Barbara: You should try to understand how it is for other people. They experience life very differently from you. Couldn't you just try once to know what it is to be somebody else?

Fritz: Ya. I would like you to go a step further. Talk to her in the form of an imperative. "Be more understanding" and so on.

Barbara: Be more understanding . . .

Fritz: All imperatives.

Barbara: Be more empathetic! Be more sensitive! Don't defend yourself so much, you don't need to! Don't be so suspicious and paranoid! Don't believe in magic, it's crazy to believe in magic! Don't always be in a double bind, where you're trying to be such a good person, such a

Fritz, Friend, and Freud

saintly person, such a paragon of the community, such a matriarch, and hating every minute of it. Don't do that!

Fritz: Now, talk like this to Barbara. Also in imperatives.

Barbara: Barbara, don't be helpless! That's crazy . . . uh . . . don't be afraid of your feelings! Your bad feelings—you have to express them. You've got to stand up for yourself! You've got to be real! Don't play hide and seek, that's a rotten game! (Starts to cry) Don't be a mess, and don't play games where other people feel sorry for you or feel guilty. Then they'll get uncomfortable and go away and that isn't what you want.

Fritz: Now go into more detail. Stick to your imperatives, and each time give Barbara some prescription—what she should do to follow up.

Barbara: Um . . . don't be a mime, a chameleon!

Fritz: Tell her how she should achieve this—not to be a chameleon.

Barbara: Figure out who you are, and what you want to be and what to do, and do it! Don't try to go around looking for other people to imitate all the time. You've imitated thousands of people and where has it ever gotten you? You still feel like an empty shell. You've got to decide who you are, and what you want to do!

Fritz: Tell her how she can decide.

Barbara: (In a scolding tone) You know what your own tastes and interests and values are. You've known for a long time. They're never . . .

Fritz: Tell her in detail what her interests are.

Barbara: Um, lots of things interest you.

Fritz: Such as?

Barbara: Such as . . . you like to work with people and it makes you feel very good when you feel that you've been useful—that you've allowed yourself to be used in a productive kind of way by other people. Do that! And figure out a way to do it in which you feel successful and useful.

Fritz, Friend, and Freud

Fritz: Come on, start figuring out.

Barbara: Well you have to develop . . . you have to do two things: You have to make a real effort to learn from other people who are much more experienced and skilled than you are and at the same time you've got to be yourself. You can't go around imitating Fritz or Virginia Satir or Dr. Delchamps or whoever the consultant of the moment is, or wherever the last seminar you went to was or the last workshop. Don't do that, that's bad! Because you're not them and you can't just go through the motions that they go through, and say things they say, and do any good for anybody. They'll know that you're a phony.

Fritz: You mentioned my name. So, tell me, what am I? What are you copying of me?

Barbara: Fritz, you're a man who works with people and lets them use him—you let people use you to grow.

Fritz: Ya.

Barbara: And I want to do that too, and I think that what you do really works . . . but I can't play Fritz. That won't work because I'm not you and my tendency would be to imitate you.

Fritz: Let me see how you imitate me. You play Fritz.

Barbara: (Laughs) All right. Shall I do it with you?

Fritz: Ya.

Barbara: All right. (Laughing)
            (Long pause) Do you want to work?

Fritz: Yes.

Barbara: Do you not want me to work? For you?

Fritz: Yes.

Barbara: I can't Fritz. I can't work for you.

Fritz: Oh yes you can.

Barbara: No.

Fritz: (With a gleam in his eye) You're Fritz, you know everything. (Laughter) You're so wise.

Barbara: It's not true. I don't know everything, and I'm not

Fritz, Friend, and Freud

that wise. You have to do the work.

Fritz: All right. I try so hard. I would like to work, but I can't. I have got a block. (General hilarity at Fritz's responses)

Barbara: Be your block.

Fritz: But I can't see my block.

Barbara: You're not listening to me.

Fritz: Oh yes, I'm listening very carefully. I just heard you say, "You're not listening to me."

Barbara: Well, let's see if we can try something else. Pretend you're out there.

Fritz: Out there?

Barbara: Uh huh.

Fritz: Where? Here, or there, or there, or there? (Pointing to different places in the room)

Barbara: Wherever you choose.

Fritz: You choose for me.

Barbara: I feel like you're making fun of me. And maybe trying . . .

Fritz: Me? Making fun of you? I wouldn't dare! You're so venerable and I just melt with appreciation. I wouldn't dare to make fun of you. How could I?

Barbara: Let's try something else then. Can you dance your veneration of me?

Fritz: Oh yes. (Laughter) Now I can't do a thing. You have to give me the music.

Barbara: Uh, try making up the music in your own head.

Fritz: But I'm not musical, you see.

Barbara: We're all musical.

Fritz: You do it. (Laughter)

Barbara: I notice that no matter what happens, the burden returns to me. No matter what I suggest, you say no, you do it for me, I don't know how.

Fritz: Of course. If I weren't so incapable, I wouldn't be here. This is my illness, don't you see?

Barbara: Talk to your illness.

Fritz, Friend, and Freud

Fritz: But my illness isn't here. How can I talk to my illness? And if I could talk to the illness, the illness wouldn't listen, because this is the illness.

Barbara: I'll listen. Did someone give you the illness?

Fritz: (Slowly) Yes.

Barbara: Who?

Fritz: Sigmund Freud. (There is much laughing among the group at this point)

Barbara: I realize that Sigmund isn't here, that he's . . .

Fritz: But for seven years I got infected.

Barbara: (Giggling) Oh, I'm three years above you because I spent ten years with an analyst. Don't tell me how bad it is! Could you talk to Sigmund?

Fritz: Oh no, I can't. He's dead.

Barbara: You've changed. That's the first time you've slipped. What are you aware of now?

Fritz: (Soberly) A great sorrow that Freud is dead before I really could talk as man to man with him.

Barbara: (Gently) I think you could still talk to him. Would you like to?

Fritz: Uh huh.

Barbara: Fine. (Pause) I'd like to listen.

Fritz: Now I'm stuck. I would like to do it. I would like to be your patient in this situation, and uh . . . (speaking very slowly) Professor Freud . . . a great man . . . but very sick . . . you can't let anyone touch you. You've got to say what is and your word is holy gospel. I wish you would listen to me. In a certain way I know more than you do. You could have solved the neurosis question. And here I am . . . a simple citizen . . . by the grace of God having discovered the simple secret that what is, is. I haven't even discovered this. Gertrude Stein has discovered this. I just copy her. No, copy is not right. I got in the same way of living—thinking, with her. Not as an intellectual, but just as a human plant, animal—and this is where you were blind. You moralized and defended

Fritz, Friend, and Freud

sex; taking this out of the total context of life. So you missed life. (There is quiet in the room for several moments. Then Fritz turns to Barbara) So, your copy of Fritz wasn't so bad. (Gives Barbara a kiss) You did something for me.

Barbara: Thank you, Fritz.

Part IV

- Excerpts from

BIRTH BOOK

by
Raven Lang

Raven Lang

Several years ago, a young artist friend—Raven Lang—asked me for any books I might have on obstetrics. She told me she was training herself to become a midwife and planned to assist a number of her friends who wanted to have their babies at home. She reported that they could get no doctor to do this. I was puzzled and not a little shocked. I asked myself why a woman who could afford a doctor and hospital delivery would want to have her baby at home, unattended by a physician. There was also the thought that these women could be just another variety of California "kook." Another reason for my concern was that I had taken pride in the high percentage of hospital births in the United States. It seemed that this previously unchallenged "good" in my set of values had been placed in question.

I talked to a number of these women, hoping to dissuade them, and what I discovered was a whole new movement underway. Their stories were remarkably similar. They wanted to be at home, attended by their husbands, children, and those who meant the most to them. They were not "kooks," but for the most part were intelligent women who were not unaware of the medical danger involved. They were willing to take the risk to gain the extreme emotional satisfaction of having their babies at home. To them, the advantages of personal growth far outweighed the risk of medical complication. The mothers- and fathers-to-be attended natural childbirth classes and studied the birth process in earnest.

When the physicians in the Santa Cruz, California, area refused to provide prenatal care, these women—all aspiring lay midwives—set up their own prenatal clinic and did it their own way. For example, their Birth Center recorded the dreams of pregnant women. Their belief was that, since our bodies and minds are one, we can learn to tune into ourselves and sense where we are "at" and what we need during times of major physical change such as pregnancy and childbirth. This belief is dramatic evidence of these women's trust in naturally unfolding life processes; and their implementation of it is equally strong proof of their sense of community. From this framework came my friend Raven's speculation that the labor of childbirth produces an altered state of consciousness that involves complex learning or imprinting forces—forces that bind together the mother, her infant, and all others present. In this regard it is important to reexamine the psychiatric studies which have showed that pregnancy produces a deviant borderline state somewhere between neurosis and psychosis. This state was attributed to the complicated hormonal changes of pregnancy and such psychological phenomena as altered body image. At the Birth Center, these various changes, with emergence of fantasy into consciousness that was previously regarded as pathologic, seemed to enhance participation in a communal spirit of sisterhood. In a related way, post-partum blues may be exaggerated by hospitalization and isolation with resultant interruption of natural social processes we are just beginning to understand. Home birth seems to markedly lower the high incidence of post-partum blues found in hospital deliveries.

Many women return to the Birth Center regularly after delivery. This is not a time-filling, "coffee klatch" pastime. The sisterhood continues. After a birth there is an awesome responsibility. The life of each woman's child literally depends on 24-hour supervision and care with no days off. The woman's relationship to her mate and to herself changes. Her sexual energy may not be directed toward the man as it was before pregnancy. Some women achieve orgasm by nursing. The process of sensing herself continues for each mother. There is much to be integrated and communicated, and social interaction can therefore be much more complicated. Some men have sensed the importance of these processes and have used the Birth Center to enlarge their own involvement in them.

Another facet of this new consciousness or style of life is seen in the Birth Center's handling of money. No one paid for any services performed by anyone mentioned in *The Birth Book*, from which the excerpts below were taken. Midwives from the center later charged only $35.00 for a delivery—and this fee was charged only to those who could afford it. In fact, *The Birth Book* itself is a prime example of the whole concept of the center, for it evolved when people spontaneously submitted their contributions to Raven.

The Birth Book is many things to many people. Raven describes it in her introduction as "a collection of intimacies." For some readers, it is a do-it-yourself manual on home birth, with much information on such subjects as the history of childbirth, Rh factor, and diet. For others, the book is an art experience because it contains fifteen photographic as well as narrative accounts of birth. Many readers share the communal joy and religious experience of home birth. I have chosen to present first the excerpt entitled "The Birth of Kyle by Doris." Her narrative was read out loud and it helped me to vicariously experience the birth process as never before. I reveled in Doris' personal growth.

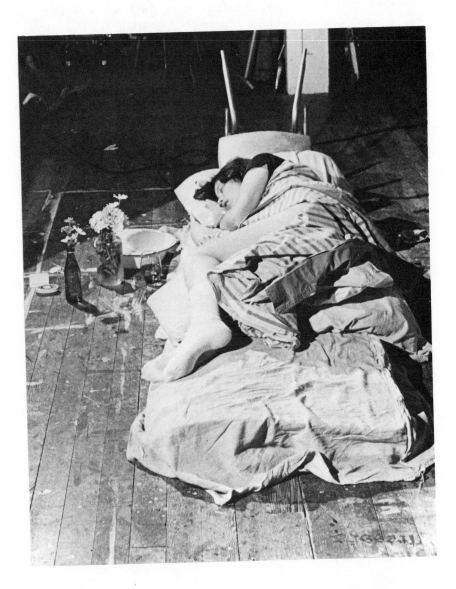

THE BIRTH OF KYLE, BY DORIS.

I'm sitting here watching Kyle, and knowing how much I love him, and I wonder how I would feel if he had been born under narcosis, or if he hadn't been beside me in bed when I woke up that first morning I was a mother and looked into his eyes so clear; fell into his eyes, and in love. I gave birth. I wasn't delivered; the difference between doing and being done to.

The decision to have a home delivery came easy to me. I feel I made the decision before I conceived. I had worked in a maternity ward in a hospital in Connecticut when I was eighteen, and at that time vowed I would never have a child if I was going to have to end up like those countless women I saw come down from the delivery room, still knocked out, not even knowing they had had a child. Anyway, I had no intention of ever doing that! My other reasons were (1) I cannot under any circumstances get along with hospital red tape and (2) I knew inside me that the bringing forth of life would be an incredible experience, and a very personal one, and the idea of being totally attended by strangers was not what I wanted either. Anyway, when I did get pregnant, there was no question about my intentions to use hospital facilities. I did feel I'd go if there was a complication, but that was all.

I began very early in my pregnancy to read every book I could get my hands on, including a nursing obstetrical textbook. I talked to everyone who had recently had a baby, and talked to pregnant ladies, and I talked, and talked . . . . All that learning was really important. While I was in labor, I flashed on how floored women must be just by the physical sensations of labor, if their only education has been a quick lecture from a doctor, and perhaps a book on motherhood with a few diagrams. That is hardly adequate preparation for the most intense experience I can imagine.

Labor is intense physically, emotionally, and usually mentally. I really had no preconceptions about what the physical sensations of labor would be. The first contraction I had, just doubled me over. It really hurt. I laughed

afterwards, because with all my studying and practicing,
I completely forgot what to do. It was painful, but it was
the only pain I had except for the movement of the coccyx
and the stitches. Emotionally, labor is intense, because it is
the vehicle that takes a woman into this other world known
as motherhood. That's bound to put you through some
changes. I did very little thinking during labor. There just
wasn't time to think. For me it was pant through a
contraction, and totally relax between, and that was all I
had time for. I don't think that this lack of thought
processes is usual. Unfortunately many times thoughts of a
laboring woman tend to be fear thoughts. Every woman
who is pregnant has fears. Will the baby have all its fingers
and toes? Did that pill I took early in pregnancy cause a
deformity? Will the baby and I be strong enough to survive
a long labor? Will the baby breathe OK? And how in the
world is a baby so big ever going to get out of there, and
will I tear, will it hurt? Not to mention fears of a
complicated delivery where hospital facilities will be
necessary. All these fears are normal, and natural, as long
as they are recognized and made verbal before labor begins.
To recognize and accept these fears before labor is really
important. If a woman starts figuring this stuff out during
labor, it causes tension, and tension creates pain. That is
what all the screaming and shouting is about. I did not find
labor to be painful, pain being defined as a lack of control
over a physical sensation. You have to relax to be in
control.

I was in labor from sundown to sunrise, about twelve
hours, and an ideal time in terms of worldly activity. It was
pretty cool, and quiet. I understand many animals bear
their offspring during the dark hours of the day. The
advantage of not having any distractions is invaluable. The
first four hours, however, I was pretty uncomfortable
because I didn't have the security of being in the studio
where I would be having the baby. The old nesting instinct
was urgently strong and made me tense because I was not
in my nest yet. Also I hadn't yet spoken to Raven, the

woman who would be helping me as midwife. Once I got to the studio and talked to Raven, I just settled down to work. For the most part of my labor the contractions had a pattern of one minute hard contraction, time for two breaths, and then a mild ½ minute contraction, with a period of 2-3 minutes in between contractions. I think I had every symptom of transition there is, including an emotional thing of being pissed off, because it seemed everyone was sleeping (it was about 4:30 a.m.) and there I was working so hard; but I had thought about what things happen in transition so often that after being angry I just thought, "Fine, that means I'm in transition, first stage should be over soon."

About twenty or thirty minutes before Kyle was born I went into a hands and knees position. I'm sure he came out faster in this position because gravity was helping out. It was an incredible experience to look between my legs, Kyle half out half in, first blue, then red and yelling. Seems real hard to imagine anything more satisfying, or beautiful. I was really high. I had done it. The strength that I found in myself during birth, makes it much easier to feel the confidence to raise Kyle.

With the birth of his head, I tore. This probably could have been prevented with perineal support and easing of the head. The tear was midline and healed in about a week. That seems to be a little faster healing than the average woman's episiotomy, but my health was probably a big factor.

I know that all that stuff about the trials of labor is ignorance, and as in any case of ignorance it can only be overcome by education. Education of doctors, nurses, and hospitals. I get angry at the entire medical profession when I realize that I couldn't find a doctor who would help me have a child in the way I wanted to. Most obstetricians, being men, really have no idea of what it's like to have a child, simply because they are men. All their education and practice in childbirth can't replace the experience of giving birth, itself. They will not listen to a pregnant woman because she isn't a doctor. They refuse to agree to such simple requests as not doing routine episiotomies, because for one thing it might entail spending more than twenty minutes in the delivery. There are advantages to episiotomies in some cases, but all too many done are totally unnecessary. Anyway, what such practices amount to, in my mind, is taking away a woman's freedom of choice concerning the welfare of her body, and that is damnably outrageous. No other field of medicine will even cut your toenails without your expressed permission. If doctors would come to respect a pregnant woman's wishes, perhaps nurses and hospitals would also come to respect a conscious beginning of motherhood.

There is no need to suffer in order to have a child. That myth has hung on longer than any myth about the nature of life. I didn't, and would love to do it again if it weren't for my concern about over population. Also, because birth was so satisfying and fullfilling, I don't feel any need to give birth again to prove my womanliness as many women seem to. But you ladies out there, we're free if we know it, and that's all that is important.

Love to you,
Doris and Kyle

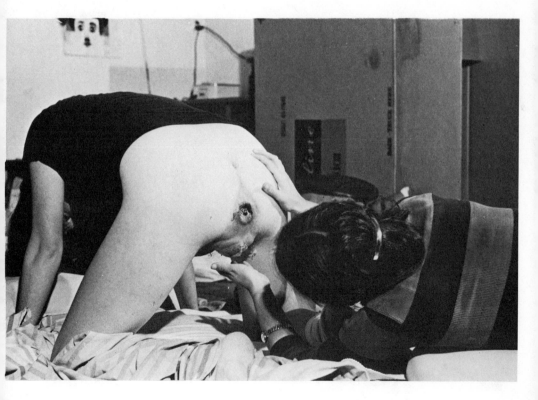

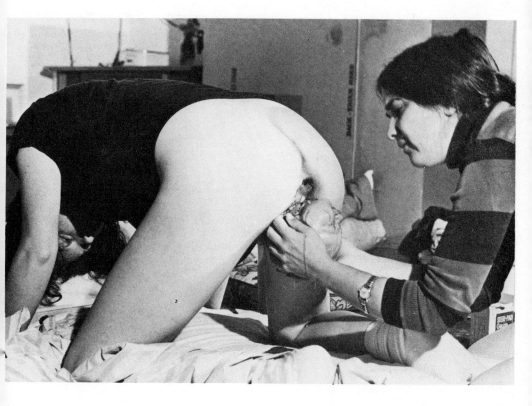

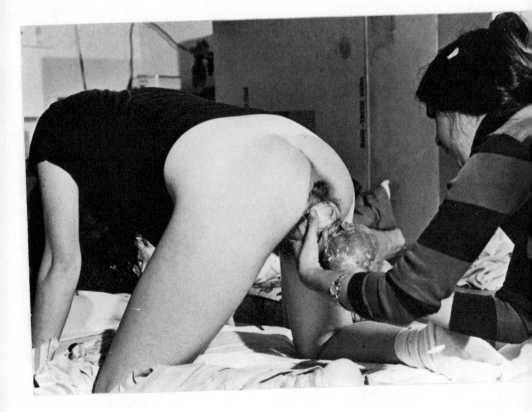

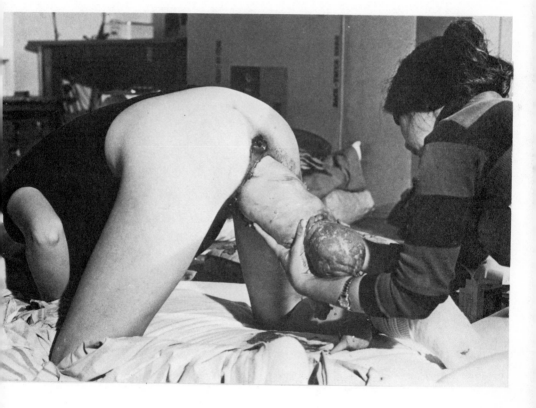

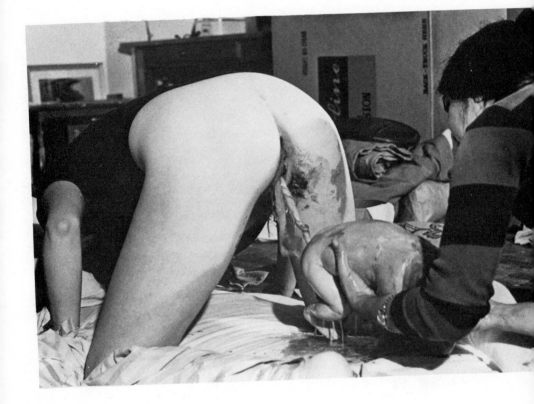

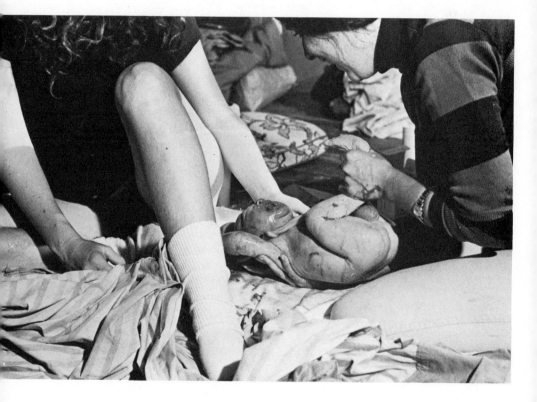

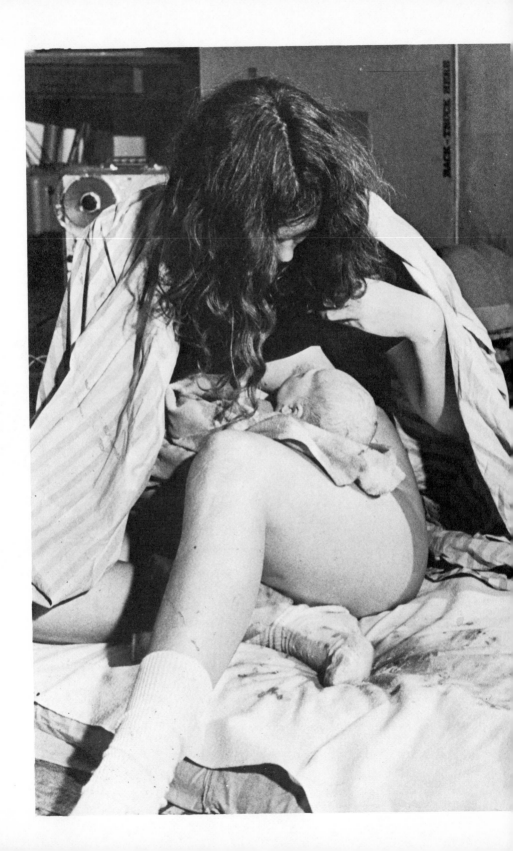

The Birth Book stresses the dangers of home birth, particularly when there has not been adequate prenatal care and communal support. Included in the book are accounts of a stillborn birth and of a birth in which complications required hospitalization. Raven's short chapters on "Confronting Fear" and "On Female Sexuality During Parturition and Lactation" are also important inclusions. I particularly admire the following extended study.

ON IMPRINTING, THE FORMATION OF LOVE, AND THEIR EFFECTS.

Recently there has been a great deal of biological research done on the effects of imprinting and motherly love among fishes, birds, and mammals. This paper is concerned with this type of research as it effects our own species, the human animal.

First let me describe what is meant by the word imprinting. It is a phenomenon which because of an early experience, determines the social and psychological behavior of an animal. It is a word which Konrad Lorenz has popularized by doing much experimenting with animals of various sorts. To describe exactly what is meant by imprinting, let me use the following specific examples.

Example 1. Take a goose setting on eggs. When these eggs hatch, the goslings form an attachment to their mother and immediately follow and stay close to her. This process of imprinting takes place within a matter of minutes. Take another batch of eggs and incubate them. When they hatch they will follow the first large moving object that they see. They begin to relate to this object as their mother. So complete is this process that if, after a few days the goslings are given a choice between their real mother and the moving object to which they were imprinted, their choice is always the moving object.

The second example of imprinting is with a turkey hen. When the eggs she has been sitting on hatch, the hen hears the chirping of her new chicks and is imprinted to this sound. The introduction of a stuffed racoon (a natural enemy) to the vicinity of the nest will move the hen to fight it. However, if a tape of the chick sounds is hidden within the body of the fake racoon, the hen will spread her wings and accept the racoon as one of her own.

The first example of imprinting with goslings is one in which vision is the mechanism of imprinting, and it also shows how this process only affects the young. In the second example with the turkey hen, the mechanism is clearly one of sound and shows how it affects the mother.

With further exploration it was found that there is a critical period in which imprinting occurs, and with ducklings for instance, a rapid decline in the capacity to imprint occurs only 16 hour after hatching.

Miltown (meprobamate), a tranquilizer, was administered to mallards just after birth when they were normally most imprintable. The results indicated that with this drug the effectiveness of the imprinting experience was greatly reduced. It seems that some degree of anxiety is necessary for imprinting and with the interference of this drug, the normal amount of anxiety was reduced, thus effecting the mallards in their ability to imprint.

Much more research has been done in this area of imprinting, but I want to move on to interesting details directly related to the human animal.

R. Fantz did experiments with human infants. These infants were tested from birth to 14 days to determine what was most exciting to them visually. It was found that they preferred the human face more than any other pattern or shape, and that patterns were of more interest than plain color. I feel the human face is preferred because it is part of the infant's survival, a recognition of one's own species; a social perception. Desmond Morris speaks of captive animals, which by mal-imprinting (being imprinted to a different species such as is done in zoos), have a susceptibility to becoming fixated on the wrong species leading to situations in which they find it impossible to adapt socially and sexually later in life.

My own pregnancy and birth experience and the experiences of women who have delivered both at home and hospital are given here to demonstrate imprinting in terms of how it effects the mother.

In my own pregnancy, I remember reading that the process of involution in primates (the uterus contracting after birth thus causing its return to its original shape) began when the primate saw her young and heard their first cry. An example

of vision and sound. I thought about this during my pregnancy. Imprinting causes involution. Far out. I wondered if
that was why so many drugged women needed a shot of
methergen or pitocin to contract their uteri.

Experience. Me. Stanford Hospital, 1968.

At the birth of my baby I was fully conscious. I remember
a head rotating to my right leg and I saw a face in which I
could recognize at least two generations of my past. A cry,
forever imprinted in my mind, as clearly this minute as
then. Heavy impressions. The baby was given to me for a
minute and placed on my abdomen—then taken away to be
wrapped and put in a plastic see-through box, far away and
in back of me—so that I had to strain my neck to even see
this little critter I had just parted from for the first time in
his life. My perineum was stitched up and I was wheeled to
maternity, my baby was sent to the nursery, my mate was
sent home. I was to see my baby in several hours.

Each time the babies were brought to their mothers they
would bring the babies first to the mothers who were at the
far end of the maternity ward. I was in the room closest to
the nursery, and so I received my baby last. Each time I saw
him he was sleeping or quietly looking around. Later when
the nursing shift changed I heard the nursery door open and a
crying baby being brought out to the mother. My uterus
clamped down as it had when I heard my newborn's first cry.
My breasts tingled and there was a definite gush of blood from
my uterus which came from the contraction caused by the
sound of the crying baby. When I realized that this was the
first baby being brought out I thought it must be a baby be-
longing to someone else and would be going down to the
other end of the ward, but with another sound of that cry
my uterus again clamped down and I felt complete be-
wilderment and a sense of demand for my baby. Within an
instant he was being brought into me by a different nurse.
My body had known this child to be mine. My self was
strongly reacting.

Had I been drugged and or unconscious, the information
that I received at the time of birth would certainly not have

registered as acutely or at all, and as a result I would have had less instinctual knowledge of my baby. I feel that when a woman first sees and hears her child at the moments of birth—which is another kind of consciousness—that she is bound to her baby already in a capacity beyond what I think we are willing to admit. I feel this is part of our survival.

Since that experience of my own involution, I have paid attention to the kinds of things women distinctly remember. Afterwards, most of them speak of that first impression as vividly as ever, and many are mentioned in the write ups presented in this book.

"The vision of that baby as seen through my legs will never leave me. Such profuse color, all purple and blue and red all at once, as she tensed expectantly in Pat's hands. John was about to introduce the syringe once more but in that second my baby burst forth in the lusty song of the newborn . . . I turned over and sat down. She was handed to me, cord still attached, covered with the yellow vernix, black hair matted in waves above her forehead. I noticed the molding of her head where she had presented and the swollen little flat features of her face. She flickered her eyes open and shut and proceeded to expell meconium all over my legs." Jodi

"It was an incredible experience to look between my legs, Kyle half out half in, first blue, then red and yelling, seems real hard to imagine anything more satisfying or beautiful." Doris

"That night I couldn't get to sleep at first. I kept looking at our baby—in fact that was my chief occupation for the next few days as well. She was just so new and perfect." Judy

There is one other aspect of the birth experience that I would like to mention, and that is the strange familiarity of birth. Birth is not totally an unknown or mysterious experience.

A woman while giving birth has her own birth as a frame of reference, even though there is no conscious memory of it. The memory is communicated through the rhythm that the organism has already experienced, the same rhythm deeply rooted in the pre-consciousness of her own birth. I myself felt when actually in labor and delivery that I knew exactly the process, that I had always known it all along my pregnancy and even before. Indeed, I knew so deeply the process of birth that when taken into delivery at Stanford and given a giant episiotomy which changed the time of my son's birth, that this was not the right time for him to be born. I remember saying to my mate, "This is not right, I am not ready yet." I remember attributing the memory of birth and the knowledge of it to the memory in my cells.

Stan Grof in his research with LSD frequently observed that female subjects reliving their own birth usually re-experienced on a more superficial level the delivering of their own children. He feels this deserves special attention.

> "Both experiences were usually relived simultaneously, so that these women often could not say whether they were giving birth or were being reborn themselves. It seems that, during the delivery of her children, a female experiences an activation of her own birth memory and is able to discharge some of the tensions bound to it. This can be explained by the fact that both experiences have many similar elements and follow the same basic pattern." Stan Grof.

Now I would like to move to the birth experience for the baby.

We can assume that certain diet and behavior of the pregnant mother plays an important role in shaping the health and behavior of the growing fetus. And we can assume that the growing fetus does have an inter-uterine consciousness, the consciousness of its mother's heart beat, movement, rhythm, emotional experiences, sounds of the external world, and so on. The complexity of its mother's environment is its only reference point. This internal environment becomes one of ever increasing restriction during labor and with the child's birth this environment changes to one of limitless space. Otto Rank calls this the birth trauma. The infant at this time of birth is a complete sensor; using sight, sound, taste, touch, smell, rhythm, and .. For the child, the time of birth is a period of great anxiety. Its world has just undergone some radical changes and the infant is feeling out for something familiar, something safe and gratifying. It seems reasonable that one of the best tools for reducing this state of anxiety is the presence of the mother. Here, with the very essence of this woman is the entire past of the child. Through the presence of the mother, the rhythms of that world and the security which those rhythms represent can be communicated. The infant should not be placed in a plastic hard edged box, isolated from the pattern of a human face, and denied the warmth and gratification that are her/his birthright.

In birds we have already considered that a sense of anxiety is necessary for imprintibility. This anxiety in humans may be related to the anxiety of being left alone. And anxiety is the mechanism which needs to be well functioning in order for complete imprintability. However, if the anxiety is kept going too long, it becomes more of a trauma than would be natural, and too traumatic an experience may no longer be valuable, but may even prove to be harmful. If we paid attention to the instinct of undrugged mothers we would give them their babies, which they so commonly demand.

And so, if this anxiety has a function, then the moments and hours after birth should not be condusive to increasing this anxiety, but toward reducing it through gratification. Adult behavior which is often anxiety ridden may in fact be directly related to a specific separation of mother and child at birth.

Effects of maternal separation and deprivation in the human have scarcely been investigated. We say we do not scientifically "know" the importance of these first few hours and days after birth, for both the mother and child. (With time and research, the consideration must also include the father and the possibility of family and friends). We say we do not scientifically "know" to what extent we are interfering with natural functions when we separate the mother and baby.

Experiments at the University of Cornell engaged in a program of research for the prevention of mental illness using sheep and goats. They demonstrated the ability of a mother to protect her offspring from environmental stress by placing twin kids in identical rooms, the only difference being that one kid was in the presence of its mother and the other kid was left alone. An artificial stress environment was created by turning off the lights every two minutes and applying a brief shock to each goat's foreleg. After the goats had been conditioned in this manner they were tested two years later by exposing them to the same environment for twenty days. The goats who had had their mothers with them during their early experience showed no evidence of abnormal behavior in response to the severe stress of this environment. The others exhibited definite neurotic behavior. Somehow the mother's presence alone protects the baby goat from the traumatic influences of the rigid pattern of tensions to which the twin in the adjoining room succumbs.

If birth is to be regarded as a trauma in which stress is either created by the compression of birth itself, or the anxiety of the organism being thrust into a completely unfamiliar environment, then the importance of the continuous presence of the mother as a means of negating the effects of this stress must not be overlooked. It is interesting to note that as a part of related experiments conditioned neurotic sheep or goats were found incapable of dealing with the situation of actual danger in realistic fashion, making their survival rate significantly less. This is because the animal's gregariousness is damaged and while other members of the herd escape together, the neurotic animal flees in panic by itself.

In light of the implications of these experiments with animals, the concept of natural home birth having importance to research in the preventive mental health field should be examined. The possibility that our hospitals through a gross oversight (as was once done with puerperal fever) may be contributing to adult neuroses through our present day rituals of birth should be looked at with much more emphasis than is done at this time. Could the separation of the baby from its mother be related to a sense of non-acceptance later in life?

The data on material like this in terms of humans is lacking, but it is coming fast. Scientists and psychologists alike feel that the infant's love for its mother is learned through association with the mother's face, smell, sound, etc. as well as her gratification of such needs as hunger and discomfort. Nursing, contact, and even hearing and seeing are also considered important in the development of the infant's love for its mother. All of these contribute to the development of the intense, loving, and profound relationship possible between the mother and child.

> "The first love of the human infant is for his mother. The tender intimacy of this attachment is such that it is sometimes regarded as a sacred or mystical force, an instinct incapable of analysis. No doubt such compunctions, along with the obvious obstacles in the way of objective study have hampered experimental observation of the bonds between child and mother." Harlow.

Other experiences demonstrate the importance of maternal contact at early ages in developing a pattern of affection in the child's social behavior, as opposed to maternal deprivation leaving them less able to form lasting ties. We know also that a child having physical contact has a greater capacity for handling stress than one who hasn't been touched, and that the ability to handle stress is directly related to shaping the personality of the adult.

> "Investigations concerned with maternal deprivation report that children raised in foundling homes develop at a retarded rate and are more susceptible to disease." Levine.

This last section of the paper is primarily made up of

comments from mothers about the experience of birth, and my own observations and thoughts on the subject.

Joan is a 19 year old woman whom I met in her 7th month of pregnancy. She had been married but was no longer living with her husband.

One day I heard a friend ask Joan what sex she felt her baby would be. Joan said it had better be a girl, and if it wasn't she would flush him down the toilet. On another occasion she said she very much wanted a girl. Some days later in conversation Joan told me that her husband wanted the baby if it was a boy but didn't care to have it if it was a girl.

At her birth which was two weeks after her statement of female preference, she gave birth to a baby boy. When she first turned around to get him, and had the sound of some-one's voice ring in her ear, "It's a boy," I felt she was suffering from a disappointment that was real. At any rate, Joan pro-ceeded to hold, examine, touch, talk to, nurse, and respond to her baby. It was the getting-to-know-you-baby time and all the gestures that go along with it. Within one half hour Joan said, "You know, it doesn't really make any difference if it's a boy or a girl." And even later she said something to the effect, "It's not really in-born, this boy/girl stuff. Babies are really all the same and it's only society that makes such changes and puts such things on the sexes." And later yet, "I will not be sexist to my son."

The next day someone came by after just having visited Joan and said she was looking beautiful, and was a beautiful mother, full of pride and love for her baby.

Now my reason for mentioning all this is to examine what might have been Joan's feeling if she had been drugged and/or separated from her baby. Would her acceptance and insights and love have been the same? And would her son's separation have increased his anxiety level? And then after returning to his mother five to twelve hours later, would he have felt the beginnings of non-acceptance and rejection, which may by routine separation be increased? We do know that when a goat kid or calf is removed from its mother at birth, and returned some hours later, there may be maternal rejection, even to the point of death for the young.

Another example: Approximately three years ago a friend of mine became pregnant. She tried to find a doctor from Santa Cruz to Berkeley who would help her have her baby at home, but she could get no one to help her. The most agreeable thing to her was to go to San Francisco's French Hospital, where the LaMaze method of birth was in common practice. Her labor was fairly fast and easy. Her husband was allowed to witness the birth, and all in all she had a very positive hospital birth. However, minutes after her baby was born he was wisked out of the room and sent to the nursery for six hours. The nursing routine was to bring the babies to the mother every four hours for fifteen to twenty minutes.

Just a month ago, this woman came to our home birth seminar and told the attending group the story of her birth. She described the post-birth experience at the hospital as the most painful thing she has experienced in her life. She told us of the four-hour periods when her son would be in the nursery, crying and crying, and how she stood on the other side of the window and also cried and cried. But her baby remained in the nursery and she on the other side of the glass. She also mentioned her sorrow that at this time she didn't simply demand her baby or physically get him and go home. But because of the vulnerability of her birth state, and her ignorance of the laws governing her, this did not happen. This incidence turned what should have been one of the highest experiences of her life into the most painful and I question the results of that kind of interference. This is not to say that all women and/or babies are as hurt by this event, but we should not assume all women and/or babies to be unaffected.

A unique experience of imprinting beyond the mother and child occurred at the birth of Trava. There was a group of eleven people at this birth. In the first two hours of Trava's extra-uterine life he was passed around from member to member of his family, all of whom were deeply moved. It was an extremely high intensity vibration birth. I, myself, felt part of this family, a kind of we-had-known-each-other-for-a-long-time-already feeling.

One day, only weeks after Trava's birth, his parents and family were all in one room quietly sitting when he rolled off the chair and onto the floor. Emily, his mother, in recounting this story told me that Gary, a member of the family and present for the birth, reacted and looked exactly as she herself felt and acted, and he looked and responded in the same manner and intensity and speed as Harry had done. (Harry being the natural father). When telling me this story Emily expressed a feeling and statement and this is a quote, "As Harry is Trava's father, and I his mother, also Gary is his father." Emily, Harry, and Gary did not fully understand this link, or how it came to be.

This kind of experience happens to varying degrees all the time at home birth. Bertrand Russell speaks of this multiple parent phenomenon amongst Trobriand Islanders who give birth in tribal situations. The most recent experience I had involving this issue happened two weeks ago at the birth center. There were two newborns present on this day. One of the newborn's birth I had attended, and the other I had not. Both of the babies were put side by side and we were looking at them together. The experience of my observation of the baby whose birth I had not attended was beautiful, healthy, full term looking baby, while the feeling I had for the other baby was of tremendous closeness to him. I felt a bond with him. This is the bond of birth which I am talking about, the same bond that affected Gary so strongly.

I would like to conclude with a few observations concerning the home birth ceremony which I have witnessed time and again at the deliveries I have attended.

The child usually quiets down when given to the mother. She/he seems to be sensing the lights of this world, its sounds, smells, air, a new sense of freedom of movement, and so on. Almost always, the baby looks good and hard at the mother, and the mother is usually glued to the splendor of her baby. Usually the mother rubs the baby's skin, starting with the face. The rubbing is done with the mother's fingertips and is always a very gentle stroking motion. I believe this is the first natural gesture made by the mother, and not necessarily the beautiful act of nursing. The baby is usually offered a nipple, but often doesn't suck right away. The most common action for the baby when given a nipple is to lick the mother's nipple over and over. I believe the infant is also smelling the mother. The infant has no trouble knowing the breast, and that it is a source of food. The baby's instinct is always to turn her or his head in the direction of the offered nipple. I feel what the mother is saying to her baby is also being recorded. If the baby is with the mother for sometime after birth, and then passed to someone else, the behavior of the child will be to cry and fuss in the arms of another. When the infant is returned to the mother, she or he will almost always quiet down and begin to lick her nipple if it is near and available. It looks to me that the infant already knows its mother and is bound to her deeply.

If there is anything valid in home birth beyond a couple's right to be free to choose the manner in which their child shall be born, it is in the areas of imprinting, where the mother's love as well as the love of all present, are important in the developing relationship between the child and these people, as well as the child's own sense of self-love.

These are some of my arguments for home birth. Midwives would most likely be more sensitive to the woman's emotional and physical state, and for this reason she would be better suited to work with the woman if she were well trained. She would be able to stay with both the mother and child for several hours after birth unlike the professional is willing to do. Mother would do more following of her own instincts as would baby. Midwives can be trained to make and record observations concerning the birth. Records can be kept during pre and post natal care of diet, emotional state, and the life style and environment in which the mother and fetus live. All of this information could be used in studying the relationship between birth and neurosis.

And so we question. We ask ourselves about ourselves in order to understand ourselves better and to correct the sometimes brutal yet seemingly innocent things that have been done to us, in order for us not to do them to our own children. A simple quest for bettering the future.

Raven. April, 1972

In February of 1974, the Birth Center was "busted" and three lay midwives were arrested for practicing medicine without a license. Many well-known civil rights lawyers, including Charles Garry and Ann Cummings, have rallied to the cause and offered to help with what may develop into a milestone case in constitutional law. Do women have the right to have their babies in the manner they choose and attended by the people they choose? Is it possible that this case will establish a precedent for the right to die at home in the manner one chooses? I agree with the statement of Dr. Michael Witte, who practices home birth in Marin County, California: "Birth is too important to leave solely in the hands of doctors and hospitals."

The Birth Book has facilitated the current trends toward natural childbirth and father-participation in hospital deliveries. My hope is that there will be widespread establishment of neighborhood birth centers—perhaps with extensive use of trained midwives, as in England. And I hope too that the midwives will be trained to facilitate the emotional growth experience for the mother and the entire family.

The actual place where birth occurs—whether it be a hospital, a neighborhood center, or at home—is not nearly as important as the attitudes of the participants and their expectations. Birth is much more than a medical procedure. It is a moment of magic that can unite all those present and enhance the formation of familial bonds.

Part V

- Excerpts from

If You Meet the Buddha on the Road, Kill Him!

The Pilgrimage of Psychotherapy Patients
Sheldon B. Kopp

Sheldon Kopp

I have never met Shelly Kopp. We have had a number of telephone conversations and have exchanged short notes, often hammering out editorial details or contractual relationships. I can understand his reputation as a brilliant but argumentative-to-pugnacious individual. Shelly knows what he wants and he fights for it. The manuscripts he submits are the cleanest we receive. It does not matter whether the content of his chapters is poetic or tempestuous—it is thoroughly documented.

I hope the following excerpts from his book *If You Meet the Buddha on the Road, Kill Him* are sufficient to convey the man to you. His approach is based on the premise that "There are no hidden meanings." The Buddhahood of each of us has already been obtained; we need only recognize it. Philosophy, religion, and patriotism are all empty idols. The only meaning in our lives is what we each bring to them. "Killing the Buddha" means destroying the hope that anything outside of ourselves can be our master. No one is bigger than anyone else. There are no mothers or fathers—only sisters and brothers.

Shelly Kopp was already a gifted psychotherapist and writer when he underwent surgery for what turned out to be a recurrent brain tumor. The threat of death has heightened his sensitivity and increased his capacity for understanding and sharing.

Pilgrims and Disciples

DIFFICULTY AT THE BEGINNING works supreme success.
Furthering through perseverance.
Nothing should be undertaken
It furthers one to appoint helpers.
                    I Ching[1]

In every age, men have set out on pilgrimages, on spiritual journeys, on personal quests. Driven by pain, drawn by longing, lifted by hope, singly and in groups they come in search of relief, enlightenment, peace, power, joy or they know not what. Wishing to learn, and confusing being taught with learning, they often seek out helpers, healers, and guides, spiritual teachers whose disciples they would become.

The emotionally troubled man of today, the contemporary pilgrim, wants to be the disciple of the psychotherapist. If he does seek the guidance of such a contemporary guru, he will find himself beginning on a latter-day spiritual pilgrimage of his own.

This should not surprise us. Crises marked by anxiety, doubt, and despair have always been those periods of personal unrest that occur at the times when a man is sufficiently unsettled to have an opportunity for personal growth. We must always see our own feelings of uneasiness as being our chance for "making the growth choice rather than the fear choice."[2]

So, too, the patient's *longing* for growth is the central force of his pilgrimage.

The psychotherapist needs only to be aware of this force, in his patient, and to keep it within his vision. Then he may enjoy

his work, and need never bog down in boredom. His task is
simply to watch, as the person in front of him wrestles with
well-nigh paralyzing conflict, for the emergence of what he knows
is there: man's inherent longing for relatedness and for meaning.
The therapist is an observer and a catalyst. He has no power to
"cure" the patient, for cure is entirely out of his hands. He can
add nothing to the patient's inherent capacity to get well, and
whenever he tries to do so he meets stubborn resistance which
slows up the progress of treatment. The patient is already fully
equipped for getting well. . . . Since he [the therapist] is not
"responsible" for the cure, he is free to enjoy the spectacle of it
taking place.[3]

Of course, like everyone else (including the therapist), the patient
is too often inclined to act out of fear, rather than out of his longing
for growth. If not, pilgrimages would always begin out of an overflow
of joy, rather than (as is more often the case) being conceived in pain
and turmoil. People seek the guidance of a psychotherapist when their
usual, self-limited, risk-avoiding ways of operating are not paying off,
when there is distress and disruption in their lives. Otherwise, we are all
too ready to live with the familiar, so long as it seems to work, no
matter how colorless the rewards.

And so, it is not astonishing that, though the patient enters
therapy insisting that he wants to change, more often than not, what he
really wants is to remain the same and to get the therapist to make him
feel better. His goal is to become a more effective neurotic, so that he
may have what he wants without risking getting into anything new. He
prefers the security of known misery to the misery of unfamiliar
insecurity.

Given this all too human failing, the beginning pilgrim-patient
may approach the therapist like a small child going to a good parent
whom he insists must take care of him. It is as if he comes to the office
saying, "My world is broken, and you have to fix it."

Because of this, my only goals as I begin the work are to take care
of myself and to have fun. The patient must provide the motive power
of our interaction. It is as if I stand in the doorway of my office,
waiting. The patient enters and makes a lunge at me, a desperate
attempt to pull me into the fantasy of taking care of him. I step aside.
The patient falls to the floor, disappointed and bewildered. Now he has
a chance to get up and to try something new. If I am sufficiently
skillful at this psychotherapeutic judo, and if he is sufficiently courageous and persistent, he may learn to become curious about himself, to
come to know me as I am, and to begin to work out his own problems.
He may transform his stubbornness into purposeful determination, his
bid for safety into a reaching out for adventure.

You may then ask, "Of what sustained value is the presence of
the therapist to such a seeker?" He can be useful in many ways. The

therapist, first of all, provides another struggling human being to be encountered by the then self-centered patient, who can see no other problems than his own. The therapist can interpret, advise, provide the emotional acceptance and support that nurtures personal growth, and above all, he can listen. I do not mean that he can simply hear the other, but that he will *listen* actively and purposefully, responding with the instrument of his trade, that is, with the personal vulnerability of his own trembling self. This listening is that which will facilitate the patient's telling of his tale, the telling that can set him free.

The therapist provides a "dreamlike atmosphere . . ., and in it . . . [the patient] has nothing to rely upon except . . . [his] own so fallible subjective judgment."[4] I have pirated this description. It was written by Carl Jung to describe the usefulness of the *I Ching,* the three-thousand-year-old Chinese *Book of Changes,* some lines from which I have used to begin this chapter.

At first, the patient tries to use the therapist, as many over the centuries have tried to use the *I Ching,* the oldest book of divination. The *Book of Changes* is made up of images from the mythology and social and religious institutions of the time of its origin. Orientals have too often searched these images for oracular guidance, just as some Christians have opened the Bible to verses picked at random in hope of getting specific advice about how to solve problems. So, too, the psychotherapy patient may begin by trying to get the therapist to tell him what he is to do to be happy and how he is to live without being fully responsible for his own life.

However, the *I Ching,* the Holy Bible, the contemporary psychotherapist and other gurus, all are poor oracles. They are instead far more significant as wellsprings of wisdom about the ambiguity, the insolubility, and the inevitability of the human situation. Their value lies just in their offering imagery that is fixed without being stereotyped, images "to meditate upon, and to discover one's identity in."[5] To these wellsprings, the seeker must bring himself, and then listen for the echo returned by the books of wisdom or by his guru. Coming to knowledge of the self is insisted upon throughout the pilgrimage. The helper provides "one long admonition to careful scrutiny of one's own character, attitude, and motives."[6]

The seeker comes in hope of finding something definite, something permanent, something unchanging upon which to depend. He is offered instead the reflection that life is just what it seems to be, a changing, ambiguous, ephemeral mixed bag. It may often be discouraging, but it is ultimately worth it, because that's all there is. The pilgrim-patient wants a definite way of living, and is shown that:

> The way that can be spoken of
> Is not the constant way;
> The name that can be named
> Is not the constant name.[7]

He may only get to keep that which he is willing to let go of. The cool water of the running stream may be scooped up with open, overflowing palms. It cannot be *grasped* up to the mouth with clenching fists, no matter what thirst motivates our desperate grab.

Starting out as he does in the urgency of his mission, it is difficult for the pilgrim to learn this patient yielding. This is to be seen in the old Zen story of the three young pupils whose Master instructs them that they must spend a time in complete silence if they are to be enlightened. "Remember, not a word from any of you," he admonishes. Immediately, the first pupil says, "I shall not speak at all." "How stupid you are," says the second. "Why did you talk?" "I am the only one who has not spoken," concludes the third pupil.[8]

The pilgrim, whether psychotherapy patient or earlier wayfarer, is at war with himself, in a struggle with his own nature. All of the truly important battles are waged within the self. It is as if we are all tempted to view ourselves as men on horseback.[9] The horse represents a lusty animal-way of living, untrammeled by reason, unguided by purpose. The rider represents independent, impartial thought, a sort of pure cold intelligence. Too often the pilgrim lives as though his goal is to become the horseman who would break the horse's spirit so that he can control him, so that he may ride safely and comfortably wherever he wishes to go. If he does not wish to struggle for discipline, it is because he believes that his only options will be either to live the lusty, undirected life of the riderless horse, or to tread the detached, unadventuresome way of the horseless rider. If neither of these, then he must be the rider struggling to gain control of his rebellious mount. He does not see that there will be no struggle, once he recognizes himself as a *centaur*.

If he ever achieves his true nature, gets beyond the point of struggle, he may wonder why the therapist-guru did not tell him at once the simple truths that would have made him free. But as a therapist, I know that though the patient learns, I do not teach. Furthermore, what is to be learned is too elusively simple to be grasped without *struggle, surrender,* and *experiencing* of how it is. As one Zen Master said to his now-enlightened pupil:

> If I did not make you fight in every possible way in order to find the meaning [of Zen] and lead you finally to a state of non-fighting and of no-effort from which you can see with your own eyes, I am sure that you would lose every chance of discovering yourself.[10]

This search for enlightenment, pursued in a secular context by today's psychotherapy patient, has in the past been cast in religious terms. Whatever the metaphors in which the pilgrim experiences his quest, any trip involving a search for spiritual meaning is an allegorical journey through life, a journey that can renew and enrich the quality of the rest of the pilgrim's daily living. The pilgrim, "strengthened by desire and hope, burdened with anxiety and fear, beset by temptations and guarded by spiritual powers, pursues his way along the Path of Life, seeking ever 'a better country.' "[11]

The early history of the pilgrimage is a variegated story of journeys made for reasons both sacred and profane to those holy places where a god resides, or where a prophet has appeared, or where a hero has been martyred. Pilgrimages were made by pagan Greeks and by the inhabitants of the ancient sites of other early Mediterranean civilizations, by orientals, Egyptians, Jews, and Christians.

The primitive Aborigines of Australia also make ceremonial trips to holy places, places whose origin their myths describe:

> The two Djanggau Sisters came across the water . . . traveling on the path of the rising sun from an island away to the northeast. They made the first people. They made the water holes and *the sacred ritual sites.*
>
> At first the sisters possessed all the most secret sacred objects, the most sacred rites. Men had nothing. And so men stole them. But the sisters said, "Oh, let them keep those things. Now men can do this work, looking after those things for everybody."[12]

And to this day, Aboriginal men still make pilgrimages to the sacred ritual sites to look after things.

In the Orient, pilgrimages have long been, and still are, common ways of fulfilling spiritual vows. Buddha himself has been called "the Great Pilgrim."[13] In Islam, Mohammed, the Prophet of Allah, proclaimed it the duty of every Muslim to visit Mecca at least once in his lifetime. As a result, Mecca, the birthplace of Mohammed, has become the center of religious life of the Muslim world.

Christians, too, have long found it rewarding to make pilgrimages. From the close of the eleventh century on, they undertook several great crusading expeditions. Taking up the Cross and forsaking their homes, thousands ventured out for the love of God, or for their own material gain. They made the far journey to the places in which the Savior is said to have walked. Whatever their motives, they went in the company of other seekers; they found community with others as they exchanged tales, made themselves known to one another, and examined the meaning of their lives.

Even before (as well as after) the Crusades, many were used to the familiar habit of journeying to the shrines of local saints. Some were sick and sought a cure. Others, now recovered, went to fulfill a vow of gratitude. Many went to expiate their sins, as a communal expression of penances. Some even went as a form of social protest, to honor a dissident hero. "To make a saint of a rebel was the most energetic means of protesting against the king."[14]

Whatever the initial motives, such a journey often gave the

pilgrims new perspective on the meaning of their lives, made them "converts to better lives, [at least] for a time."[15] The metaphor of his journey is a *bridge,* and as the pilgrim crosses it, "a fiend clutches at him from behind; and Death awaits him at the farther end."[16] But there are companions and helpers along the way as well. One pilgrim may help another as when a blind man carries one who is lame upon his back, so that together they may make a pilgrimage that neither could make alone.

By acts of devotion, the crossing of this bridge may be undertaken. But the call to the difficult life of pilgrimage may be ignored or denied. Christ admonishes:

> Enter ye in at the strait gate: for wide *is* the gate, and broad *is* the way, that leadeth to destruction, and many there be which go in thereat:
> Because strait *is* the gate, and narrow *is* the way which leadeth unto life, and few there be that find it.[17]

And a journey may be a flight, rather than a search. James Joyce, the Irish expatriate, went to find his place in Paris, and spent the rest of his life in exile there, writing about life in Dublin, the home from which he had escaped. Someone once suggested that his God-term should have been a *pier,* rather than the *bridge* of pilgrimages, for a pier is a bridge that goes nowhere.

Search we must. Each man must set out to cross his bridge. The important thing is to begin. "A journey of a thousand miles starts from beneath one's feet."[18] But, remember, setting out does not by itself guarantee success. There is beginning, but there is also persevering, that is, beginning again and again and again. You are well advised to set out with a *professional pilgrim as a guide.* Such men of lifelong calling (or penance) are easily recognizable, "adorned with many tokens, the witness of many wonders, the hero of many adventures."[19]

And remember, too, you can stay at home, safe in the familiar illusion of certainty. Do not set out without realizing that "the way is not without danger. Everything good is costly, and the development of the personality is one of the most costly of all things."[20] It will cost you your innocence, your illusions, your certainty.

The Healing Metaphors of the Guru

> He finds a comrade,
> Now he beats the drum, now he stops.
> Now he sobs, now he sings.[1]
> *I Ching*

Some men undertake their pilgrimages in solitude, others in the company of other seekers. Even those who set out alone may find helpful companions who join them along the way. But for most of us, at the troubled time at which we set out on the search for the meaning of our lives, it seems wise to turn to a helper, a healer, or a guide who can show us the way (or at least can turn us away from the dead-end paths we usually walk). "Priests and magicians are used in great number."[2]

Such a spiritual guide is sometimes called a *Guru*. This special sort of teacher helps others through the rites of initiation and transition by seeming to introduce his disciples to the new experiences of higher levels of spiritual understanding. In reality, what he offers them is guidance toward accepting their imperfect, finite existence in an ambiguous and ultimately unmanageable world. Gurus may at first appear to be "the ideal bearers of final truths, but [in reality, they are] simply ... the *most extraordinarily human* members of the community."[3] Even the contemporary Western guru, the psycho-therapist, can only be of help to that extent to which he is a fellow-pilgrim.

The guru will appear in different forms. He may wear the garb of a simple teacher or an itinerant healer. Or he may come upon the scene with the dramatic force of a prophet, a sage, or even a wizard, depending upon the time and place of his appearance. He will fit the cultural expectations, even though he may be responded to as much with distrust and fear as with confidence and respect.

Both the awe that he commands and the distress that he engenders are, in part, responses to his radical, even charismatic, strangeness to all rules and traditions. Arising in a revolutionary context, he sets himself against both the traditional authority of patriarchal domination and the bureaucratic legalistic defining of power. Unintimidated by cultural expectations, he is his own man, piercing the group's conventional wisdom and overturning the usual ways of understanding the meaning of life.

His impact comes in part from his speaking the forgotten language of prophecy, the poetic language of the myth and of the dream. "If the myth is the outer expression of the human condition's basic struggles, joys, and ambiguities, then the dream is its inner voice."[4] The guru teaches indirectly, not by way of dogma and lecture, but by means of parable and metaphor.

Instruction by metaphor does not depend primarily on rationally determined logical thinking nor on empirically objective checking of perceptual data. Instead, knowing metaphorically implies grasping a situation intuitively, in its many interplays of multiple meanings, from the concrete to the symbolic. In this way, as the Sufies demonstrate with their Teaching-Stories, these inner dimensions make the parable capable of revealing more and more levels of meaning, depending on the disciple's level of readiness to understand. By way of example, here is the Sufi Teaching-Story of the Water-Melon Hunter:

> Once upon a time, there was a man who strayed from his own country into the world known as the Land of Fools. He soon saw a number of people flying in terror from a field where they had been trying to reap wheat. "There is a monster in that field," they told him. He looked, and saw that it was a water-melon.
>
> He offered to kill the "monster" for them. When he had cut the melon from its stalk, he took a slice and began to eat it. The people became even more terrified of him than they had been of the melon. They drove him away with pitchforks, crying, "He will kill us next, unless we get rid of him."
>
> It so happened that at another time another man also strayed into the Land of Fools, and the same thing started to happen to him. But, instead of offering to help them with the "monster," he agreed with them that it must be dangerous, and by tiptoeing away from it with them he gained their confidence. He spent a long time with them in their houses until he could teach them, little by little, the basic facts which would enable them not only to lose their fear of melons, but even to cultivate them themselves."[5]

The Truth does *not* make people free. Facts do *not* change attitudes. If the guru is dogmatic, all that he evokes in his pilgrim/disciples is their stubbornly resistant insistence on clinging to those unfortunate beliefs that at least provide the security of known misery, rather than openness to the risk of the unknown or the untried. That is why that Renaissance Magus, Paracelsus, warned that the guru should avoid simply revealing "the naked truth. He should use images, allegories, figures, wondrous speech, or other hidden, roundabout ways."[6]

The earliest form in which the guru appeared was that of the shaman, who arose in the hunting and gathering societies of the paleolithic era (and among their contemporary Eskimo and Indian progeny). Before the advent of God and His priests in the more stable agricutural societies of the neolithic era, the shaman acted as spiritual leader to the nomadic, Stone-Age hunting band.

Such a guru starts out on his own tortured pilgrimage as a deeply troubled, misfit youth. In mastering his personal afflictions, he gradually comes to the position of being able to help others on their spiritual trips. Unlike the later priests who were ceremonially trained in ritual acts and verbatim incantations, the shaman has been inspired by the visions that arise during his own pilgrimage. The power of his growing self-awareness and the spontaneity of his improvisations fit the hunters' needs for daring and imagination (just as the priests' ritual intonements and predetermined social proscriptions fit the planters' needs for stability, achieved by the sacrifice of the individual to the greater good of the group).

The source of the shaman's moving inner vision is a journey deep into the self. Usually in a trance-like state, he experiences the struggle within his own soul as an encounter with the spirit world. In the religion, myths, and literature of every culture, the personal motives and conflicts that men would disown are represented by gods and ghosts, by spirits and visions. A young Eskimo neophyte shaman tells of his own transforming experience while out on the pilgrimage of a lonely wilderness vigil:

> I soon became melancholy. I would sometimes fall to weeping and feel unhappy without knowing why. Then for no reason all would suddenly be changed, and I felt a great, inexplicable joy, a joy so powerful that I could not restrain it, but had to break into song, a mighty song, with room for only one word: joy, joy! And I had to use the full strength of my voice. And then in the midst of such a fit of mysterious and overwhelming delight, I became a shaman, not knowing myself how it came about. But I was a shaman. I could see and hear in a totally different way. I had gained my enlightenment, the shaman's light of brain and body, and this in such a manner that it was not only I who could see through the darkness of life, but the same bright light also shone out from me, imperceptible to human beings but visible to

all spirits of earth and sky and sea, and these now came to me to become my helping spirits.[7]

After his pilgrimage, the shaman then returns to the community of his tribe, "reborn" by way of his self-healing process. Now he is able to liberate the ordinary hunters of the band by revealing to each of them his own personally enlightening inner vision.

The shaman can also bring spiritual calm and confidence to a troubled tribe by helping them to work out the merited misfortunes that have befallen them. He will usually go into a trance at such times, his helping spirits speaking through his mouth in those poetically cryptic ways in which spirits (and gurus) speak. They ask the troubled ones what is causing the unhappiness. The power of the shaman's personal presence leads the troubled person to acknowledge that his thoughts have been bad, and his actions evil. The helping spirits of the shaman then make veiled references that evoke the whole story.

For example, to a woman who has caused "bad blood" among the men by her seeming infidelity, the spirits may say: "I see a gleaming object, broken in your lower body." With the encouragement of the communal audience, the sufferer believes that she has been seen through, purges herself with an outpouring of confession of her misdeeds, and then talks out and settles the troubles between herself and other members of the tribe.

This purging brings peace to the tribe through constructive human interaction mediated by the inspiring power of the shaman's confidence in his own inner vision, and by the metaphorical evocation of the troubled seeker's own tale.

Another powerful example of the guru who instructs by metaphor may be found in the Zaddik, the spiritual leader of the Hasidim. The Hasidic phenomenon was "a Jewish mystical movement of the eighteenth and nineteenth centuries, a movement which brought a charm, a vitality, and a personal relevance that touched and renewed the lives of a despairing people."[8]

Devastated by Cossack oppression, the hope-starved Jewish people had turned in vain desperation to the false messiahs who arose, and to the cultist esotericism of the masters of the Kabbalistic mysteries. They struggled to retain their faith in the covenant with God, the faith that their suffering had meaning. They found themselves fooled, betrayed, lost in a spiritual desert, and unable to understand the mysterious prophecies of the Kabbalists in which they had hoped to be able to believe.

It was in response to this desperate search for guidance that the Baal Shem-Tov, the first Zaddik, appeared. No longer would men have to depend on the magical authority of the priestly keepers of incomprehensible secret truths. Instead, this new guru promised that truth would be open to all men, that each would be able to renew his faith by joining the Zaddik on a personal pilgrimage. This guru would acknowledge his own human fallibility, yet trust his feelings, and expect a like commitment from those who would seek his guidance. They would no longer be bewildered pilgrims standing like children before the gates of the temple. The meanings which they sought would be accessible to all. No longer would there be a distinction between the sacred and the profane. Everyday life would be hallowed, and each man would be responsible for that bit of existence that God had entrusted to his care.

The guru of Hasidism would join the other pilgrims in their search, rather than offering them the authoritarian teachings of the high priest or wizard. One such Zaddik describes his leadership by likening his Hasidic pilgrims to a band of wanderers who have become lost in a deep, dark forest. They chance upon their guru, who has been lost even longer. Unaware of his helplessness, they ask him to show them the way out of the woods. He can only answer: "That I cannot do. But I can point out the ways that lead further into the thicket, and after that let us try to find the way together."[9]

Like the shaman, the Zaddik instructs by metaphor, by indirection, not by teaching the pilgrims to be more like him, but to be more like themselves. Rather than offer dogma to his followers, he offered himself. He was the teaching. His trembling before God inspired faith, and his risking being foolish gave the Hasidim the daring to be themselves. His stories instructed each pilgrim by way of what the seeker brought to it, rather than by laying down instructions on how to live.

So it was that when the Hasidic pilgrims vied for who among them had endured the most suffering, who was most entitled to complain, the Zaddik told them the story of the Sorrow Tree. On the Day of Judgment, each person will be allowed to hang all of his unhappiness on a branch of the great Tree of Sorrows. After each person has found a limb from which his own miseries may dangle, they may all walk slowly around the tree. Each is to search for a set of sufferings that he would prefer to those he has hung on the tree. In the end, each man freely chooses to reclaim his own personal set of sorrows rather than those of another. Each man leaves the tree wiser than when he came.

The metaphorical teachings of the Hasidic guru sometimes took the form of his own personality being a substitute for dogma, of the pilgrim's relationship with him being the vehicle for salvation. Whatever the Zaddik was doing at any given moment was what mattered most to him, and he did it with his whole soul. Thus it was that his followers would come to him, not to be taught great truths, "but to watch him tie his bootlaces."[10]

As a final example of the guru who instructs by metaphor so that his disciples may learn what they already know, let us consider the Zen

Master. The original Buddhist teachings first appeared in Southern India where they helped to free men from the imprisoning Hindu social caste system and the Yoga emphasis on control of mind and body. As the teachings were passed northward through China, they allowed men to see through the tradition-bound social conventions that held them fast. And then in Japan, the spirit of Zen imbued the Japanese penchant for ceremonial elegance with an absurdity that undid its own restrictions.

A favorite method of Zen guidance is the Koan exercise. The disciple is given a problem on which to meditate, a problem that is insoluble by conventional or intellectual means. With it the Zen pilgrim must struggle until either he *gives up* in despair or he *gives in* and is enlightened. A classical example is for the master to direct him to concentrate on "the sound of one hand clapping."

Such conundrums are often offered in response to the young monk's demands for clarification. Ironically, it is these very demands with which he confounds himself. So it is that when he asks: "How can I ever get emancipated?" the Zen Master may answer: "Who has ever put you in bondage?"[11] Or, consider this exchange:

> A monk asked: What is the meaning of the First Patriarch's coming from the West?
> Master: Ask the post over there.
> Monk: I do not understand you.
> Master: I do not either, any more than you.[12]

Only by such indirection can the Master lead the pilgrim to turn back to the here-and-now moments of his everyday life, to learn that there is no truth that is not already apparent to everyone. This sense of immediacy without struggle comes across in the sad/lovely parable of the Zen Master who, while out walking one day, is confronted by a ferocious, man-eating tiger. He backs away from the animal, only to find that he is trapped at the edge of a high cliff. The tiger pursues the Master whose only hope of escape is to suspend himself over the abyss by holding on to a frail vine that grows at its edge. Above is the tiger who would devour him. Below is the certain death of a long fall onto the jagged rocks. The slender vine begins to give way, and death is imminent. Just then the precariously suspended Zen Master notices a lovely ripe wild strawberry growing along the cliff's edge. He plucks the succulent berry and pops it into his mouth. He is heard to say: "This lovely strawberry, how sweet it tastes."

By speaking to him in metaphor, the guru turns the pilgrim in upon himself. He offers the seeker only what he already possesses, taking from him that which he never had. What the guru knows that the seeker does not is that *we are all pilgrims.* There is no master, and there is no student. At its worst, the fundamental humanity of the guru may be expressed in his inevitable corruptability. The grace of the guru and the disciples who take his place are subject to the same eventual decay that is the other face of all human forms of growth. The charisma of the guru may become as self-serving as the very Establishment against which it arose, as it is routinized by efforts to sustain its power. The arrogance of the guru may tempt him to self-elevation, or he may be done in by his followers' needs to make more of themselves through his apotheosis. Empty ritualistic parodies may eventually be all that are left of teachings that were once spontaneous and alive. The reification of his metaphors by those who take his place may lead to the hollow appearance of continuity, without the original life-giving substance of inspired teaching.

The teaching mission of the guru is an attempt to free his followers from him His metaphors and parables make it necessary for the pilgrims who would be disciples to turn to their own imaginations in the search for meaning in their lives. The guru instructs the pilgrims in the tradition of breaking with tradition, in losing themselves so that they may find themselves.

Disclosing the Self

Contemplation of my life
Decides the choice
Between advance and retreat.[1]

Hidden dragon. Do not act.[2]
I Ching

The guru instructs by metaphor and parable, but the pilgrim learns through the telling of his own tale. Each man's identity is an emergent of the myths, rituals, and corporate legends of his culture, compounded with the epic of his own personal history. In either case, it is the compelling power of the storytelling that distinguishes men from beasts. The paradoxical interstice of power and vulnerability, which makes a man most human, rests on his knowing who he is right now, because he can remember who he has been, and because he knows who he hopes to become. All this comes of the wonder of his being able to tell his tale.

When the great Rabbi Israel Baal Shem-Tov saw misfortune threatening the Jews it was his custom to go into a certain part of the forest to meditate. There he would light a fire, say a special prayer, and the miracle would be accomplished and the misfortune averted.

Later, when his disciple, the celebrated Magid of Mezritch, had occasion, for the same reason, to intercede with heaven, he would go to the same place in the forest and say: "Master of the Universe, listen! I do not know how to light the fire, but I am still able to say the prayer." And again, the miracle would be accomplished.

Still later, Rabbi Moshe-Leib of Sasov, in order to save his people once more, would go into the forest and say: "I do not know how to light the fire, I do not know the prayer, but I know the place and this must be sufficient."

Then it fell to Rabbi Israel of Rizhyn to overcome misfortune. Sitting in his armchair, his head in his hands, he spoke to God: "I am unable to light the fire and I do not know the prayer; I cannot even find the place in the forest. All I can do is to tell the story, and this must be sufficient." And it was sufficient.

God made man because He loves stories.[3]

The contemporary pilgrim is a person separated from the life-infusing myths that supported tribal man. He is a secular isolate celebrating the wake of a dead God. When God lived, and man belonged, psychology was no more than "a minor branch of the art of storytelling and mythmaking."[4] Today, each man must work at telling his own story if he is to be able to reclaim his personal identity.

Should he start out on a psychotherapeutic pilgrimage, he sets out on an adventure in narration. Everything depends on the telling. The "principle of explanation consists of getting the story told — somehow, anyhow — in order to discover how it begins."[5] The basic presumption is that the telling of the tale will itself yield good counsel. This second look at his personal history can transform a man from a creature trapped in his past to one who is freed by it. But the telling is not all.

Along the way, on his pilgrimage, each man must have the chance to tell his tale. And, as each man tells his tale, there must be another there to listen. But the other need not be a guru. He need only rise to the needs of the moment. There is an old saying that whenever two Jews meet, if one has a problem, the other automatically becomes a rabbi.

But sometimes it is not enough for there simply to be another to listen. A man not only needs someone to hear his tale, but someone to care as well. This universal human need is touchingly revealed in the metaphor of the Legend of the *Lamed-Vov.*[6]

According to the ancient Jewish tradition of the Lamed-Vov, there are at all times thirty-six hidden Just Men, thirty-six secret saints upon whom the continued existence of the world depends. When one dies another takes his place. The Lamed-Vov are indistinguishable from other human beings, except in the heartbreaking depth of their caring. And only so long as the Just Men exist, only so long as their special caring continues, just so long will God allow the world of ordinary men to continue to exist. So inconsolable are the Just Men in their anguish about human suffering, that even God Himself cannot comfort them. So it is, that as an act of mercy toward them: "From time to time the Creator, blessed be His Name, sets forward the clock of the Last Judgment by one minute."[7]

The story is told about a young boy whose aging grandfather informs him that the last Just Man has died without designating a successor. The boy is to take his place as one of the Lamed-Vov. He can soon expect to attain the glow that is the aura of his coming ascendency. The boy is awed, but bewildered as to what he should do in this life as a Just Man. The old man assures him that he need only be himself, that he need not *do* anything to fulfill his destiny. In the meanwhile he need only continue to be a good little boy.

But the child worries about his role, becoming obsessed with the idea that if he learns how to be a Just Man, perhaps God will be satisfied and spare his aging grandfather from dying. He fantasizes the grand self-tortures and self-sacrifices that may be required of him. Will he have to be dragged along the rough ground clinging to the tail of a Mongol pony, or would it be of greater merit if he were to be consumed by purifying flames while being burned at the stake?

He is terrified, but ready to do whatever is required of him. He decides to work his way up, beginning by holding his breath as long as he can. When this does not seem enough, he holds a match to his hand, burning his palm to a painfully satisfying stigmatic char. His grandfather is deeply upset and yet touched when he learns that the boy has been training himself to die in order to save the old man's life. He teaches the boy the nature of his monstrous error by explaining that as a Just Man, he will not be able to change anything. He will save no one. A Just Man need not pursue suffering. It will be there in the world for him as it is for each man. He need only be open to the suffering of others, knowing that he cannot change it. Without being able to save his brothers, he must let himself experience their pain, so that they need not suffer alone. This will change nothing for man, but it will make a difference to God.

The boy wanders off trying to understand, but not seeing the sense or the worth of it all. His epiphany comes later that day when he catches a fly whose life he holds in the hollow of his hand. He knows a sudden sympathy for the terror and the trembling of the fly. The fly's anguish is suddenly his own as well. Releasing the fly from his own trembling hand, he suddenly feels the glow of becoming one of the Lamed-Vov. He has become one of the Just Men. Love is more than simply being open to experiencing the anguish of another person's suffering. It is the willingness to live with the helpless knowing that we can do nothing to save the other from his pain.

As a psychotherapist, I am no longer willing to accept anyone as my patient to whose pain I do not feel vulnerable. If someone comes to me for help whom I do not experience as the sort of person who is likely to become personally important to me, I send him away. I am no Lamed-Vov. I do not live for God's sake, but for my own. Every hour spent treating a particular patient is an hour of my life as well. Much of my life is over. Some of what is left is already filled with the emptiness of my loneliness, that pain in each of us that can from time to time be eased, but from which there is no final escape, save death. And too, in my life there are disappointments that I cannot evade, frustrations that I do not choose, and losses that I am helpless to do anything about. Some troubles, of course, I bring on myself, but others fall out of the skies onto my unprotected head, shattering my joys and darkening my pleasures. It seems foolhardy not to try to take what care of myself I can, and so I choose to work only with patients about whom I feel hopeful in sharing my time. There are some patients whom I believe I could help, but whom I send away nonetheless, feeling that being with them would not be good for me. If I am not able to be open to their pain, I may perhaps find professional satisfaction in working with them, but no personal joy. It's a bad bargain, and one I am no longer willing to make.

When I work with a patient, not only will I be hearing his tale, but I shall be telling him mine as well. If we are to get anywhere, we must come to know one another. One of the luxuries of being a psychotherapist is that it helps to keep you honest. It's a bit like remaining in treatment all of your life. It helps me to remain committed to telling and retelling my tale for the remainder of that pilgrimage that is my life. Research in self-disclosure supports my own experience that the personal openness of the guru facilitates and invites the increased openness of the pilgrim.[8] But I operate not to help the patient, but to help myself. It is from the center of my own being that I am moved to share my tale. That it turns out to be so helpful to the patient is gravy. Whenever I make the mistake of giving a piece of myself *in order to* get the patient to share more of himself, he balks at the shoddy, self-righteous manipulative quality of my efforts. In recent years, most often instead I trust my feelings, and do what I feel like doing without trying to control its effect on the patient. When an untrusting patient speculates on whether I am being genuine or just using psychotherapeutic techniques, he finds me totally uninterested in the distinction. I have not wondered whether I am being genuine or technical for almost as long as I have given up wondering whether I am being selfish or unselfish. What's the difference? How can the answers to such questions possibly help me? I try to be guided by Carl Whitaker's advice to feed the patient not when he is crying that he is hungry, but only when I feel the milk overflowing from my own nipples.[9]

The mutual exchange of self-revelations between guru and pilgrim do, of course, give priority to those of the seeker. I am in some ways an expert paid to offer services. The patient, though he may not realize it, always knows better than I just where we should begin each session. Because of this, each session begins with my silent attention to his coming initiation of the hour's interaction. I have not begun a session myself since I was a patient. I operate as a counter-puncher, each movement being a response to the patient's words, gestures, or postures. Yet it is not simply a game, and I cannot move with confidence in the healing power of my metaphors without being firmly centered in my own inner feelings. I must begin by joining the patient in "the transparent way"[10] we are to walk together, by being transparent to myself.

In a non-selectively accepting way, I must allow my own changing being to be continuously disclosed to my consciousness. I must be ready to confront feelings and ideas within myself that are ugly, evil, and discrediting, if I am to receive the lovely, tender, decent aspects of myself. All of the good/bad, strong/weak, divine/ridiculous Janus faces must be seen, if I am to have any time to live with my mask off. And should I wear my mask too long, when I take it off and try to discard it, I may find that I have thrown my face away with it.

If I am transparent enough to myself, then I can become less afraid of those hidden selves that my transparency may reveal to others. If I reveal myself without worrying about how others will respond, then some will care, though others may not. But who can love me, if no one knows me? I must risk it, or live alone. It is enough that I must die alone. I am determined to let down, whatever the risks, if it means that I may have whatever is there for me.

My own free decision to be transparent is a commitment to never-ending struggle. Before a man can be free, first he must choose freedom. *Then* the hard work begins. But if this commitment invites a like commitment in my patients, we can offer each other courage to go on, joining each other along the pilgrim's way, foregoing semblance for openness, and solitude for community.

As in all problems between myself and the other, I must begin by trying to straighten myself out. As with every other significant human interaction, "the most effective way to invite authentic disclosure from another is to take the risky lead and offer it oneself, first."[11] Though I believe that the only real danger lies in that which is hidden, disclosure of myself to myself must precede disclosure to the other. Often I reveal to the other without any certainty as to what I am getting into. I may be just as surprised (horrified or delighted) as the other at what emerges.

Yet in some basic way my awareness of what emerges from within me has the primary function of giving me the freedom/responsibility of choice as to which feelings I choose to move on (and which I do not) in any given instance. I am *not* committed to the encounter group ethos of random openness at every point. I reserve a right to privacy at any given moment, and I respect that right in others (including my patients). I do not wish to engage in the brutality that masquerades as indiscriminate frankness. The "philosophy of the here-and-now," of "you do your thing and I'll do mine," is not my thing unless I am willing to face the consequences of my acts, to eschew needless hurting of others, and to know that no matter how into myself I am, from time to time I will surely act like a fool.

Within those ambiguous parameters, I would come to know the other and come to be known to him. We will tell each other our tales, and we will be moved by the tales of others. As a child, I was so often lonely and out of it that if I had not found the tales of others in the books I read, I believe I would have died. Partly out of gratitude, I am regathering some of these tales that enabled me to survive. In these stories the pilgrim appears in varied contexts, wearing many guises. And as testimony to my own continued seeking, I have included an epilogue of the dreams that recount the story of my own continuing pilgrimage.

Tale of a Spoiled Identity

Women are to blame for all the trouble in the world. The Bible tells us so.

When God confronted Adam in the Garden of Eden, He thundered the accusation: "Have you eaten of the tree, of which I commanded you not to eat?"[1] And Adam, trembling and ashamed in his nakedness, copped out: "The woman whom thou gavest to be with me, she gave me the fruit of the tree, and I ate."[2]

Because Adam had listened to the voice of his wife, instead of harking to the commands of the Lord, God was angry and condemned him to live from then on by the sweat of his brow. He would no longer take care of a man who had yielded to female domination. Eve was to suffer punishment as well, and additionally was to endure man's political domination forever. To the woman, God said: "I will greatly multiply your pain in childbearing; in pain you shall bring forth children, yet your desire shall be for your husband, and he shall rule over you."[3]

But there is an apocryphal interpretation of the myth of Creation, which suggests that Eve's formation from the rib of the lonely, sleeping Adam, was God's *second* attempt at finding him a helpmate. When God first "created man in his own image, in the image of God he created him,"[4] at the same time, "male and female he created them."[5]

An old Hebrew tradition holds that this first creation included a female called Lillith. She was the very first defender of the cause of women's liberation. When Adam told Lillith that she was to obey his wishes, she replied: "We are equal; we are made of the same earth."[6] So saying she flew up into the air and transformed herself into a demon who ate children. Even that early, women who would not subjugate themselves to the will of men were seen as witches.

To this day, women have remained the most consistent object of man's inhumane political and social oppression. Other groups rise and fall, but females remain oppressed, even when they no longer constitute a minority.

The female pilgrimage is an attempt by women to regain their status as full-fledged human beings, to be accepted as the natural equals of men, and no longer to be used as a repository for the projected evil that males thus disown. As a man, at times I am certainly a part of the conspiracy that has kept women degraded and unhappy. I no longer relish my part in this alleged supremacy. I am committed to the struggle toward freedom that the success of the female pilgrimage would provide for both men and women. But for all my good intentions, I am still more a part of the problem than of the solution. Though I support the Women's Liberation Movement, I will not attempt to speak for it. Women are no longer voiceless. They now speak out strongly for themselves.[7]

As a psychotherapist, I am particularly interested in that part of women's spoiled identity that is fostered by destructive family relationships. The roots of most of women's problems are political and social. The solution to such political problems must be revolutionary rather than psychotherapeutic. Psychoanalysts in particular have been justly accused of encouraging women to adjust to, rather than change, oppressive cultural conditions. They have suppressed the dissent of understandably unhappy women by classing them as "neurotics," in a way that makes no more sense than it would to impose such a diagnosis on ghetto-trapped blacks.

In my own work with female patients, I try to encourage them to sort out those parts of the problem that belong to all women, to seek the support of their sisterhood, to explore Women's Liberation Movement meetings if they wish, and to find political solutions for the political problems. Then, as I can, I work with them on the personal psychological aspects of their identity struggles.

My work with Willo has been a rewarding opportunity to join and to guide an unhappy young woman along the way of her pilgrimage toward freedom, self-respect, and appreciation of her personal worth. We have helped each other, and she has taught me to understand something of·the nature of a woman's ordeal in the struggle to become whom she might be. I will let her speak for herself. She has learned to do that in ways that are both touching and powerful.

At Willo's request, I have not guarded her identity by giving her a fictitious name. She is proud of what she has become and generous in her willingness to share the moving experience of her own painful struggle with other spiritual pilgrims. Willo grew up feeling unsupported by her mother as she was thrust into the role of an enigmatic decoration for a father who was deeply committed to the pursuit of his own professional achievements. As an adult she was too often a self-discrediting support for her husband, helping him to do his thing, while settling for the meager reward of "security" for herself. Needless to say, she made him pay. For years she engaged in all of the self-degrading, secretly spiteful ways that women have developed to subtly victimize their oppressors. It is much like the passive resistance to white domination that Negroes so long practiced as "niggers," before they stood up to become blacks.

Early in therapy, for the most part Willo concentrated her struggle on new ways of defining her relationships with men. As part of her quest for an identify as a grown-up woman-person, she had to give up defining herself as some man's good girl or lovely wife. She had to wear a face of her own. There was much to be learned, and perhaps even more to be unlearned. But at least the enemy was clear, first as the cruelly insensitive Male, and then as her own stubborn need to be taken care of by Daddy.

She labored long and hard to emerge from the slime of an identity spoiled by the oppression of experiencing herself as a non-person, born to be a helplessly trapped disappointment to a father who was not really interested in any child who could not immortalize his maleness. Though this is the family link most often emphasized in Women's Liberation Movement analyses of the degradation of the female ego, a young girl's sense of who she is in her mother's eyes is also a crucial parameter in the development of her stigmatized self. Willo's growing awareness of her resentment and longings in connection with being her father's daughter arose more readily than the more subtly stifled, insidiously vaguer self-dissatisfaction implied in having been her mother's girl.

The congested feelings deadened the joy in her. She could not scream them out. She did not own her rage. In order to facilitate a more vivid experience of these elusive feelings of hurt, of anger, and of longing, I suggested that she write a letter to her mother, a letter she need never mail. It was to be an attempt to make a claim on her mother, to speak out in that anguished voice that no one had ever heard.

For weeks, Willo stalled, panicked at the thought of experiencing her own dreaded feelings, which the writing of such a letter promised to unleash. She claimed that what was stopping her was the hopelessness that she would ever be heard. Should she write and send such a letter, the only response she could imagine receiving would be more of the same self-sorry, evasive denials and pap that had met all earlier attempts to reach out to her mother. Her inability to have any impact on her mother had been transformed into a sense of her own powerlessness, a paralyzing drain of futility.

I suggested that since this never-to-be-mailed letter was only a fantasy trip, rather than a political act, Willo was free to write mother's answering letter as well. She might be able to release herself from the ambivalence on which she usually relied, if she could somehow separate her desperately tender longings from her depressing expectations. I recommended that she consider writing two separate replies from mother. The first would be the sort of response that had felt so devastating every time she had tried to get close to mother in the past. If she could get that out of the way, then perhaps she could write a second letter, the sort of reply that she had always wanted from her mother, but had never gotten. In any event, even fantasizing the possibilities of these two separate sorts of replies might free her to write her own unspoken cry to mother.

Finally, one day Willo began her individual therapy hour by handing me copies of these three letters, which she had finally managed to let herself write. I had not recommended this experiment as an attempt to garner more clinical information for myself, but rather as a way of providing an opportunity for Willo to get into more direct touch with her own feelings. And so, I turned the letters back to her without reading them. If she would be willing to read them aloud to me, she would come to know the feelings in still a new way, and I might share in her experience of reclaiming this lost part of her soul. She trusted me once more, and began to read the first letter, stopping only when, from time to time, she was crying so hard that she could not speak. The first letter began:

Dear Barbara:

I started to write "mother" out of habit . . . but Barbara seems more appropriate, as you never really have been a mother to me in the ways that I think are appropriate. A mother should nurture and protect her young, not eat them. A mother should touch and love her children physically and emotionally. We always had a thing in our house where we did not spank the kids. . . . I used to think that this was a great thing, that hitting a kid was a breach of trust . . . however, I realize in our house it was just an extension of our not touching at all . . . not in anger or in love. Instead we were disciplined by a quiet sullen anger that would erupt in tirades that were isolating and destructive, and indicted the whole person. To this day if someone gets angry at me I equate it with their feeling me totally worthless and with their wanting to cut things off with me. I experience a panic on the edge of which I have lived all my life.

I used to think that you were the victim and such a weak, ineffectual woman whom life had dealt some cruel blows. You were really a goddamn slut who was manipulating everyone with your supposed helplessness. When I look back you sure were the

victor who ended up with the spoils. Your possessions always
meant more to you than anyone else . . . that's funny, I said
"anyone" . . . but to you they were animate . . . at least as
animate as you were. You always lavished such care on the house,
the car, your boat . . . and of course your poodle . . . but he
offers no threat . . . time time time . . . time and money and
things . . . that's your life. I could never understand why you
were always running around saving time . . . it never seemed to
me that you did anything with it . . . you don't read, you don't
think . . . what is important to you . . . not your new husband,
Bill . . . he is just another non-threatening object in your life that
gives you the impression that you are not alone . . . but you are
ALONE AND IT'S YOUR OWN GODDAMN FAULT. . . . It
could have been different . . . when I was little I really needed
you and if you could have been there for me instead of sacrificing
me at the altar of my father . . . we could have a beautiful
relationship now. A mature mother and daughter relationship
instead of this.

When I think of you I get all squirmy and ughc . . . it's like you
were completely decayed inside and if I really gave you a warm
supportive loving hug . . . your walls that are a facade would
crumble . . . you are a variation on Dorian Gray only yours is
happening inside. . . . You are like bacteria that cannot live in the
presence of warmth and love . . . and real concern. I have paid too
high a price to pretend that I have a mother . . . I don't . . . and I
do not want to sacrifice my own daughter at your altar.

It was a while before she could go on beyond her gasping,
anguished rage, before I was able to listen to more. The second letter
was delivered as a mocking, openly cruel parody of all the empty replies
her mother had ever offered. The reading began in a disturbingly nasal
whine:

Dear Willo.

I was very disturbed by your recent letter. When you are a little
older, Willo Ann, I think that you will understand more of the
kinds of things that I did. It is not as easy as you younger people
would like to think that it is. When your children are older you
will find out what it is really like.

Bill and I went down to the boat for the weekend. . . . I baked a
chocolate cake and 60 dozen cookies. I froze some of the cookies
in little bags so that I can take out a dozen at a time when I need
them. We have bought a new refrigerator for the boat and it is
wonderful. We can take enough food down for the whole weekend. We took a cruise at night to look at the harbor lights.

Bill is going to take off the month of August so we can take a
cruise. He has worked very hard this year and really needs the
rest. We have been working in the yard every night when he gets

home, trying to get it in shape. It was such a mess, you know, since we haven't gotten much rain.

I told you that we had the complete house repainted. It really needed it. It looked so awful. I have put up lovely ruffled curtains in the guest room ... it was very expensive, and the painters worked so slowly. I could have done it faster myself and probably better but I just don't have the energy anymore. Anyway, It is really nice to have it done.

We haven't heard anything from your brother. I guess he is still up in Maine.

I have discovered a new recipe for Marshmallowed Marshmallows. It is really terrific. If I can find the recipe I'll send it to you. It's very quick to make and you can freeze it.

It's almost time to go back to school again. I am not looking forward to it. The kids just aren't the same. The town isn't like it used to be. They don't come from the nice families that they used to here. So many Mexicans and colored now, you know. If I can just get assigned to Home Ec., it's so easy because I have done it before, and hang on a few more years, I can retire.

Well, say hello to the kids for me.

Love,
Mother

Willo and I laughed and snickered in the new-found intimacy of a conspiracy of naughty children. Our snide vengeance spent, we turned toward the final fantasy letter, the reply Willo had always hoped for, and would never ever receive, the one she would have to do without. She read this one softly, with quiet tenderness:

Dear Willo,

I was very sad to receive your letter because it said so many things that I have known but have tried to hide from myself. I know that I was not a very good mother ... I cannot even say that I tried very hard. I was so scared most of my life and was not really ready to be a mother or even a wife. I suppose I was only doing what I had seen my mother do and experience but someone has to stop the cycle. I am sorry that I could not be the one to do it. I am glad for you that you are trying to find something real for yourself ... I am afraid that it may be too late for me. I am locked into a job and a marriage that are not satisfying for me but they do give me financial security. I grab onto things because I am terrified that I will be poor, old, ugly, stupid and alone.

You were such a cute little girl. I regret that I did not enjoy you when you were small. Your own daughter reminds me so much of how you were. You should value this time with her because it will never come again. I know.

Young people seem to be fortunate today. They have so many

choices that I didn't think were possible when I was young. Maybe that is just rationalizing why I didn't take more control of my own life in a real way. You are right that I sold out to the wrong things. In many ways I was more in control of my own life because I never let it happen; I always manipulated the situation. It only left me with a very empty, lonely life. It's ironic but in fact all the things that I feared have really come to pass.

I hope that it is not too late.

Love,
Mother

We cried softly. I thanked her for letting me come so close, for teaching me so much.

As Willo came to know and to value her own wishes during the course of psychotherapy, she began more and more to put her deadening security on the line. She reached out for her freedom. How delighted she was to be warmly received by a sisterhood of compassionate pilgrims. As her considerable creative imagination came to flower, one of the ways in which she asserted her rights was in the search for a career of her own. The piece that follows is part of her *Statement of Purpose*, an essay required by the graduate studies program to which she was applying:

I managed to get a bachelor of arts degree by pasting the right number of stamps on transcripts and turning them in at an accredited institution which awarded me the degree. It was a meaningless, directionless, end-gaining experience. In applying to be accepted as a graduate student, I am asking that you take a leap of faith with me. As a weaver, I am very improvisational, planning only the warp and allowing the design to take shape from the dynamic tension between the threads as I build up the weft. I trust that in the environment which this program would provide, my intellectual and emotional growth would create a dynamic tension and I, WILLO, would be in the real sense my own thesis.

I am going to begin my essay with that about myself which I feel will most hinder me because the essence of my statement of purpose is to overcome my feelings of inadequacy as a woman and in so doing, develop a system whereby I can help others accomplish this also.

The beginning of my handicap has its roots in the social structure but for my personal development it has its beginnings in my name, Willo. For years whenever anyone met me they would ask the origin of my beautiful and unusual name. "I was to be my father's first son," I would reply glibly, "and when I arrived they had to change it from Willis, Jr." My parents might have feminized it to Willa but they neuterized it to Willo. It took me years to experience the irony and anguish in that anecdote which

I tossed off so quickly. I have struggled so many years as the "neutered son" of an emotionally impotent father. I have raged against others because of the gnawing self-hatred that I have felt. I have diminished myself in most ways because of what my parents and society taught me was my worth as a woman and my perception of myself as a second-class man.

My audacity in applying for this innovative graduate program makes me realize that I have begun to lift myself out of the morass of feelings of inadequacy and worthlessness. However, I have come to recognize that the pain which I have and will continue to experience in coming to love myself will prove my greatest asset.

The graduate training at the Institute, with an emphasis on the symbiotic understandings "that individuals cannot be understood apart from the social contexts in which they live and that an understanding of social structures and processes depends in part on knowledge of personality dynamics," is crucial for me. I feel that I must understand the "essential core of psychology" and from this distill the myths that have enslaved and confined women in their own minds. My graduate study will be a personal odyssey of self-understanding and self-acceptance. I will then apply these perceptions in a therapy situation working with women and men as individuals and groups helping each to confront his or her own peculiar dilemma.

Tale of a Quest for Love

During the Middle Ages, everyone knew that it had been in the spring that the earth was first created. And so spring was a good time of the year to begin things, and a most fitting time to start out on a venture as holy as a pilgrimage to Canterbury.

Then too, with winter ending, it was a relief to be done with dark castles, too little heat, and a dull diet of light foods. It's little wonder that:

> When in April the sweet showers fall
> . . . .
> Then people long to go on pilgrimages
> And palmers long to seek the stranger strands
> Of far-off saints, hallowed in sundry lands.
> And specially, from every shire's end
> In England, down to Canterbury they wend.[1]

Chaucer's fourteenth-century *Canterbury Tales* form the last of the medieval pilgrim literature, with the pilgrimage itself serving as a framework story, which binds together the individual tales. Twenty-nine other pilgrims, and Chaucer himself, start out at an easy pace, riding fifteen miles each day of their three-day journey. To amuse and enlighten one another, each is to tell one story on the way, and another on the return.

Among the pilgrims are many types of people, representatives of almost every social class. They include, among others, a knight, a miller, and a cook, a man of law, a shipman, a nun and a monk, as well as a physician and a friar, a yeoman and a clerk. Each is described and comes alive through the earthy perspective of Chaucer's own tough-minded yet highly civilized realism. Our host is a man who accepts all that is human, "enjoys everything and respects nothing."[2] He apologizes to the gentry and to the church, lest he has offended, but only as a further bit of political irony.

The characters themselves often take out their dislikes by derogatory stories about the jobs and positions of one another. It is out of the clashes of the personalities on the trip that some of the stories grow. And so it is that this literal pilgrimage mirrors the pilgrimage of human life. Geoffrey Chaucer's "wise, sure-eyed, and sensitive selection of daily detail, mellowed and harmonized by a humane and often amused approval, qualified . . . by an ironical wit"[3] make his pilgrims live even now.

The most memorable of them is The Wife of Bath. This lusty woman, Dame Alice, has spent her life engaged in the dance of love, with five husbands, "apart from other company in her youth," those "cocky lads." On her way to Canterbury, she is even then dressed for her primary pilgrimage in scarlet stockings "gartered tight," a big floppy hat "broad as . . . a shield," a flowing cloak over her large hips, and "ten pound" of colorful kerchieves.[4]

She is glad to have the opportunity to tell of the misery and woes of marriage and of the delicious joys of love-making. Experience is authority enough for Dame Alice. She has little use for celibacy. Religious mores of the time are misleading.

> Had God commanded maidenhood to all
> Marriage would be condemned beyond recall,
> And certainly if seed were never sown
> How ever could virginity be grown?[5]

Besides, virginity was intended only for those who wished to lead the perfect life. It is advised, not commanded. As for herself, Dame Alice is unwilling to forgo the honey and the flower of life for some senseless ideal.

She has always been a willing wife, since the age of twelve, always happy to offer her *"belle chose . . .* whenever he wanted it."[6] Her first three husbands (to each of whom she was unfaithful) were old when she was young, rich at a time when she was poor. She received their money and their lands, had her fun, did little to court their favor, and treated them to shrewish nagging. She would only be sweet to them once they had submitted to her domination.

Burying each in turn, she married a fourth, a playboy whom she thinks she loved best because he was "disdainful in his love."[7] And when he died, at his funeral, she was attracted to a young Oxford clerk. Marrying for this fifth time, it was now *her* turn to be the older, the wealthier, and the more abused of the two. She was forty and he only twenty, but he was most unamorous, preferring to spend his time reading anti-feminist literature. Finally they had a fistfight over his neglect and contempt. She pretended he had killed her, "coming to" only once he showed remorse. Because he gave in, from then on she was kind to him.

Such exquisitely tortuous struggles between the sexes continue to be played out most elaborately in the lovely/awful, long-term compact called "marriage." Nonetheless, lifetime commitment to monogamous union seems to me the most rewarding alternative available in our present culture. I certainly wish to be open to the other alternatives, which are being suggested by the articulate spokesmen and spokes-women of the sexual revolution, women's liberation, and communal living, but I do confess to finding it hard to believe that new solutions will not engender new problems. At present, I see monogamous, life-long marriage as our most viable solution to loneliness, as the best setting so far available in which to raise children, and as the most practical contract for mutual support and freedom in a world so difficult for any one person to manage within.

Of course, marriage is also limiting, frustrating, and periodically terribly painful. Part of this, I believe, simply reflects how incredibly difficult it is to share the center of one's life with another completely separate, self-of-his-own human being. I am not even sure that the rewards ever clearly outweigh the difficulties. But with marriage, as with working for a living, there is little point in tallying up the credits and the debits to find out whether or not you are satsified, unless there is another live possibility for solution. Certainly, you can (and in some cases it is wise to) find a new job or a new mate. But at the moment, long-term commitments to being out of work, or to remaining single, seem to create greater problems than they solve.

Many of the people who seek my help as a psychotherapist are troubled by the pain of marital difficulties. Ironically, in these willful struggles, a spouse often complains bitterly about having to live with a mate who is acting in just the ways that he (or she) found most attractive during courtship.

The wife, for example, once delighted to have found such a mate, now feels disappointed and lonely. When she first met her husband, she was attracted by his stability, his capacity for self-control, and his sensibleness. It was clear and pleasing to her that he could not be easily upset, that he was "objective" in outlook, and that he was very, very practical. His considered detachment made it seem that he could be counted on to protect her from her own hairbrained impulsivity, and to see to it that she did not make an awful mess of things. What a terrible disappointment he turned out to be! Now she finds that he is cold, ungiving, and stodgy; he stubbornly ignores her feelings, and is no fun to be with.

This pejorative description of shortcomings that were once seen as virtues is not at all restricted to the female side of the struggle. Her husband once considered himself both wise and fortunate to have discovered a woman who was so alive and free emotionally, so enthusiastic, affectionate, and overflowing with energy. Now he is fed up. She has turned out to be impractical and impossibly demanding, asking more than anyone could give, never satisfied, and carrying on irrationally when she doesn't get what she wants.

He, of course, meets this onslaught first by trying to be "reasonable," and then by withdrawing into prolonged, thoughtful silences. He cannot understand why his detachment does not calm her down, any more than she can understand why he does not respond to her loneliness when she expresses it by crying pitifully, or by screaming, "All you ever do is watch the damn ball games on T.V." Each wants to get his (her) own way without being vulnerable, lest he (she) be seen as "giving in."

What people look for in marriage, at least in part, is the other half of themselves. Each of us is in some measure incomplete, with some aspects of our humanity over-developed and others neglected. What we do not claim for ourselves, we look for in the other (for example, aggressiveness, tenderness, spontaneity, stability, and so on). This is most extreme in the marriages of neurotics whose own self-image is so skewed that they seek out mates who are caricatures of the other end of the personality spectrum (such as the timid, self-inhibiting woman who searches for a glamorous, super-adventuresome epic-hero of a man, while he in turn seeks a woman too scared to let him get into trouble).

To some extent, each of us marries to make up for his own deficiencies. As a child, no one can stand alone against his family and the community, and in all but the most extreme instances, he is in no position to leave and to set up a life elsewhere. In order to survive as children, we have all had to exaggerate those aspects of ourselves that pleased those on whom we depended, and to disown those attitudes and behaviors that were unacceptable to them. As a result, to varying degrees, we have each grown into disproportionate configurations of what we could be as human beings. What we lack, we seek out and then struggle against in those whom we select as mates. We marry the other because he (or she) is different from us, and then we complain, "Why can't he (she) be more like me?"

If we married spouses who were like ourselves to begin with, other sorts of disasters might well ensue. For example, two timid souls would bolster each other's cautiousness till neither ventured to try anything new, while an adventuresome pair might escalate each other's recklessness into a spiral of catastrophes. Like it or not, these same differences between spouses are both the strengths of a good marriage and the hazards of a bad one.

In working with a struggling couple, I may point this out by asking the adventuresome husband: "Just what would happen if your wife said, 'Fine, go ahead!' every time you spun out one of your impulsive flights of fancy?''; or to the cautious wife: "Where would you get if your husband met your doubts with doubts of his own, so that you could stay stuck, instead of being encouraged to proceed, no matter how reluctantly?"

One way of conceiving the origins of these struggles is in terms of how children shape their identities in their relationships with their parents. What I am about to say about a boy's identification with his parents applies to the emergence of a girl's personality as well. And, too, obviously the identifications need not be with the parent of the same sex. Granting these variations, consider the oversimplified example of a boy identifying with a detached, passive, overly controlled father. His mother is likely to be aggressive and dramatically emotional. When the boy grows up, he will marry someone who is like the parent with whom he did *not* identify (aggressive mother). Soon the very qualities that attracted him will seem oppressive, and he will insist that she become more like the parent with whom he did identify (the passive, detached father). Ironically, should she try to comply, he will complain about the changes as being too little, or too late, or somehow not quite what he had in mind.

I used to wonder why there is so much marital difficulty. Now that I am more aware of the willful ways in which we are all tempted to struggle spitefully to get our own way, it amazes me that we are so often successful in our quest for love.

The Wife of Bath's autobiographical account of multiple marriages is merely a prologue to her chosen pilgrimage tale. The story she tells to the other pilgrims is another recounting of a struggle for sexual mastery in the quest for love, this time proceeding from rape, to marriage, to everlasting devotion. In this tale, "the world-wide scene of the quest dwindles to the marriage-bed of the dilemma."[8]

The tale begins in the good old days when King Arthur ruled, before the elves and fairies of the land gave way to the purging holy friars. One of Arthur's young knights came upon a lovely young girl in the woods and "by very force he took her maidenhead."[9] For this rape, he was condemned to have his own head forcibly removed. The Queen and her ladies-in-waiting pleaded for his life, and so Arthur agreed to let the Queen decide the young knight's fate.

The Queen set up a condition under which he might be pardoned. She set him a task to be fulfilled in a year and a day, saying:

Yet you shall live if you can answer me:
What is the thing that women most desire?[10]

If not, then he must die!

For almost a year he searched the land, knocking at every door, asking his question, and receiving many, many answers, none of which he could count as right. What it was that women want most, he was told, is "wealth and treasure . . . honour . . . , jollity and pleasure . . . , gorgeous clothes . . . , fun in bed . . . , to be oft widowed and remarried . . . , [to be] flattered . . . ," and "freedom to do exactly as we please."[11] Near the end of the year, he felt no nearer to the secret truth than he had been at the beginning.

Finally, his time almost up, he rode home in dejection. As he came to the edge of a wood, he spied twenty-four ladies dancing on a green. He hoped that this might offer one last chance for him to learn the answer to the Queen's question, but as he approached, the lovely dancers vanished. In their place, there remained only an ugly old hag. She asked what he was looking for, and he told her of his quest. She promised him the answer to his question if, when he received it, he would swear to do whatever she should next require of him. Overcoming his revulsion, he took the old crone's hand, and agreed, upon his honor. And so it was that she revealed the secret to him.

The old woman and the knight rode to the Court together. The Queen asked the knight whether his search had been successful, and if so, commanded that he speak the answer. He spoke out, saying:

A woman wants the self-same *sovereignty*
Over her husband as over her lover.[12]

All the ladies were delighted with his answer, and agreed that his life would be spared.

The old woman sprang up and told the assemblage of her compact with the knight. She then turned to him, saying: ". . . keep your word and take me for your wife."[13] The young man was horrified and begged to be let off, to be subjected to some other demand instead. "Take all my goods, but leave my body free," he pleaded. But, alas, "he was forced to wed."[14]

On the joyless bridal bed, the young knight writhed in anguish, in "torture that his wife looked so foul."[15] The old woman felt hurt when he told her that he could not stand her because she was so old, and so ugly, and so low-bred. She insisted that all these matters of appearance counted for nothing. In fact, she went on to point out that, given all this, he would not have to worry about her being unfaithful.

Nonetheless, she would compromise, if need be. She offered him two choices: *either* he could have her old and ugly and faithful till she died, *or* she could change herself into a young and pretty and faithless wife. He needed only to choose.

He could not choose between two such grim alternatives. Instead he gave himself over to her sovereignty, leaving it to her to make the choice. At the moment when she knew that she had won mastery, she demanded that he kiss her. And just as he submitted, she turned all at once into a lovely young woman. Not only that, but she relented and swore to be faithful forever. And to his kisses,

> . . . she responded in the fullest measure
> With all that could delight or give him pleasure.[16]

Like Dame Alice, many of the latter-day seekers, now on psychotherapeutic pilgrimages, are also much preoccupied with the struggle between the sexes. Psychoanalytic theorists tend to understand the plethora of sexual problems among patients as an expression of the unresolved infantile meanderings of the libido (that hypothetical fundamental sexual energy, the alleged instinctual basis of all behavior). I have no idea what proportion of the problems of sexual *struggle* may be instinctual. It is, however, clear that there are other influences afoot. The long-needed contemporary Women's Liberation literature, for instance, points up the oppressive politics of sex, the brutal oppression of women, the reciprocal entrapment of men in their own power-perversity, and the destructive counter-ploys that women have had to develop.[17] It may be that, if a man or a woman grows up in a culture as oppressive as ours, he (she) can no more be completely straight about sex than any of us can be about relationship between the races. Even as I dare to write about such issues, as a man, I must keep in mind that there are many ways in which I can never hope to really understand what it is like to be a woman in our culture.

Another set of parameters crucial to the sexual struggle is the expression of personal rather than social interactions. That so much human struggle seems to take place in sexual terms is somewhat misleading (by "sexual" here I mean a whole range of relatings between men and women, not simply the explicit pleasures of the bedroom). The ambiguity and uncertainties of fulfilling oneself as a man or as a woman sometimes mask the more profound anguish of simply being human.

The ubiquity of such struggles occurs, *not* because of some fundamentally *problematic quality* of sexuality, but on the contrary, because sexuality has qualities that draw other problems to it as *people seek sexual solutions* for the never-ending conflicts and ambiguities of the hassle of living life as a human being, whether male or female. The entangled relationship between the sexes is the site of attempted solutions, which give the appearance of "problems." only because the solutions are unsuitable. *Sex is an arena* within which other kinds of problems get played out.

The first factor underlying the ubiquity of sexual conflicts within and between a man and woman is that sexual longings are to some extent instinctual, and therefore *dependable*. That is, they can reliably be expected to occur in everyone.

Second, sexuality is an *expendable* instinctual need. Hunger and thirst, for instance, though dependably present in everyone, cannot be messed with. These instinctual needs cannot long be denied without our destroying ourselves. They lack the logistical malleability of sex. Imagine trying to "hold out" on a partner by giving up food and drink for weeks!

A third fortuitous quality, which makes sex a likely instinctual arena for the acting out of other (non-sexual) conflicts, is that of all the instincts, sexuality seems to be the only one that is somehow fundamentally *interpersonal*. Even masturbation usually has an interpersonal quality in that it brings with it (or facilitates) fantasies in which our wishes regarding relationship with another can be fulfilled. Because of this interpersonal parameter, sex often invites the expression and attempted resolution of nonsexual struggles around polarities of personal relationship. These include dominance and submission, parenting and dependency, persecuting and playing victim, power and helplessness, and tenderness and violence.

The fourth parameter of sexuality, that which pivots the *dependable-expendable-interpersonal* qualities full tilt into the arena, is its *vulnerability* to subtle shifts of mood, attitude, and behavior in the self and in the partner. Men and women are so easily "turned on" and "turned off" by a gesture, a word, a facial expression that sexual interplay becomes a most tempting battleground on which to carry on the nuances of unresolved longings and resentments, feelings that arose in other human contexts that were not primarily sexual.

Willfulness, stubbornness, spite, and other petty insistences of maintaining the illusion of being in control of that which we cannot control, run rampant in the relationship between the sexes. The unwillingness to be vulnerable, to be helpless, to give up control, to trust, is deployed in a mad attempt either to get one's own way, or failing that, at least to make sure that the partner does not get his (her) own way. *Getting our own way,* that which Dame Alice says is what women want most, is, God help us, as often what men want most for themselves as well.

My Pilgrimage to the Sea

> Water flows on uninterruptedly and reaches its goal.[1]
> Quiet return, Good fortune.[2]
> *I Ching*

At least once in each year of my life, for almost as long as I can remember, it has been necessary for me to return to the sea. The living waters draw me back to their shores again and again. They seem to wish to show me that though they are ever changing, yet they never change. The ocean is both endlessly calm and disruptively turbulent, alternately quieting my own inner turmoil, while yet insistently warning me of the dark powers that lie unquiet beneath the water's surface, and my own.

Inevitably, if I remain open to the tidal rhythms, the sea puts me in touch with the ebb and flow of my own inner area of unrest, my rising struggles and intermittent surrender and release. My romance with the sea helps me to know both the importance of my own singularity, and the meaninglessness of my trivial being.

> As the [Hasidic] saying goes, a man must have two pockets into which he can reach at one time or another according to his needs. In his right pocket he must keep the words: "For my sake was the world created." And in his left: "I am dust and ashes."[3]

For many years now, I have undertaken this pilgrimage with my wife, Marjorie, and our three sons. In order to mask the power and the mystery of the venture, we sometimes talk of the trip as if it were only a pleasant summer vacation on Martha's Vineyard, one of Cape Cod's lovely off-shore islands. But secretly we all know (even the children) that the journey to her magic island and to my great surrounding water ritually reconsummates our marriage.

Ever since we first came together, I have been for her an island on which she could be free from the distractions of a soul-devouring world. At the same time, she has provided for me the sea's life-giving depth and nurturance, an eternal female "thereness" through which the forces of nature flow. Her female wisdom is a fulfilling reciprocal, which matches and completes my parameters. As a man I must struggle against nature, carving out a definition, tearing it away from life itself. During our pilgrimage, she becomes the island unto herself, just as I for a time enter and merge with the sea. At such times, it is as if we each complete ourselves. Ironically, we can then offer more to the other, simply because it is no longer required.

The powerful beginning of the pilgrimage is a rite of passage, which masquerades as a four-mile, forty-five-minute ferry crossing of Nantucket Sound from the Cape to Martha's Vineyard. Waiting for the ferry is always difficult, because of the fear that this time maybe it won't arrive. But each time it finally *does* pull in at the dock, and each time we board with the same maiden-voyage excitement. Standing at the rail of the upper deck, I pretend a naturalist's curiosity about the screamingly greedy sea gulls so as to distract myself from worrying about the overcast sky, the threat of weeks of stay-indoors weather. The boat's whistle blasts unexpectedly, always a shade louder than I remember it.

We begin to move out into the channel. I explain to myself that it is the boat that is moving, that it only *seems* as though it is the everyday world of the mainland that is drifting away. In mid-channel there is once more the sense of being suspended in permanent limbo on the angry choppy waters of the Sound. And as if in a recurrent childhood dream, it is at this point that the change begins.

During this suspension from the disappearing mainland, the unvarying gray of the sodden sky begins to break up into a textured crazy-quilt of all the kinds of partly-cloudy/partly-sunny meteorological categories into which the skies can be sorted. Time is compressed as the day changes expression more rapidly than I can read it. I can no longer make judgments. I begin to become frightened by the loss of landmarks. And then, without my ever being able to name the moment when it occurs, the sunlight emerges with soothingly penetrating warmth.

All at once I am aware of how brilliantly the water sparkles. The air, once an impenetrable barrier, is now a lens for eyes till now unaware of their myopia. Everything stands out in a brightness and clarity that make the world seem almost theatrical, more real than real. I am sure that I can see as far as I like. I am disappointed to find that, to the stern, the mainland is out of sight. Then I remember. I turn away from the ship's wake, and there before me, out of the water, thrust the green island hills. The excitement and the relief make me cry joyfully again. I am coming home!

The island itself is typical of those formations plowed out ten thousand years ago by the southward movement of the glaciers, having a long central moraine from which the land descends on either side. The terrain is uneven, alternately thrusting up and dipping down in what are called "knobs" and "kettles." Glacier-tossed boulders and stones are scattered about. The natives use these "erratics" to build low stone walls, which separate one man's land from the next. The island is well-wooded, and fringed with beaches. And everywhere, there are the living waters. Not only is Martha's Vineyard bounded by the Sound and by the Atlantic Ocean, but it is spotted with smaller bodies of water.

Brooks abound, and great salt-water, kettle-hole ponds attract me now as they once drew the Indians who lived along their perimeters. The Indians camped on their banks, feeding on the shellfish and other pond life that are still to be found there. I am drawn to the ponds to feel once more a part of this primitive existence. But too, it is the *stillness* of the pond that calls to me. Looking into the mirror of the unmoving waters, I see the reflection of my own face. The quieting water confronts me with an image of myself that does not flatter. The stillness within me, which its calm elicits, provides an escape from the usual frenetic struggle to adorn my image. The mirroring water reflects the true face, the face behind the mask. It is always something of a disappointment. And yet in a way, it's a relief to see myself as less than I might like to be, but yet, for better or for worse, just as I am.

Though I return to the mirroring ponds again and again, I cannot remain at their quiet edge. Always in the background is the hypnotically rhythmic siren-pounding of the great surf beyond the dunes. As in a dream, empty of my own will, I walk like a somnambulist drawn helplessly back to the Great South Beach. It is on these sands that the winter of my life is revealed in lunatic perspective.

Once on the beach, I am totally engaged by this world's simplicity. Endless blue sky, hung with just enough of soft unthreatening clouds to relate it to the earth; its mythic vastness is more than my gaze can take in. This blue, the ocean's changing greens, and the yellow of the sands, these are the colors of time's beginning. The air is clear enough to crisp my vision, and it has a pure sweetness, scented by only the salt-water smell of life. There is no sound, save for the steady breaking of the surf, the whisper of the windblown sand, and the nasal "criii" of the fish-hungry, sky-arcing sea gulls.

The input of sound and sight and smell is so simple that I cry out with the surprise of sudden relief. It is as though all through the rest of my daily life, without my being aware of the noise, someone else's radio, tuned too loud, had been blaring in my ear. Standing on the beach, I only now become aware of the oppressive cacophony, only now that it has been switched off. My mind is emptied, and I am openly transparent once more.

I walk the wild, empty beaches, past dune-grass-tufted, mountainous sand hills, in the shadow of great, crumbling, ocher clay cliffs, along deserts of sandy flatness. I pocket colorful beach pebbles collected as a hedge against the too unmarked openness of sea and sky. The foaming edge of the breakers teases at my feet with playful unpredictability.

I survey the sea. My vision defines the world. I am the master. Then, perhaps through God's eye, I look in on myself, as if high on hashish. The ocean's vastness is beyond belief. I see myself as a pitiful speck at the edge of a cosmic puddle, a miniscule moment deluding himself that he is in charge of Eternity. It is terrible to be so helplessly alone. Longing burns in my aching chest, my eyes mist over.

At the edge of the sea, I am the last human being left. And too, I am the first man ever created. It is *my* ocean and *my* sky. I feel the power of my sovereignty. It is heartbreakingly lonely. It is only a moment, this time-out. Yet I cannot bear the awful feeling that it will last forever.

Each year this happens. I know that this experience is coming, without ever quite remembering how much anguish it will bring. Yet this is part of why I return to the sea, to put myself in touch once more with my terrible loneliness, to learn again that I must bear this. To remember that this pain is the same for us all, that it is each man's weakness and his strength.

Last summer came close to being my final pilgrimage to the sea. The winter preceding it I had undergone the tortured ordeal of brain surgery during which I almost died, and after which I was psychotic for a time. I was grateful to have survived, though part of the tumor could not be removed and my future was ominously uncertain. My hearing in one ear was lost. I was left with precarious physical balance that I experience as a loss of grace as I move through the world. And pain had become my unwelcome companion, dogging me with two or three headaches every day. If only I could have one day without the pain, it would be like coming up for a gulp of sweet, fresh air, after having been submerged too long beneath the water's surface.

But that winter and spring, shortly after the operation, it was different. Sure, I felt in some ways like a dilapidated wreck on fugitive status from the terror of the hospital. But more than that I felt I had won because I was still alive, with but a few handicaps to overcome. The crisis called forth in me all of the old crazy "I can handle anything that comes along" attitudes that I learned so long ago when my mother would tell her trembling child: "You're not really frightened. You're brave enough to do anything you want (I want you) to do."

The first thing I did while recuperating at home was to write a paper about my ordeal.[4] I was half-dead, scared to death and what did I do but write a Goddamn paper about it. It was a wise reaching-out to tell my story, to get myself together, to announce that Lazarus had arisen. It was also a patently absurd undertaking for a sick man. I had been cut down, and tried to make of my tragedy a challenge. I did not see the dark humor in calling a brain tumor a "growth experience."

I got myself together, thrust myself forward toward life, went back to work (too much and too early), even wrote a book. I was in a manic high, denying my losses, my pains, my fears. Friends and patients, who had been generous in their sharing of my anguish up till then, were relieved and happy. I was no longer the pariah who would remind them of their own vulnerability. In good faith, they applauded my courage, and celebrated my return to life. Only my wife, Marjorie, who had taken care of me and had saved my life, was both wise and loving enough to tug at my sleeve and repeat softly, "Be careful, darling. There's something crazy about what you're into." After a while she was even able to save herself by being openly angry at my being so irresponsibly high.

Then last summer, on my pilgrimage to the sea, I crashed. All the madly denied sorrow and hurt caught up with me as I paused, away from the distraction of my work, vacation-vulnerable once more. The undistorted pond-reflection of my real face and the clarity-bringing simplicity of the seascape, combined to put me in touch with my hidden despair. I felt a depth of helplessness and hopelessness that I had not experienced for more than twenty years, not since I was teen-aged, worthless, and lost.

Fear that the remaining sliver of tumor would begin to grow again left me feeling that, rather than someday simply dying, I was to be killed off. Or, worse yet, I felt the terror that I might not die, that instead I would become paralyzed. What would it be like to be trapped alive, imprisoned for years in a dead body? What if I could do nothing for myself, and if no one else would be there to bother to do for me, except out of burdensome pity?

I felt deeply sorry for myself. It seemed to me that I could not stand being so out of control of my life. My wife was there, with her own pain, and sorely open to mine. She later described it as "the summer we cried on the beach." But I was so into myself, so frightened, so determined to reassert my will and to have my own way that nothing else seemed to matter.

I spent many hours huddled on the empty beach, alone and brooding. Again and again, I decided that this was to be my final meeting with the sea, that I would swim out as far as I could, leaving my painful life, like a bundle of old clothes on the shore. And each time, I chose not to kill myself, explaining to myself that my wife and children needed me, would miss me too much. But it was not out of any sense of fairness to them that I did not drown myself. In my nearness to suicide, I really cared about nothing but escape from my own helplessness and anxiety. Recalling what I was up to, even now I still feel ashamed.

When we left the island to go home, I was still very depressed, unsure as to whether I was fit to help anyone else. It was time for me to get some help. But it was so very hard to face. I was feeling so down that the idea of going back into therapy as a patient once more made me feel like my life had been a fraud and a failure. And yet, if I would not go and ask something for myself, then everything I had tried to offer to my own patients was a lie.

There was an older therapist in town — a man whom I trust. He had supervised my work years ago, during a period when my father was dying. I used to go for supervision and cry every time. He had helped me then, and I hoped he would be able to help me again.

I phoned and told him briefly about my illness, and about how bad I finally realized I was feeling, hoping that he might have time free to see me. I was grateful and deeply moved when he told me he would "make time." The day I went to his office, I felt frightened, but was grimly determined to work things out. I told him my story in a detailed and well-organized account, and stated that I wanted to get to work right away, to get past this depression, to get back on my feet. Though sympathetic to the pain of my ordeal, his wry answer to my impatience was: "How come a big tough guy like you is thrown by a little thing like a brain tumor?"

That lovely bastard turned me round in a way that helped me to laugh at myself for thinking that I should be able to handle anything, without sorrow, rest, or comfort. He put me in touch with my own longings when he pointed out that I had resisted going through with drowning myself, *not* because my family needed me, but because *I needed them*. He said softly: "If you kill yourself, you'll never see your wife or your kids again, never. Think how much you'd miss them."

After much crying, and some raging, I came to begin to accept how sick I'd been. This tumor was no existential challenge. I had been cut down, without reason. I was in some ways helpless, and perhaps still in danger, but I was alive, and could have what I could have if only I would surrender to things as they were.

This summer I have returned to the sea, no longer feeling any temptation to swim out and never return. I enter the water to play at fighting the great torrents. My balance remains impaired and my stamina is limited, but my courage has returned. Soon I go with the power of the surging seas, happily body-surfing, allowing each newly breaking wave to return me to the shore where I belong. I merge with the sea only briefly, knowing that I am from the water but not of it. The sea renews me with its dark powers, but I am I, and She is She. My pilgrimage of repeated return to the sea will not end so long as I live. And now I know that I *shall* live, for as long as is given to me. And should my body be battered even more, then I will live as I can, enjoying what I might, having what joy is available to me, and being what I may to the people whom I love. I must continue my pilgrimage, for it is my only way of remaining open to this vision. It is to this end that I must struggle for the remainder of that pilgrimage that is my life.

Along the way, like everyone else, I must bear my burdens. But I do *not* intend to bear them graciously, nor in silence. I will take my sadness and as I can I will make it sing. In this way when others hear my song, they may resonate and respond out of the depths of their own feelings.

We will call out to each other in the darkness of the Great Forest, so that we may not be lost to one another. Then, like the innocent Forest People,[5] for a moment we will live in a world created by a God so benevolent that, when there is trouble, we will know that He must be asleep. And, like the Hasidim, just when life is heaviest with pain and anguish, that is the time when we will dance and sing together to waken the sleeping God of our own lost hope.

Part VI

Toward a Family of Man

by

Robert S. Spitzer, M.D.

Toward a Family of Man

Orwell's *1984* and Huxley's *Brave New World* exemplify traditional dramatizations of catastrophic expectations. I want to dramatize a happy ending, not just because we all like happy endings but because I think a good case can be made for such a future. Usually when we think about the world getting better, we do so only in abstract terms. We are too caught up in the day-to-day crises that panic us—an energy crisis, oil embargo, hijacking, kidnapping, inflationary trend, strike, or whatever. I think we need a wider-ranging dramatization of where we see ourselves going in the long run, particularly since we know that our expectations will surely influence the outcome.

By 1984 America will be experienced much differently by us and by the rest of the world. It will be very clear that America learned significant lessons in foreign affairs, especially in Vietnam. Humility will have entered our national image and added maturity to our idealism. It will be generally accepted that we can best help other countries by being an example to them— a model. It will be necessary first to get our own house in order. Then, when other countries approach us with specific problems, such as wanting help in controlling their population growth or developing their agriculture and natural resources, we can help them fulfill their purposes. A trend already exists toward working through international agencies rather than dealing unilaterally with countries because we have found that obligations often end in suspicions. We are learning that it is not wise to dominate foreign economies nor to try to change foreign life styles.

In ten years we will feel good about the likelihood of peace continuing, and it will be evident that for some time we have had no irreconcilable differences with any country. We Americans will recognize that we stand to profit, in the broadest sense possible, from the prosperity and happiness of other countries. My own guess is that in ten years we will be very friendly with China and Russia. It is hard to guess about the timing of such changes, as we still know little about the internal workings of both Russia and China and equally little about the successors to their present leaders. I think it is often overlooked that Russia and China have shown considerable restraint and maturity in foreign affairs in the past two decades. Russian soldiers have not been involved in wars since World War II, whereas we have had extensive involvement in Korea and Vietnam. Some Russia-watchers may disagree, but I interpret Russia's takeovers in Czechoslovakia in 1948 and 1968 and in Hungary in 1956 as essentially defense moves to protect its sphere of influence.

I think it is likely that Khrushchev's exposure of the tyrannical injustices under Stalin will be seen by historians as a turning point in Russian national and international affairs. I am impressed by the apparent popularity of both the Chinese and the Russian governments with their own people. It is likely that continued growth and material progress will take place in both countries. Skirmishes along the Siberian-Manchurian border could erupt and lead to widespread fighting and conceivably to a deterrent nuclear attack by Russia. However, it seems to me that the peak of danger in this regard is past. As each year goes by, China's nuclear strength increases. Already it is probably impossible for Russia to be certain it could attack China without significant retaliation. The important fact is that both countries are involved in their own growth and making progress about which they have every right to be proud.

I think there is every possibility that in ten years Russia and America, and probably China, will have shared many successful projects of increasing magnitude in such areas as developing natural resources in their own and other countries as well. It is likely that Russia and America will supply the finances and technological skill to help implement worldwide population control and agricultural projects to feed existing populations.

On the domestic scene, the various liberation movements will have developed to the extent that we will feel a real sense of brotherhood by 1984. We will have outgrown our fear of differentness. I think we will finally allow ourselves a natural sense of joy in encountering other people. We will recognize the dignity of each individual, and it will not embarrass us to acknowledge that each of us is—in a very real sense—quite beautiful. I believe we will see the development of a variety of small, informal, inexpensive neighborhood centers—perhaps utilizing television tapes as described in Part I, Chapter Six. These centers will be fun to go to, and will serve as a place for people to comfortably come together and share their humanity.

In ten years we will be able to see how suspicious and defensive we once were in many areas of our lives. We will see how easily we were scared and how easily we were duped by such dramas as Orson Welles' "War of the Worlds," which was based on the threat of invasion from outer space. We will see this kind of fear as anthropomorphic—realizing that if life exists out there in space and it is less intelligent than we are, it is hardly likely that these space people would be able to come to earth. And if there are beings with superior intelligence out there it is unlikely that they would want to come to earth. It might be interesting for them to observe us from a distance, but they would prefer to see us in our natural habitat rather than following our practice of putting animals in zoos. Our underlying fear is that some unknown Martian or other spaceman will want to rape our women or, perhaps, go to Disneyland. We have assumed that what we consider beautiful or interesting would appeal to someone of superior intelligence and of a different culture, and if that were the case, he would try to take it from us. This kind of fear of a foreign take-over made sense during World War II but it no longer does.

The trend of experiments in education which has already begun will branch out in even more directions during the next ten years. There will be much more emphasis on early participation. We will recognize that we learn by doing, and all kinds of apprenticeships will be built into education. We will see education as something that goes on throughout life and new resources will be developed for allowing more people to discover that learning is a joyous activity.

Our insecurities about sex will have dropped from our attitudinal patterns by 1984. We will allow ourselves to recognize and use more colorful clothing. There will be more music and more dancing. It will become apparent how puritanical we had been and how very little we had let ourselves experience joy. And there will be other moods that will also be more fully expressed—moods and meditation and contemplation and of simply being comfortable by oneself without a feeling of being left out.

I think 1984 will see marked intermarriage. In reality, probably very few pure Africans are found in America. The vast so-called black population is really a product of intermarriage with whites, a continuum from the few pure black Africans to the so-called white population—itself a composite of many different peoples. At some point it will become evident to people that the color line has been a very arbitrary one, much like the situation of the untouchables in India. Someday we shall look back on the distinctions we based on skin color as ridiculous, much as we now look back on the days when women did not have the vote.

Many technological breakthroughs will occur in the next ten years. Alton Ochsner predicts that we will have a cure for cancer within ten years. It is not possible to state when and how the actual breakthrough will occur, but Ochsner points out that this is the kind of medical problem that research has solved in the past; and with the expected logarithmic increase in manpower and resources tackling the problem, the outcome is predictable. And it is likely that we will develop cleaner energy sources and that smog and other forms of environmental pollution will be markedly reduced.

Insecurity about death will be greatly diminished in ten years. In England there is already a successful experiment—a new kind of hospital nursing home called a *hospice*, for people with incurable disease, particularly cancer. Hospices are comfortable, informal places where patients regulate their own use of pain medication. It has been found that most people require much less medication if they take it before their pain becomes too severe. There are now sixteen such hospices in England. Visiting is encouraged and no one dies alone. Death is experienced as a natural process—even as a potential learning experience.

In ten years we will probably live longer and have much fuller lives, even in old age. Aging, for most people, is largely a matter of expectations anyway. Other animals do not deteriorate until very old age unless their activity is restricted. Several places exist in the world where apparently a number of people live to ages of one hundred and even one hundred thirty years. These communities are being studied to determine whether longevity is related primarily to diet, heredity, or other influences. What seems common to all these places is that people lead outdoor, physically active, uncomplicated lives—lives that they value; and that are valued by their communities. People in these places are happy, and there is little fear or stress. This kind of life style will be recognized as a valuable goal in ten years, and much progress will be made toward attaining it.

Breakthroughs will also take place in psychological areas, in the form—for example—of new insights into our thinking processes. For some time, to students of semantics and more recently to students of Eastern thought, it has been apparent that the very nature of our language almost forces us to categorize. If someone asks me who I am, I am likely to say my name—Bob Spitzer—and that response sets me off from everyone else. If I am again asked who I am, I may reply that I am an American, again setting myself apart from other nationality groups. Or, I might answer that I am a man—a response that refers to a larger group but still sets me apart from women and children. If I reply that I am a human being, the group is again enlarged; but my answer emphasizes my differentness from other animals rather than my membership in the whole animal group. A progressive enlargement of reference takes place as we go from a *human being* to *the human animal*, and from there to *a living entity*. it is likely that our language has forced us to emphasize differences and to value the various boundaries, or ego states, of different stages of organization. Although these are beautiful and intricate, perhaps they have no intrinsic value; and if we weren't thinking in words, we would be more in touch with the flow. It is likely that our ways of thinking and our language cause us to ask such questions as "What was there before the beginning of time?" and to be overly concerned about our own individual deaths.

In the coming years, we will find that our gratifications are much more direct and immediate, rather than symbolic as they are today. We will find that it's fun to grow our own food, prepare it, and perhaps even build our own homes. It will become apparent to us that the more we express ourselves directly in these various ways, the happier we are—provided that we are confident that we will come out with something that fits us and is what we want.

In a decade, attitudes toward money and career choice will be much different. People of my age—48 and older—have been markedly influenced by the Great Depression. Money was of vital significance to my grandmother. Savings made it possible for her to emigrate to America. In her day, money determined whether one could get medical care, education, entertainment, and even food. These basic needs will be taken for granted in ten years. Henry Kissinger is reported to have said that power is the greatest aphrodisiac of all. Young people will respond to that kind of remark by saying, "Fine, if that turns you on." They will not put down the person who becomes an executive of a huge corporation, but they will not particularly envy his vocational choice either. It will be seen as just one of many different life styles—each one valuable in its own way.

Ten years may seem like a very short time for all this to come about. The title of this chapter, "Toward a Family of Man" may seem like a mere literary device. But upon reflection, these projections don't seem unrealistic to me. The Stockholm International Peace Research Institute reports that the sums spent annually on armaments in the period 1970-1973 by the major powers is equal to the total national income of the poorer half of mankind. These monies will become increasingly available for worthwhile domestic and international programs as it is clearly recognized that the threat of war is negligible. It may take us five years to develop this realization, but it seems inevitable. Never before in the history of man has there been such a realistic basis for lasting peace. And there are far-reaching and equally unrecognized effects of the liberation movements. It is an exciting thing for a member of any oppressed minority—whether it be a woman, a black, a child, or a senior citizen—to define himself in a new way. It involves risk-taking, consciousness-raising, and development of organizational know-how to implement social changes. I think that success in redefining oneself in one area of life leads to hope and increased ability, one develops willingness to view life freshly, to take risks, and to implement changes.

In ten years we will be in an "age of identification," as opposed to the current period which could be called the "age of anxiety" or the "age of alienation." The new age will be characterized by increased empathy and ability to identify with others. At the same time, there will be increased individuality. People will want to know as much as possible about their pasts and will value their heritages, not in the sense of considering themselves "chosen" or superior to others but in the sense of enjoying their own uniqueness. We can see this happening now in Mexico, where anthropology has become the "national pastime." Great influxes of people have come to the cities there, with resultant homogeneity. But there is a healthy counter-trend, and city dwellers maintain an active interest in the arts and culture of their ancestors.

Already in the developed Western countries, a very rapid dissemination of meaningful information exists on many levels, with vicarious participation through television, films, and newspapers. Typical of this phenomenon, of this age, is the fact that the first man who went to the moon was accompanied by television and therefore anyone watching television anywhere in the world could identify with him. A very different kind of dissemination of information took place in the past. For example, I remember studying Einstein's theory of relativity in school. I even got an A on a paper describing the theory, although I paraphrased the encyclopedia! Even after studying it, the theory had little meaning for me! However, when the atom bomb was explored and we saw it on television or in the movies, then $e = MC^2$ took on a new and different significance. Suddenly isotopes, uranium, the chemical nature of elements, protons, electrons, and the possibility of a hydrogen bomb, all had real meaning. Every intelligent person realized that he had to cope with this new phenomenon in some way. This has been taking place over and over again. At an early age, children see a man on the moon, jumping around in a much-reduced field of gravity. They see how the earth looks from a satellite. No one needs to arouse their curiosity about gravity or convince them that the earth is round. This kind of dissemination of information is part of our lives today and is applied to facts that were not available even to a Ph.D. twenty or thirty years ago. Almost everyone knows something about the complicated matter of the origin of life. It is fairly common knowledge that man can breed hybrid species and improve plants. Most of us know about artificial insemination. Most of us know about chromosomes and genes and RNA and DNA. We realize that experimentation may take place in the future that will affect the genetic makeup of plants, animals, and even man. It will soon be generally accepted that the universe extends indefinitely in all directions. Every school child knows that we have not only sent men to the moon but have also sent rockets to distant planets. He knows, too, that beyond our solar system and galaxy, billions of other galaxies exist. Children realize that there is apparently no limit on how far we can ultimately go, how much we can discover—only the temporary limitation of the current state of our technology. Similarly, children know that scientists can probe inward as well as outward; that solid objects such as wooden chairs are composed of molecules of wood atoms, that these atoms are in turn composed of protons and electrons, and that each of these is like a tiny solar system.

Wendell Wilkie wrote about "one world" in 1940, and for him this meant breaking out of isolationism. He pointed out that each country was affected by every other country in foreign affairs. Today the concept of one world has been extended to thinking of the entire world as one economic unit. Soon—as a result of the dissemination of information and its integration through vicarious participation—a worldwide body of information and life experience will emerge. In the past each culture had its private myth of origin and fated destiny. Soon all cultures will share a common myth—a myth based on factual, reproducable evidence and including the fact that we don't have all the answers.

All of this points to the future general acceptance of ideas that have been the basis of most religions throughout the history of man. Each one of us is very much like every other one of us. Enough food and shelter for each can be provided, and we can live in a more comfortable world. As our ability to identify with one another increases, it becomes increasingly uncomfortable to enjoy the affluent life when elsewhere there exist pain and discomfort which we know could be alleviated. The age of identification will be characterized by a growing altruism, which we will gradually come to appreciate as enlightened selfishness.

Books of Interest

Peoplemaking by Virginia Satir. Drawings by Barry Ives. ($5.95 paperback, $7.95 casebound)

The Gestalt Approach & Eye Witness to Therapy by Fritz Perls. ($6.95)

The Birth Book by Raven Lang. "The Birth of Kyle" photos by Don Ferrari, Phil Lake. ($6.00)

If You Meet the Buddha on the Road, Kill Him by Sheldon Kopp. ($6.95)

The books (excerpts of which are included in this anthology) may be purchased at a book store or ordered by direct mail:

Science and Behavior Books, Inc.
P.O. Box 11457
Palo Alto, California 94306

Jacket Design by Warren Talcott

Typeset by Vera Allen Composition, Castro Valley, California